DISMANTLE

First published 2014 by Thread Makes Blanket Press
Philadelphia, PA USA

www.threadmakesblanket.com

Dismantle: An Anthology of Writing from the VONA/Voices Writing
Workshop

© 2014 Edited by Marissa Johnson-Valenzuela for Thread Makes Blanket
Press

This edition © 2014 Thread Makes Blanket Press, Philadelphia

ISBN 978-0-9897474-1-7

Library of Congress info forthcoming

Cover artwork "The Structure" by Damon Locks
Book layout by Maori Karmael Holmes

Printed in Canada

DISMANTLE

An Anthology of Writing from
the VONA/Voices Writing Workshop

EDITED BY
Marissa Johnson-Valenzuela

POETRY EDITOR
Andrea Walls

NONFICTION EDITOR
Adriana Ramirez

FICTION EDITORS
Camille Acker
Marco Fernando Navarro

Thread Makes
Blanket press

Philadelphia, PA · USA

TABLE OF CONTENTS

Outword

Elmaz Abinader & Diem Jones

Introduction
Junot Díaz

1

When I was in my mid-twenties I decided to apply for an MFA in creative writing. Part of it was I wanted to get *serious* with my writing—whatever that meant. Part of it was that my body was getting worn out from delivering pool tables. Part of it was a worrying sense I had that I was going to need a lot more sophistication if I was ever going to be any good at writing. And part of it was I didn't know I had other options.

These days there are all sorts of writing workshops: part-time, full-time, low-residency, and more resources online than you can shake a stick at. These days you got *fifth graders* that can talk your ears off about MFAs. This is the Age of the Writing Program—but in the early 90s none of that had come to pass. I barely knew what an MFA was. My professor told me some stuff, but these things are like the Matrix—no one can really *tell* you what they are; you have to experience them for yourself. Still, I was pretty dumb about the whole thing. I never visited the schools I applied to, didn't look up their faculty or try to communicate with any of their students. I went after it with about the same amount of foresight that my parents brought to their immigration— which from my perspective seemed to be none.

I applied blindly and not very widely.

Six programs, and out of some blind pocket of luck that the Universe reserves for total fools I got into one: Cornell. I was excited, but not as excited as I planned to be when I got into my history PhD program (which in those days was my ultimate dream). But until then the plan was to spend two years in workshop, learning all I could about fiction in what I assumed was going to be a supportive environment.

I should have known better but hey I was young; I was naive.

2

Lots I could tell you about my time at Cornell, good, bad, crazy—and one day if I get a chance I'll try to write some of it down but for now I'll keep it simple and say only this: I didn't have a great workshop experience.

Not at all. In fact by the start of my second year I was like: *get me the fuck out of here.*

So what was the problem?

Oh just the standard problem of MFA programs.

That shit was *too white.*

3

You ask: *Too white . . .* how?

Too white as in Cornell had almost no people of color in it. Too white as in the MFA had no faculty of color in the fiction program—like none—and neither the faculty nor the administration saw that lack of color as a big problem. (At least the students are diverse, they told us.) Too white as in my workshop reproduced exactly the dominant culture's blind spots and assumptions around race and racism. In my workshop there was an almost lunatical belief that race was no longer a major social force (it's class!) and yet white people and their point of view were still supposed to be the default for everything. In my workshop we never explored our racial identities or how they impacted our writing—at all. Never got any kind of instruction in that area—at all. Shit, in my workshop we never talked about race except on the rare occasion someone wanted to argue that "race discussions" were exactly the discussion a serious writer should *not* be having. In my workshop, the plurality of students and faculty didn't believe that the lens of race was relevant to the evaluation or understanding of *anything.* From what I saw the plurality of students and faculty had been educated exclusively in the tradition of writers like David Foster Wallace, Jayne Ann Phillips, Lydia Davis, or Alice Monroe -- and *not at all* in the traditions of Toni Morrison, Maxine Hong-Kingston, Arundhati Roy, Edwidge Danticat, Alice Walker, or Jamaica Kincaid. Students in my workshop could quote what John Gardner had to say about writing but not Fanon or Anzaldúa. In my workshop the default subject position of reading and writing—of *Literature* with a capital Gothic L—was white, straight and male. This white straight male default was of course not biased in any way by its white straight maleness—no way!—in fact it was not even raced! Race was the unfortunate condition of nonwhite people that had nothing to do with white people and as such was not a natural part of the Universal of Literature, and anyone that tried to introduce racial consciousness to the Great (White) Universal of Literature would be seen as politicizing the Pure Art and betraying the (White) Universal (no race) ideal of True Literature. In my workshop "white consciousness . . . assumes a universality that is denied the consciousness of people of color and their reality... the consciousness of people of color is not the equal, but the exception, and therefore does not necessarily need to be acknowledged." In my workshop "the presence of people of color and the indication of their presence is always the exception to the rule; they are perpetually "other" and must be indicated as such."[1]

In my workshop the baseline assumption (despite abundant evidence to the contrary) was "that none of the white people in the class are racists or consciously or unconsciously subscribe to any elements from an ideology of white supremacy." In my workshop any attempt to raise the possibility that this was at best problematic was viewed "as blasphemy, as an act of aggression.[2]"

In my workshop what was defended was not the writing of people of color but the right of the white writer to write about people of color without considering the critiques of people of color.

Oh, yes: *too white* indeed. I could write pages on the unbearable too-whiteness of my workshop—I could write folio, octavo and duodecimo on its terrible whiteness—but you get the idea.

Simply put: I was a person of color in a workshop that was not interested, philosophically or pedagogically, in trying to account for my racialized ontology. I was a person of color in a workshop whose theory of reality did not include my most fundamental experiences as a person of color—that did not in other words include *me*.

The consequences of my white workshop's whiteness—by which I mean its deeply held assumptions about itself and about the nature of reality (no race) and literature (no race) and me—were devastating for a writer like me. My workshop's whiteness more or less barred my reality, my voice, from its conversations. It ensured that I was not witnessed in class, not by the faculty or by the majority of my peers. It was an act of silencing, of erasure, of negation—of violence.

". . . the MFA student of color experiences in a predominantly white institution is not simply an obscure or numerically insignificant occurrence. Instead it is symptomatic and revelatory of the ways the voices and consciousness of people of color are suppressed in our society."[3]

No wonder I was unhappy in workshop. No wonder me and some of the other Calibans in the program—my Diné buddy, Ichabod, and this Caribbean-American sister, Athena—talked constantly about the workshop's race problem, about the shit our peers said to us (shit like: Why is there even Spanish in this story? Or: I don't want to write about race. Or: I want to write about *real* literature.) No wonder we all talked at one time or another of dropping out.

---

1 All quotes in paragraph from David Mura in his essay "Reading and Writing Race." Honestly he's the man to read in this area and many more.

2 All quotes in paragraph from David Mura's essay "The Student of Color in the Typical MFA Program"

3 Again Mura's "The Student of Color in the Typical MFA Program"

Some of you are probably saying: Fool, what did you expect?

That's a good question. I guess I assumed that a graduate program full of artists dedicated to seeing beyond the world's masks would be better on the race front—that despite all my previous experience with white-majority institutions the workshop would be an *exception*. I guess I misjudged how conservative the arts are, underestimated the ferocity with which arts spaces are organized to obscure and protect the mechanism of elite power. What can I tell you? I was young. In those days I must have needed that little fantasy, that little hope that somewhere shit might be better. Hard for any of us to face the pervasive toxic density of coloniality's power, its utter inescapable ubiquity. Easier to imagine it otherwise.

Like I said: I was young.

4

It's been twenty years since my workshop days and there are workshops everywhere and AWP brings in over 10,000 participants and yet from what I gather a lot of shit remains more or less the same. I've worked in two MFA programs and visited at least 30 others and the signs are all there. The lack of diversity of the faculty. The students lack of awareness of the lens of race, the vast silence on these matters in workshop. Also, I can't tell you how many students of color seek me out during my visits or approach me after readings and presentations in order to share with me the racist nonsense they're facing in their programs, from both their peers and their professors. A lot of these MFA-heads are usually the only people of color in their workshop and a lot of them admit to feeling wounded by their experiences. In the last 17 years I must have had at least three hundred of these conversations, *minimum*. Some of the students talk clinically; some with tremendous rage; others seemed resigned and more than a couple have broken into tears during our conversations. It's all so familiar—and terrible. I remember one young MFA'r describing how a fellow writer (white) went through his story and erased all the 'big' words because, said the peer, that's not the way 'Spanish' people talk. This white peer, of course, had never lived in Latin America or Spain or in any US Latino community—he just knew. The workshop professor never corrected or even questioned said peer either. Just let the idiocy ride. Another young sister told me that in the entire two years of her workshop the only time people of color showed up in her white peer's stories was when crime or drugs were somehow involved. And when she tried to bring up the issue in class, tried to suggest readings that might illuminate the madness, her peers shut her down, saying *Our workshop is about writing, not political correctness*. As always race was the student of color's problem, not the white class's. I could go on; these little anecdotes are as horrid as they are common. The racist micro-aggressions directed at people of color in these

writing programs when combined could, I suspect, X out the sun. Many
of the writers I've talked to often finish up by telling me they're considering
quitting their programs. Of course I tell them not to. If you can, please hang
in there. We need your work. Desperately.

Sometimes they say: You did an MFA. Did you ever think about
dropping out?

All the time.

Why didn't you?

5

Another good question. I'm not sure I have a real answer. Answers yes but
An Answer: no. Maybe it was immigrant shit. I already knew a whole lot
about surviving white people craziness, had put up with crap like this in my
youth and, even though I'd tried to forget it, knew what it was to live under
that kind of constant low-grade assault, to feel unsafe *for years*. Maybe it
was characterlogical—I was just a stubborn fuck. Maybe it was the fact that
I didn't want to move back to my mother's basement for anything. Maybe I
just got lucky, I didn't snap or fall into a deep depression or get completely
demoralized.

In all honesty I probably would have blown it, the way I was drinking and
acting out, but then at the start of my second year something happened. A
massive Latino student movement sparked up on campus. That shit almost
never happens but there it was, the real deal and, desperate for anything like a
community, I jumped right the fuck in. That solidarity more or less saved my
life. Made everything in workshop bearable because I suddenly had a group
of people on campus who pulled for me, a group of people who *saw* me. Not
a bad movement either—we scored some solids against the University and
that also gives you a ton of heart. (One of our crowning triumphs, something
I still take pride in, was that we were able to push through our first fiction
faculty of color in the MFA program, Helena Maria Viramontes—how
perfect is that? If I wrote it in a book no one would believe it—too pat—but
that's exactly what happened. Helena came to campus too late for me but not
for all the other students who have since benefited from her genius. Helena
was exactly the faculty I had dreamed about during my MFA; she came out
of the tradition of Chicana artists, of women of color artists, the tradition of
resistance to the silencing forces of the larger culture and in her workshop
you better believe race existed and was not an interloper or an aberration from
True Literature; it's a social force which all of us must learn to bear witness to;
but best of all in Viramontes' workshop a writer like me could exist fully.)

I think in the end it probably *was* the organizing. Got me refocused, gave me hope and energy and in the end even though my thesis chair refused to give me a letter of recommendation (she had disagreed with hiring Viramontes and wanted to punish me), I did it; I graduated. My boy, Ichabod got through too—mostly by spending nearly every weekend away at the various upstate New York reservations. Athena, though, did not make it.

Talk about tragedy. Athena was a truly gifted writer. Wrote about her Island and its diaspora, their beauty and agonies with a clarity and sympathy I've never seen matched. She was also about the only ally I had in my actual workshop and one of the people in workshop who had the greatest impact on how I write today. She taught me important lessons on how to narrativize the Caribbean, exposed me to a whole suite of techniques and most importantly of all corrected a lot of my bullshit. Wasn't until many years later that I fully appreciated what I owed her.

She was tough and she was smart and she'd read loads but in the end, the whiteness of the workshop just wore her out. These people are killing me, she told me repeatedly.

Word, I said. Word.

I thought that she was in the same place as all of us but one day she announced that she was quitting for real.

I'm done, she said.

Maybe she just decided to do other things. Maybe there were problems at home. Maybe she was tired.

I cannot honestly say.

Of course I tried to get her to stay. Shit, I would have gotten on my knees if I thought it would have changed her mind. Selfish shit really; I just didn't want to be alone in that workshop but she didn't change her mind. When push came to shove, none us Calibans were close enough, I guess, to really make an intervention. Instead of pulling together we Calibans had all descended into our own spaces, taking the bus home every chance we got.

Early that fall (I think) Athena moved home; and I have never heard from her again. Shortly after a second writer of color left our workshop but I didn't know him at all (see how awesomely close we were) so I'm not going to speculate on the reasons. Still. The fact that we lost two writers of color in less than two years should tell you something.

Every now and then I search for signs of her on the internet but her name never shows up. I don't think she ever published anything. Breaks my heart because she was amazing.

6

Twenty years since the workshop and what I'm left with now is not bitterness or anger but an abiding sense of loss. Lost time, lost opportunities, lost people. When I think on it now what's most clear to me is how easily ours could have been a dope workshop. What might have been if we'd had one sympathetic faculty in our fiction program. If we Calibans hadn't all retreated into our separate bolt holes. If we'd actually been there for each other. What might have been if the other writers of color in the workshop—the ones who were like I don't want to write about race—had at least been open to discussing why that might be the case. I wonder what work might have been produced had we writers of colors been able to talk across our connections and divides, if we'd all felt safe and accounted for in the workshop, if we'd all been each other's witnesses. What might have been.

7

We founded the Voices of Our Nation Workshop in 1999 because all the founders, having survived the kinds of workshops I described above, were haunted one way or another by "what might have beens."

And because we saw a deep need for a space where writers of color from all backgrounds could gather to develop their art in a safe supportive environment. We saw the need for a space where, as writers of color, our ideas, critiques, concerns, our craft and, above all, *our experiences* would be privileged rather than marginalized; encouraged rather than trivialized; discussed intelligently rather than exoticized; a space where the stories we tell (and how we choose tell them) are considered cornerstones to the project of literature. We saw a need for a *decolonial* space where writers of color could deliberate critically on matters of race, ethnicity, self-hate, colorism, _____ (etc) freely and without fear.

From its inception Voices has aspired to be the kind of space where all the above would be possible -- all the above and more. We founders conceived the workshop as a revolution. A place where the Empire struck back[4]—where all stories were equally authorized, where all stories were the Universal and the dominant story that afflicted so many of us had no sway. Voices was to be an example of how a workshop *should* be. A workshop where people of color from all different backgrounds and experiences could talk to each other, learn from each other, explore affinities and filiations that lay outside the generalizing categories of our hyphenated identities: affinities and filiations that are the first words in the language of our collective future. Voices aspired to be a workshop where our differences would be opportunities

4   One of the editors asked, upon reading this line, Isn't this where the Jedi returns? I was referring to Paul Gilroy's co-authored classic T*he Empire Strikes Back: Race and Racism in 70s Britain.*

to *connect,* opportunities for *communion.*

(Pretty lofty goals for a group with no real funding, that meets only two weeks out of the year -- but hey, in a culture like ours, which works overtime to collapse people's utopian horizons, you got to dream if you want to be free.)

At our core Voices shares the conviction of Morrison, of Anzaldúa, of Moraga, of Momaday, of Roy, of Silko, of Hong-Kingston, of Said, of Hongo, of Chin (both Frank and Marilyn), of hooks, of Jones, of Rosal, of Ellison, of Goldman, of Walker, of García, of Rodríguez, of Alexis, of Castillo, of Álvarez and a thousand *thousand* other artists of color who have shown us by their courage, their humanity and their art that without the information (to use Audre Lorde's term) that people of color have about the world there can be no true reckoning of who we are as culture, as a nation, as a planet, as a race. Without us, in other words, there can never be hope of a We.

The truth is that the 'information' we people of color have about the world is information necessary for us all. To think, to be, to survive. Information without which no better future is possible. And without which literature, too, is not possible.

Voices was designed to be a space where the literature of the *all,* as opposed to the literature of the few, could be born.

8

We're fourteen years into Voices and it's become a lot of things. It's a fantastic workshop with the best faculty English has to offer. It's a week of beautiful brilliant inspirational learning and solidarity. It's a safe harbor for those of us who have never had one. It's a think tank for those who want to describe realities that the mainstream does not consider real. It's a counter-song to our post-racial derangements. It's love medicine. It's my favorite week of the year.

But it's deeper things, too. Silent things we almost never talk about. For me it's an attempt to do-over that lousy MFA I had. To create in the present a fix to a past that can never be altered.

Voices is about Athena. First and foremost. In many ways it's all about her—created in her honor, in her memory, in her hope. I guess there's a simplistic foolish part of me that believes that if Athena had only had Voices she would never have quit. The workshop would have given her enough light to make it through. And we'd all be reading her today.

I hope that one day she'll find us. And if there are other Athenas out there—which I know there are—I hope they'll find us too.

Preface
Marissa Johnson-Valenzuela

So often, when we want something, we have to do it ourselves. This is part of why this book exists, and it is why VONA was founded.

VONA/Voices is a writing workshop where people of color, for lack of a better term, gather for shared education. In the classroom, in conversations in the workshop's lounge, and in those moments when we comfort a writer who is shaking and shedding wounds—we learn together. It is a thriving writer's workshop/intentional community because so many of the people who have found it need it. We come to VONA to learn to better tell our stories, to push language, and to push ourselves.

We know that literature reflects reality, and we know that we can do better. *Dismantle* is a celebration of the lives we live, and the lives we want to live. It is an insistence that the construction of identity is complex, and that creative work should be as far reaching as our experience. Cultural racism says stories need to fit expected molds, that the quotas have already been met, and insists on "bridge characters" and explanations for an assumed kind of audience. Such expectations arrive subtle and blatant, are internalized and are all around us. Like all writers, writers of color are rewarded, read, and even ignored based on how well they fit the game; on whether their writing has the right kind of color.

I sometimes jokingly call the Latino equivalent of this sort of expectation "tortilla literature" (with a jazz hands accompaniment). And while such narratives are real and important—are vital—and some versions do speak to the experience of my ancestors, they are not my story. I grew up with tortillas, but it was the 80s so they were often flour tortillas warmed in the microwave. The tortillas, bought in bulk, transported for four hours, and kept in the freezer until needed, were from El Perdico, a tortilla factory in Garden City, Kansas where my mother had grown up. This was around the time that that western Kansas town had the highest percentage of people with Mexican heritage in the United States. (Also notable: so much in Garden City is in three languages: English, Spanish and Vietnamese because of meatpacking and post-war targeted immigration.) And so, stories later, I ended up in the highlands of Chiapas, living in Zapatista communities and the indigenous women, who were not taught Spanish, giggled and otherwise clearly communicated without language how terrible my tortilla making skills were.

Ultimately, our stories cannot be simplified, and audience must be entertained *and* challenged. We must trust that readers understand such complications because they too live them. The writers included in *Dismantle* do this work. VONA does this work.

I had the idea for this anthology about 6 months before I hesitantly voiced it to others. I wanted to help VONA reach the world, and I wanted every alum to have a book they could be proud to be a part of, but most of all, I wanted to do VONA justice. To this end, I assembled an editorial team of alum who I loved and trusted, and who each brought a wealth of expertise and perspective. As a result, I have ever so much gratitude and respect for Andrea Walls, Adriana Ramirez, Camille Acker and Marco Fernando Navarro. Additionally, I am honored by Elmaz's, Diem's, and all of VONA's support—this book would not exist without them. All along—I knew this anthology had to be beautiful. I thank everyone for making it so.

While I always took this endeavor seriously, I had no idea of what we were getting into, and it's been a long road. In the process of compiling *Dismantle*, we learned a lot, and, in that, we made some mistakes. I now have a greater appreciation for editors who go through submissions (who are forced to break hearts), and who dance careful dances in assembling a balance of established and new voices.

This book is a celebration of VONA, and more than that too. It is my earnest hope that every reader, VONA alum or not, published here or not, recognizes the power and possibility—the humanity—that is documented in this work.

To the white woman on the plane who doesn't understand my discomfort when she asks if she can touch my hair

Torrie Valentine

What will you do now
your hands in the dark thick of my hair

tracing the spine of a curl.
Your sleeve brushing my face.

If I were your lover I would begin
to undress you, unbutton your blouse

the warmth of you suddenly there.
And you surprised at how easily we give in,

search my eyes for something
more than your face

something more than you
fingering a coil near my ear.

Wake
Ashaki M. Jackson

In this light

her skin: resplendent The missing
breast returns like a runaway
child The chest expands
opens:
        a bird-speckled sky In this light
her laughter startles
birds from the canopy   At once
a billow of bodies wild bodies
troubled   unsure of why
they propel themselves up and up in fury   why
the trees seemed to hoist   why
the air seemed to crowd so

quickly

Grandmother Dies on the Curanja River
Ashaki M. Jackson

We strip our walls
of axes and machetes for her
final undressing   The flesh is like this –
disarmed and bare   We hew her walls   open
the body

wait

When Asked How to Remember
Ashaki M. Jackson

When asked how to remember
her, we find every rite
empty (threaded mouth prosthetic breast Mother hollow)
How she pleaded
not to be left alone No
box   nor toothless memory

Let us carry her   the weight
of a child on hip   the loving harry
when grown folk are talking   The conversation returns
to her like seasons

Or let us suspend the smallest
bells in her room   wait
for small winds: her breath
rushing through our closed spaces

Or tuck her throughout this house
Plant her many bodies
beneath the Cordyline   admire marrow red
leaves stretch

stretch

Hailu's Heart
(an excerpt from *Beneath the Lion's Gaze*)
Maaza Mengiste

The human heart, Hailu knew, can stop for many reasons. It is a fragile, hollow muscle the size of a fist, shaped like a cone, divided into four chambers separated by a wall. Each chamber has a valve, each valve has a set of flaps as delicate and frail as wings. They open and close, open and close, steady and organized, fluttering against currents of blood. The heart is merely a hand that has closed around empty space, contracting and expanding. What keeps a heart going is the constant, unending act of being pushed, and the relentless, anticipated response of pushing back. Pressure is the life force.

Hailu understood that a change in the heart can stall a beat, it can flood arteries with too much blood and violently throw its owner into pain. A sudden jerk can shift and topple one beat onto another. The heart can attack, it can pound relentlessly on the walls of the sternum, swell, and squeeze roughly against lungs until it cripples its owner. He was aware of the power and frailty of this thing he felt thumping now against his chest, loud and fast in his empty living room. A beat, the first push and nudge of pressure in a heart, he knew, was generated by an electrical impulse in a small bundle of cells tucked into one side of the organ. But the pace of the syncopated beats is affected by feeling, and no one, least of all he, could comprehend the sudden, impulsive, lingering control emotions played on the heart. He had once seen a young patient die from what his mother insisted was a crumbling heart that had finally collapsed on itself. A missing beat can fell a man. A healthy heart can be stilled by nearly anything: hope, anguish, fear, love. A woman's heart is smaller, even more fragile, than a man's.

It wouldn't be so surprising, then, that the girl had died. Hailu would simply point to her heart. It would be enough to explain everything.

He'd been alone in the room, the soldiers smoking outside. He could see their shadows lengthening over the bare and brittle lawn as the sun swung low, then lower, then finally sank under the weight of night. It was easy to imagine that the dark blanket outside had also swept into the hospital room, even though the lights were on. It was the stillness, the absolute absence of movement, which convinced him that they, too, this girl and he, were just an extension of the heaviness that lay beyond the window.

She'd been getting progressively better, had begun to wake for hours at a time and gaze, terrified, at the two soldiers sitting across from her. The soldiers had watched her recovery with relief, then confusion, and eventually, guilt. Hailu could see their shame keeping them hunched over monotonous card games.

It hadn't been so difficult to get the cyanide. He'd simply walked into the supply office behind the pharmacy counter, waved at the bored pharmacist, and pulled the cyanide from a drawer that housed a dwindling supply of penicillin. Back in the room, Hailu prayed and made the sign of the cross over the girl. Then he opened her mouth and slipped the tiny capsule between her teeth. What happened next happened without the intrusion of words, without the clash of meaning and language. The girl flexed her jaw and tugged at his hand so he was forced to meet her stare. Terror had made a home in this girl and this moment was no exception. She shivered though the night was warm and the room, hotter. Then she pushed her jaw shut and Hailu heard the crisp snap of the capsule and the girl's muffled groan. The smell of almonds, sticky and sweet, rose from her mouth. She gasped for air, but Hailu knew she was already suffocating from the poison; she was choking. She took his hand and moved it to her heart and pressed it down. He wanted to think that last look before she closed her eyes was gratitude.

It was only Almaz who'd recognized the vivid flush of the girl's face, the faint hint of bitter almonds, and known what had happened. She'd walked in just as Hailu was explaining to the soldiers how the electric shocks she'd received had damaged her internally.

"Oh," she said, "yes." She collected herself. "It was too much for her. Too much infection."

The soldiers were agitated. They paced back and forth. They asked Hailu again and again to explain exactly what had happened.

"The infection was climbing from her feet to her heart," he repeated. "There was no way to stop it. She was too weak to fight it."

"But she was waking up, getting better."

Hailu's palms were sweaty. He heard a ringing in his ears that seemed to get louder as he talked. He cleared his throat. "It was a surprise for all of us."

The girl's body was still in the bed, covered completely in a sheet. They hadn't filled out the necessary forms, the soldiers had yet to acknowledge these next steps.

"You have to do something," the deep-voiced soldier demanded. He grabbed Hailu's arm and shook it. "We reported she'd be able to leave in a few days. People are expecting her." He tightened his grip. "Do something."

The skinny soldier sat back down in his chair and began to rock. "What are we going to say? They'll send us to jail." He shrank back against an imaginary blow.

"I'll write up the death certificate," Hailu said. "Everything will be explained there."

"I'm a witness," Almaz said. "There was nothing we could do."

The soldier stopped rocking and looked at his partner. "We can't say anything for a few days." He nodded to the girl. "Just yesterday we told them she was fine."

The other soldier nodded. "We should wait." He looked at Hailu, his eyes growing cold. "They'll want to ask you more questions, I'm sure of it. She was an important prisoner."

So it was that the girl was still in the hospital room tonight, dead, being watched by two frightened soldiers who could do nothing but stare in front of them and shudder at the reaction their report would bring. Hailu had wanted to stay, to sit with the girl, but Almaz had ordered him home.

"Nothing changes," she advised. "I'll be here anyway." She'd handed him a small brown paper bag just before he walked out of the hospital. "It's the girl's. She had it on when she came here and I was keeping it for her." She squeezed his arm. "Keep it." Inside the bag, in the brown hollow of space entirely too large for it, was a slender, delicate gold necklace with an oval pendant of Saint Mary holding her child. He held up the necklace and watched as it swung daintily under the glow of his lamp. Cold, bright light caught the pendant and shot glints against the windshield.

. . .

Hailu sat at his desk in the dark. He'd been summoned to the jail officially. His presence was requested in writing, delivered to him by three skinny soldiers who spoke in unison. They'd walked into the hospital and gone to his office. They stood in a straight line, their shoulders even. Their identical uniforms, the way they each planted their feet the exact same width apart and had their hands folded in front of them, fingers plaited together, made Hailu think he was looking at triplets, though they were nothing alike in appearance. One was darker than the others, another was heavier, and the third had strange see-through eyes that looked like chips of stained glass. Watching them address him had been as confusing to Hailu as the order itself, handed down by a man most only knew as "the Colonel."

"You were told to come in, we spoke to your friend. Here is a written order. Come to the jail tomorrow, arrive by dawn," they said. "The Colonel wakes up early."

They kept their eyes lowered, but even then, Hailu felt their indifference to his status and age.

"What's this about?" He looked at the inked signature at the bottom of the letter and tried to imagine the man whose hand moved across the page with such jagged sweeps of the pen. "I have to work tomorrow morning, I'm scheduled for surgery."

Two of them turned to look at the third soldier. He stepped forward. "Please don't disobey orders," he said. His eyes were the color of a pre-mature leaf, his pupils black coins floating in a pool of green water.

"Should I bring a suitcase?" Hailu asked.

Most prisoners were ordered to bring a suitcase of clothes under the pretext that they'd return home eventually. Soldiers took the suitcases and added to their wardrobe, many of them wearing to bars and parties the clothes of those they'd executed.

"You won't need to," the third soldier said.

Hailu tried not to think about the fact that no one he knew ever returned from a summons to jail.

"Tomorrow," they said before walking out of the office. "Don't disobey this time."

Now, Hailu was in his chair with the lights off. He sat with his back straight as a tree and waited, though for what, he wasn't sure.

My White Wife ™
Adam Balm

Part I.

I cannot completely be who I'd intended to be, married as I am to My White Wife ™. I was put here—possibly by God, certainly by my parents—to rub black excellence in the face of white people, everywhere I go. And I do a pretty good job of it. But literally sleeping with the enemy adds an uncomfortable footnote to the message.

More uncomfortable is the indictment I face from my own people for My White Wife ™. Yes, even in our post-racial age. It is far more damning than the Being Black charge that is filed daily by strangers. No district attorney on earth would even bother charging me with Being Black if they also had a viable White Wife charge. They'd dismiss the Being Black and go after me balls-out on the White Wife. The best I could hope to do is cut a deal and plead to one count of Selling Out.

My White Wife ™ is, apparently, my "darkest" secret, my deepest, most shameful act. It completely upstages my love of mild kink, my childhood bedwetting, or my fondness for playing with loaded guns in the house. Unlike those bits of trivia, and a thousand others, My White Wife ™ is apparently a deal-breaker.

Which is weird, because back in New York in the 80s I wasn't exactly beating the sistas off with a stick. I suppose it is unknowable how much of that earlier circumstance was due to me, and how much was due to something else.

I still harbor a suspicion that, at 5'7", I am simply not tall enough for a lot of black women, including many black women 5'6" and shorter. In support of this suspicion I cite the "all the black men are either married or gay or on crack or short or in prison" scene in *Waiting to Exhale*. I also cite the times I was told so point-blank by sisters, sometimes while on what I'd thought was a date. In contrast, My White Wife ™ dated all sizes of men but, if anything, prefers men my height. Her celebrity boyfriend is Ruben Blades. I suspect that I was not living up to my culture's standards. Clearly, when I was single, I was not *something* enough for most of the black women I was interested in.

(In fairness, it may have also had something to do with all the hard rock and my sometimes white-sounding voice and all the white pop culture references and the occasional Yiddish.)

(Or the skateboarding and the frisbee and the hackey sack and all the white friends and the no black friends but that's circular.)

(Or, for a while, all the weed and beer and malt liquor and tequila and vodka and gin and hash and the public urination and the vomiting and the passing out and the occasional–I think occasional–blackout.)

This seems relevant: I have never fit in. Ever. Even when I was just another peasy-headed little black boy in the South Bronx I was fighting bullies. I had a small crew, but we were a crew of outcasts.

Following is a partial list of what I am afraid that some black people think of me and My White Wife ™. Many of these are on this list because from time to time people have come out and told me that this is what they think:

- That she calls me a n****r during fights and/or sex.
- That she thinks I'm white.
- That I think I'm white.
- That she thinks she's black. This is confusing.
- That she doesn't get me, and doesn't want to, and I'm OK with that. Like, if I get dissed while we're out, I don't say anything and she acts like she didn't notice.
- That I am a security risk: I am leaking classified black intel to a deep-cover white operative in exchange for sexual favors.
- That we are like almost every other black/white couple I have ever known.

I admit it: I can barely think of any other black/white couple that didn't creep me the fuck out at least a little. Either they both hate black people, or the brother is one of those real mild constantly smiling "Hootie" types, or the chick is just straight-up racist and the brother makes excuses for her. Once, I expressed some vague solidarity (regarding our treatment by cops, or maybe it was cabbies) between myself and a brother named Scott to his White Wife ™; her response: "Oh, Scott's not like that." I didn't bother to ask what she meant by that.

And those are the couples I've known! With strangers, I make all the same assumptions about them that others make about us. So it's tough, to expect people to know that we are the one black/white couple that isn't creepy. It's tough.

If I had known that there were some black people like me out there, whom I would meet eventually and who might accept me as I am, and that some of them were female and cute and single and possibly interested in me—if I had known all that, would I have gone on that fateful first date with My White Wife ™ 17 years ago? Maybe not. Maybe now I am supposed to divorce MWW ™ and go out and find somebody just like her, only black, so that I can be as happy as I am now but also do the face-rubbing thing 24/7. Maybe. Honestly, that's not showing up real high on my to-do list.

But, know this: I concede that I have let my people down by acting on my persistent feelings of attraction and affection for You-Know-Who. I completely understand the disappointment. I kind of couldn't help it.

Part II.

Okay. My first wife was white too. God damn it!

This is how I met my first White Wife™. She accompanied a black woman named Glenda to my apartment. We were all in law school together. I was pursuing Glenda, but she was putting me through my paces. She was in an on again/off again thing with some white guy twice her age and was reluctant to give us a try, or even go on a decent date. I don't remember why they came over, but Glenda specifically asked my first White Wife™ to cock block while they were there. She did. I courted Glenda around her chaperone and they stayed for about an hour.

After they left, I was later told, while walking down the stairs of my building, my first White Wife™ stopped Glenda, looked her in the eye, and said: "If you don't take him, I will!" Exact quote. The fact that my first White Wife™ turned out to be a flaming asshole has no bearing on the point I am trying to make here. I'm just saying, if Glenda had taken me off the market, this all would be moot. Sisters had the right of first refusal. A brother plays the hand he's dealt. One woman's trash and all that.

Interestingly, at least one sister has straight-up told me to my face that the above story is a lie. Not sure what to do with that.

My girlfriends started out pretty multicultural. And from nursery school (Nancy) to maybe the summer before 7th grade (Jackie Watkins), they were all black. No—in 6th grade I had a girlfriend who looked and acted like a very young Jodie Foster; she went on to marry a billionaire. Jackie Watkins went on to date LL Cool J. That should get me something.

In the 7th and 9th grades (I skipped 8th) I don't think I had any girlfriends per se, but there was a very active make-out community on my block. My crew (call it four black, two Jewish white, one white white, two Puerto Ricans, two Filipinos) had sort of a sister crew, and each of us made out with each of them as many times as we could manage. I'd say: two black, one Jewish white, one white white, one India Indian, and one Puerto Rican. Still a virgin this whole time.

I stayed with cousins upstate and had a very brief summertime makeout thing with a chick who was kind of trailer trash. At the time I didn't think anything of it.

High school. On again/off again with a sister, Wanda, through high school and college. One time we were fooling around in my room and that song "Too Hot" came on the radio and Wanda sang along but modified the lyrics like so: *At fourteen we fell in love...* So I'm going to take her word for that as the start point. During one of the off-again periods, shortly after college, she got married. I'm not positive we stopped fooling around right away.

I fell in with the theater/stoner crowd. Enter the aforementioned frisbee and hackey sack. I'd been skateboarding since '75. Lots of parties. I remember a toga party at the Waldorf. Not a lot of black people around.

First serious relationship: Senior year of high school. Jasmine was half India Indian and half Puerto Rican. Her mom was polite enough, but I'm pretty sure she hated me. She kept a very traditional Indian home, and Jasmine was a pretty traditional Indian. Remember the movie *Mississippi Masala*? I lived it, which makes me Denzel, baby! But, serious: I'm married twice now, and I'll still tell you that that was the real thing.

Freshman year of college I got with Donna, a black Valley Girl. She was perfect for me. But shortly after that the weed and hash and beer and rum and vodka and mescaline and tequila got going in earnest. I don't remember a whole lot about college, but what I do remember, except for Donna, I hate.

I pledged a frat. Rush Week was a big deal. We all got recruited pretty hard.

Okay—you tell me. Where do you pledge: a frat where you have to march around single file terrified and not speak and dance on command and study study study and probably get your ass beat and *definitely*, at the end, get *branded?*

BRANDED!

Or, a frat where all they do is drink and smoke weed and try to have sex with sorority chicks?

I was 16 when I went to college. But I'm well into my 40s now and, looking at just those facts, that's still a no-brainer.

Also, did anyone catch the whole "white girls are all slutty freaks; sistas don't play that" vibe of that era? Maybe it was an East coast thing. But I definitely saw and heard that expressed all around me. And on some level I was like, *Note to self: Get white girls.* I understand politically where that party line or mood came from, but that was the particular effect it had on me.

I guess 16 matters because I took it all at face value. I now have reason to suspect that folks were partying pretty hard at the black frats too. But the hype at the time was how we were all so "serious." It was the 80s. We took blackness very seriously then. There were a lot of rules. I was 16 and just out from under my dad, a high school dean. So I wasn't really feeling rules. And my folks split up. Do I get anything for that?

Obviously, pledging the same frat as Ronald Reagan was a bad idea, and the whole thing had completely blown up in my face by the beginning of sophomore year.

I saw few options. To just up and start being black the following Monday was not feasible; I had burned many a bridge by trying to be happy. Also I lacked the wardrobe, although it now appears that I, in my flannel shirts and Timberlands, was only ahead of my time. So I stayed high until I graduated. Cheap thrills with those freaky slutty white girls and the occasional weekend visit from Wanda kept me going. Also, weed.

After graduation, I spent two years working and getting myself together. Some flirting and some near-misses (sisters and others), but no girlfriends of any denomination.

I went to law school. I guess this means that I have to tell you the Prince tickets story.

I entered law school in August 1988. I did so with 2 tickets to see Prince at the Garden in October—the Lovesexy Tour—in my possession. To recap: it was 1988 and I had two (2) tickets to see Prince at Madison Square Garden. The seats were in the nosebleed section, but still.

I thought I was a genius. Everybody says you don't just ask a woman if she wants to go out "sometime"; you have to have a specific thing. Boy, did *I* have a specific thing. And since the show was still about 6 weeks off, I could take my time and make friends before I started trying to date.

I started school with my heart and mind open. Law school actually had black folk who were kind of like me. I was active in the Black Law Students Association—the parties anyway. I no longer drank or got high. At any given time there was a rotating roster of two or three women, all sisters, with whom I felt some chemistry and was getting to know, and, when the time came, was asking out.

I got nowhere. Granted, in hindsight, many of the women I tried to talk to were lesbians—it was, after all, law school—but at least some of them had to be straight. They were all single as far as I knew. And, frankly, even the lesbians—a lesbian can't go see Prince with me? In 1988? The hell?

I ended up taking a friend from my dojo. German. Damn! Our subsequent grope session obviously was Prince's fault, not mine.

Then I met Lisa, away from school. Sister, mostly; probably some Latin, probably some white, maybe some other stuff. Whatever you want to call her, Lisa was fine. To this day, my friends that knew her will say, Lisa was *foine*. (Picture Heather Hunter in her prime.) I almost flunked out, running down to Brooklyn every day. When I wasn't in Brooklyn I was parading Lisa around the law school: *Fuck y'all*. It lasted exactly 9 ½ weeks.

The next thing that happened after Lisa dumped me was I got interested in Glenda.

I no longer know what this all was supposed to tell me.

Part III.

So, My White Wife ™ is but a symptom. Of a larger—what? Problem?

Over the years I have been tight with some white boys. It is a waste of time. We can have a similar take on the world or common interests or whatever. But, invariably, they say some dumb shit, and then I've got to let them go.

I don't cause it. I don't make them say that dumb hillbilly shit they grew up with, that they think having a black friend suddenly makes OK to say in civilized company. I used to have some sort of 3 Strikes rule, but white boy dumb shit is like roaches, or N-bombs in a rap: if there is one, there are always more. So it starts off cool, and it's cool for a while, then it's Dumb Shit Day, and that's it for me. And yet my quest for the mythical Down White Boy continues. What's up with that?

Joel, one of my best friends growing up, was Jewish. We were a 14-year-old Crockett and Tubbs. For a while, some psycho was killing nurses with a sword over by Bellevue. Yes, the mental hospital. So one night Joel and I got drunk and walked over to an alley near Bellevue where one of the murders happened, and we went looking for the serial killer in the dark psycho murder alley with our knives out. It doesn't get any better than that.

So maybe I'm trying to recreate me and Joel. Also, my Dad's best friend for much of my childhood was white. "The Greek," they called him. Fuck. Why does everything have to go back to father issues?

So I blame my Dad. And TV. And music. Music is huge. Music is loaded. I've always had a music problem. Listening to AC/DC and Cheap Trick and Styx. My mom tells me they used to stand at the bottom of the stairs listening to that shit coming out of my room and just shake their heads.

Pop quiz. Following is the playlist that accumulated on my mp3 player yesterday. This is what I listened to on the way to work, at work, and on the way home from work yesterday, in the order that I listened to it. I don't know what it means; I just have a feeling that it's going to be really embarrassing, and therefore potentially valuable. (Though if I had known I'd be doing this today I might have made some different choices yesterday.)

Next to You - The Police
Mystery Achievement - Pretenders
Come Together - Beatles
TV-Glotzer (White Punks on Dope) - Nina Hagen
Bucky Done Gun - M.I.A.
Tennessee - Arrested Development
Glorious Pop Song - Skunk Anansie
Funny How Time Slips Away - Al Green
They Call Me Flavor - Public Enemy
The Warmth of the Sun - Beach Boys
Dead Souls - Joy Division
Surfin' Bird - The Trashmen
Biding My Time - Pink Floyd
The Phuncky Feel One - Cypress Hill
Cold Lampin with Flavor - Public Enemy
Back to the Scene of the Bass - Terminator X
Beat It - M. Jackson
Hot for Teacher - Van Halen
The Lords of Salem - Rob Zombie
Complain - King's X
Rock Hard in a Funky Place   Prince
Chantilly Lace - Jerry Lee Lewis
California Love - Tupac and Dre

God damn—that's a nice-ass playlist. I think if I had three wishes, one would be for the email address of everyone else who listened to all of those songs yesterday. Or even just Jerry Lee and Tupac. That feels like my people. Well, Kid Rock probably listened to Jerry Lee and Tupac yesterday, so, never mind, I guess. Oh my God, music is so fucking loaded.

Like every other dude my age, I played at being a rapper for a while in the 90s. In '96 or so I decided to write a song about how they like to act scared of me at odd times—for example, when I'm at Whole Foods buying tofu and bok choy. I say "act" scared because I don't think that a moderately sane person of even average intelligence would behave so aggressively towards someone they were genuinely afraid of. There is much flinching and cringing and grasping of purses, but not nearly enough getting the fuck out of my way. They appear panicked and intrigued at the same time. It seems insane.

Anyway, I knew exactly where I wanted to go with the song, but I was having trouble finding the first few lines. They came to me in the wee hours. Suddenly I was awake, writing on whatever in the dark:

> Mace in my face!
> Nice move, wrong place
> I'd been thinkin' 'bout bouillabaisse
> Excuses came at a manic pace
> I guess you stressed about my race

> I remember you from before
> making eyes at me across the store
> I was not impressed
> Your psyche is a mess

> It's either one trip or another
> It seems you want to fuck a brother
> But if I fail to see your charms
> then that must mean I mean you harm

The song took off from there. It's one of my all-time favorite creative moments. My White Wife ™—then My White Girlfriend™—was snoring on the other side of the bed.

Seventy-five percent of my band was black. (The guitar god was Jewish.) We did very political rap over very hard rock, years before it was cliché. A typical gig consisted of me basically cussing out a bunch of drunk white people over blazing guitar riffs. Good times.

***

A while back, MWW™ and I went to the Rob Zombie show at The Warfield. Just before The Guy That Got Stabbed At Altamont became The Guy That Got Stabbed At Altamont, he was The Only Black Guy At Altamont. This fact is often overlooked, and it may have been lost on me too, the day of the Zombie show. Or not. I guess I decided to be primarily guided by the fact that Zombie mother fucking rules.

My White Wife ™ and I were apparently the only people at the Zombie show who had not been released from prison that morning. We were definitely the only people who did not have a tattoo on our neck. I was pretty much the smallest guy there. Out on the floor, second row, three feet from the stage, there were tiny rocker chicks, big skinheads, huge bikers, and us. The skin standing immediately behind me was wearing a T-shirt that bore the image of a bald eagle perched on a baseball bat in front of an American flag. Nice. I was starting to wonder what I'd gotten myself into, not to mention MWW™, who was only there because of me. But then Zombie came on.

He started with some new stuff, which was cool, then went from the *Educated Horses* album all the way back to *Devil Music Vol. 1*. Motherfuckers went crazy. Zombie kept it going with "House of 1000 Corpses," "Living Dead Girl," shit like that. I think I started to lose my mind during "Never Gonna Stop."

At some point, I became aware of a lot of jostling in the crowd and realized that I was in the mosh pit. It had moved over to where we were. MWW™ was edging away, staying just beyond the edge. I was differently inclined. So, for a while, I moshed. At one point I got sandwiched in by three stocky frat-looking boys and just Samsoned them all the fuck off me.

It got really crazy. They did "Superbeast." I lost it. There was a moment when, in the center of the chaos, I became still. Nothing touched me. And I lifted my head and cocked my ear and listened to something that wasn't there. Something in my head. I don't remember what it was.

I remember, I think it was during "More Human Than Human," I looked up at Zombie and our eyes met and I just *roared* at him. "GAAAAAAAAAAAAAGGGGHHHHH!!!!" I was *gone*.

Then they went into "The Lords of Salem" and it got *really* crazy and I got out while I was ahead. Only then did I see what I think was my own specially assigned security: a brother who looked an awful lot like Eazy E, wearing an All-Access Pass, just off the floor, very near. I gave him sweaty love. Props to The Warfield for special Black Guy at the Zombie Show security, if that's what that was.

Walking home in the aggro afterglow, I asked My White Wife ™ if she had ever seen me so amped before. She thought about it. "Yeah. When you were rapping." *Orale*.

The funny thing is that I feel pretty black. Not quite as black as I felt when I was rapping—I was being black for a living back then—but, overall, a damn sight blacker than I felt in my teens. Exactly how black I feel, quantitatively, is of course impossible to say. But it feels quite black. Call it, maybe almost as black as a black person who never wonders how black he feels.

Part IV.

I will close with two stories.

1. Several years ago, My White Wife ™ brought home that romantic comedy starring Queen Latifah and LL Cool J on DVD. I agreed to watch it with some reluctance. Even greater than general romantic comedy reluctance was the fact that I'd sat through Latifah's buddy movie with Steve Martin on DVD just a year or so earlier.

The Steve Martin movie was, at best, a tired *48 Hours* knockoff; at worst, it was a minstrel show. For the entire movie I had trusted the Queen to make the "white people do everything normal/black people do everything wild" theme of the film make sense and be worth it. Like, maybe, she was a billionaire genius who had a bet going with Oprah that she could make Steve Martin act a fool. Something. *Anything.* To the very end, I was certain that there would be some twist that explained and justified all I'd seen and heard. This was, after all, the Queen. Obviously, she would make it right.

I remember watching the credits roll up my TV screen. Sometimes there's a little bit more movie after the credits are done. I sat and watched the credits and waited. The DVD ended. Nothing. That was the whole thing.

And now, just a year later, I was faced with another DVD and I was tempted to watch it. This was still the Queen we were talking about. The Queen! *WHO you callin a .... U-N-I-T-Y! Yoouuu In Eye Tee Why, a-that's a-unity!* My turquoise/teal/maroon/gold argyle Kid & Play sweater is in a Webvan box in my closet. And so I agreed to at least start the romantic comedy with LL. We started the DVD after dinner and watched for about a half hour, until I fell asleep.

The next day, I announced stiffly to MWW™: "I cannot continue watching that movie. Do you know why? Because I am going to die one day."

***

2. One Saturday afternoon a couple of years ago, I was walking down the street in downtown San Francisco running errands. I was alone. I think, based on where I was, that I was going to the hardware store. Anyway, there was a woman sitting on a milk crate on the sidewalk. A black woman in maybe her 60s, or maybe just some hard 40s. She *seemed* homeless, whatever that means, but I saw no cup or sign. I kind of looked at her as I went by, but our eyes did not entirely meet, and we didn't speak as I passed.

But after I passed, when I was about 10 feet away, she called after me. "Boy, somebody put the love on you!"

I don't know what she saw. I was going to the hardware store. I was not strutting down the street holding a bouquet of daisies out in front of me. I was alone. I was not singing "My Girl." I was just walking down the street. Maybe she was psychic.

I stopped and went back. It had not been a question, but still I had to answer. I had to acknowledge.

"Yeah," is all I said. And we just looked at each other for a second. I was probably smiling. "Yeah." And then I went on.

I guess I'll keep doing whatever this is I'm doing.

Confessional: Hijacked
Ching-In Chen

1.

dear body invasive *notes from city march 19, 2003:*
linguists   *sister, the sky*

breathing here   *above us unstitches*
the boats
breaking
    I
don't like   *the morning the US began*

goodbyes stamped
    eyes restricted

ash-colored buttons
down   *the bombs and our brothers and sisters*
tongue   *need*
scratch *us*
        that

divination // erasure bird

naked   I *live in a house underground*
    eye burnt hurt // black
throat sea of gold *Lolita LeBrun lemonade, frybead, fried rice*
    urine *from the liberation lounge*

my tongue if *Oakland* her song

the canal   across my street, your   *bodies blocking the SF highway offramp*
figure slow where I *mob the Chinatown streets* made a map

of our incisions. that morning, your organ

my own unwillingness to give

2.

Eight years since I lived
in the Brownfist
Collective house, West
Oakland.
Collapsed collective
experiment.
Rolling revolutionary
spring rolls, listening
to the anti-war march on
the underground
kitchen radio.
I desired the flush
of crowds moving
forward on concrete,
banging gongs
with the Chinese
Progressive Association
elders, watching the
tango dancing against
war. I wasn't ready then
to hunker down
in my house, sliding
plates through the
kitchen wall.

Now, a new city, Milwaukee, with three socialist
mayors in its lineage. Emergency lights flashing,
familiar crisis, pack buses to the capital, early
morning coffee going down the lists, which category,
black marker legal, roll call chanting, highwire
voices. Bon Jovi blasting to the crowd on speakers,

firefighters erupt the crowd.

Solidarity, what it means, wind through your fingers,
icy mouth chant. Solidarity pressed up against the
window. Red hearts everywhere, classroom cutout
reminders, the labor of teachers.

What can we eliminate, what can we make do, what
can we scrap together. February 15, 2011.

3.

songs in the city with the fiery sheen:

in my pocket, i could
have kissed you deeply,
your teeth hooked

because you were here before they could remember
because they could not take no for an answer, because because bitter trade route
your heart is a transit station, I write down my esophagus,

face melting into *what printed on the chant sheet*

gutter, now your   *arrests*
song – blue river cloth *at the military recruitment station*

4.

Floating signs in the air
Imperial Walker
on the man's shoulder, left quadrant.
Gathering on Madison mud. Farmers and movie
stars, Kill the Bill tractors. Later, faces, clapping
hands, megaphone mouths set to a soundtrack

but every time you close your eyes Lies!

Plug ourselves into wireboard, keyboard, consensus.
Roll call in the meeting room, donated bagels, pizza
boxes amass, sleeping bag bodies underneath the
desks of fleeing senators. Door blockage, bodies
bodies bodies against the security guards who want
to take off their uniforms

but every time you close your eyes Lies!

Used-up fuel becoming litter, we do not want to be
dirty in the eyes of the camera. Put it in the bag, put
it in the bag, a small army of trash-pickers.
State officials say $7 million, cordon off speech zones
to the 1st floor. Young boys decide to hold their
space, issued a ticket.

but every time you close your eyes Lies!

5. *war profiteers* cut halfway by a dull *Neptune Orient Lines Ltd.'s APL unit*
Remembering the voices of America knife — takes up camp *Part of Oakland anti-war*
demonstration in the back of the throat. *Oakland police* All *inch-thick wooden dowels*
the voices lie with you down *concussion flash-bang grenades*
there where the still *tear gas*
birds migrate. my mouth *sting balls*
a door where i keep *projectiles*
my safe secret lovely. *grapefruit-sized welts*
small girls sit *refuse to disperse*

there keeping score. Note

6.

A Manifesto for Action

i've since left by   what we want

the window, waiting for silver

Promises are not enough

flame.

Notes:

Confessional 4: *"but every time you close your eyes Lies!"* is a line from Arcade Fire's "Rebellion (Lies)," a song used in Matt Wisniewski's "Wisconsin 'Budget Repair Bill' Protest" video.

Confessional 5: Italicized text borrowed from news coverage of the anti-war Port of Oakland action on April 7, 2003.

Confessional 6: "A Manifesto for Action," "what we want" and "Promises are not enough" are phrases borrowed from the Milwaukee Graduate Assistant Association's "A Manifesto for Action," published April 26, 2011 at http://mgaa.org/the-manifesto/

(Previously published in Conversations at a Wartime Cafe: a Decade of War, CreateSpace, 2011)

Painting a Body of Loss and Love in the Proximity of an Aesthetic
Chris Abani

1.

Everyone forgets that Icarus also flew.
–Jack Gilbert

And so as with many things, it begins with a war.

We had been traveling for days when that little plane touched down in Lisbon with only two out of its three wheels working. It listed to a stop and we emerged, a fat priest, a young photojournalist, my mother in her one faded African print dress and five children in little more than rags. The nuns met us with bristling beards and the warm embrace of old aunts and took us to a convent where it was impossible to hush the noise of four boys bouncing balls down hallowed halls. They loved all the attention I think, these women who had given their lives to God and silence unperturbed even by my baby sister who cried and cried because my mother's breasts were too dry and emaciated to make milk for her. And all those people in the street staring at this bedraggled white woman in a faded African print dress, worn flip flops and crazy white hair who trooped her black brood through the city center because she thought, why not see the sights while we wait for a plane to England. And the many, many old women who pushed sweets and their sadness into the hands of us grateful boys and bounced my crying sister on their laps trying to coax her to take her feed from a bottle all the time singing softly in Portuguese, silencie bebê pequeno, while my mother smiled and sipped gratefully on the free coffee strangers bought her in street cafes. And every night, in the convent after a meal of rice and pork too rich for hunger-taut bellies, we threw up contentedly while my mother washed and rewashed the same old dress, hanging it to dry from the convent balcony, her nude body singing to the night.

2.

All agree that it began with tracing an outline around a man's shadow
–Pliny the Elder

The quote above comes from a larger piece within Pliny the Elder's book, *Natural History*, and alludes to Pliny's attempts to trace the mythical origin of sculpture as an art-form; its very conception, when allegedly a potter's daughter traced a human figure on a wall from its shadow and began to mold a clay form from it. The myth, as Pliny recounts it, locates the impetus to make this work, this mark, to capture this shadow in the fact that the potter's daughter's lover was leaving to go abroad, perhaps to fight a war. That much remains obscured.

So it seems that the desire to make art, to draw the limits of the body, to create a simulacrum has its roots in loss; or at least, the possibility of loss. The need to remember, to create (or re-create) a body out of loss, but also against loss, and against forgetting, is what drives the artist. This intervention in the world is repeated through time and culture and place, regardless of the truth of this or any other myth. It can be argued that the creative process is a ritual of remembrance.

Consider the Catholic order of mass, as the priest raises the communion wafer and the chalice of wine, the moment he seeks, and the magic he is working is that of transubstantiation, the turning of bread and wine into the body and blood of Christ. More than the transformation of matter, is the transformation of the imagination; its very transubstantiation. The act of the ritual of mass is an elaborate ritual of remembrance, a mnemonic device that reminds us of the essential message of the Christ: my peace I give you. The idea of religion, of any religion, of a belief in deity or doctrine, is not what is important in this moment. It is just that the ritual of reclaiming loss has found expression most often within religion. In a sense, religion is a complex language for melancholy and nostalgia. What is important is the ritual, which helps orchestrate these creative interventions.

Perhaps in this age of photography and film, of being able to record images and videos on our cell phones, we overlook the importance of the rituals of making. Perhaps because we no longer carve plastic representations of these simulacra of loss with our very hands, with our sweat, we forget. But there is nothing sadder than a photograph. It is a reminder of that which we no longer have. Perhaps this sadness is the root of the instinctual fear that pre-technological cultures harbored for photographs. Not so much that their souls would be stolen, but rather that they realized upon seeing a photograph that its lifelessness reminded them that memory and its truth, its deeper value lies in what we bring to representation, not what the representation offers us. Denied the ritual of making, the recognition of loss becomes even more acute, but there is nothing to staunch the wound. It is no accident that most early photography was the recording of the dead.

It may be deliberate in Pliny's tale that it is a woman who stands at the liminal moment of birth, of the knowledge that ties remembrance to its physical double. Perhaps that kind of melancholy, that deep sorrowful knowledge is too much for men to bear. In his extended essay on memory, *Memoirs of the Blind,* Jacques Derrida writes about this desire we all have to mark loss, to record memory physically. Derrida argues that it is not that we desire to mark the moment of trauma, of the wound, but rather that we often need to and want to record the moment just before it. In all those trains that rode to the camps in Germany, people frantically drew, made marks in the wooden cattle cars. On Angel Island in San Francisco, we can see the same markings in the timber beams that held up the roof and in the frames of the double bunk beds made by early Chinese immigrants held there in limbo between the China they had left and the new land of promise just miles across the small bay. Marks made as talismans against loss. In this I think that Derrida and I agree; that to create the memory is to turn away from the moment, to remove one's gaze from the trauma and turn it instead to transubstantiation. We know it is through this ritual, however tangentially or deeply obscured the lens, that we can even begin to bear witness to these histories, these shadows of love and loss that we carry within us.

This raises the specter of art as witness.

3.

There is no evil angel, but love
–William Shakespeare

My mother is standing by the stove in the fading daylight. The kitchen is small, an adobe addition to the rest of the house. Its floors and walls of pounded earth that smelled damp and full of promise after a rain, and warm and crinkly when she baked cakes, the very pores of the floor and walls heavy with nutmeg.

There is one small window above the stove and the sun is slanting in at an angle, framing her hair in a halo. She is stirring a pot of stew, or soup, perhaps. I no longer remember the exact details of the food; I was five or thereabouts.

Around her on the floor, crunching underfoot every time she moves is glass, shards from the oven door, broken by my careless football.

She is crying and her face is swollen where my father's fist has hit her. An eye is half closed and there is blood from a broken lip. On the radio on the table by the eggs, Jane Birkin and Serge Gainsbourough are whispering through "Je T'aime."

Mom, I say softly, afraid to startle her, afraid of the look in her eyes. If she hears, she doesn't respond.

When I broke the glass on the oven, I ran and hid and wouldn't come out when my father called. So in anger at my defiance, he beat my mother. I watched from the cupboard under the sink. I didn't move, didn't come out to defend her, and didn't speak up. I am a coward.

I am not sure if she is crying from the beating, from loving him, or because of the broken oven that had survived a civil war but is now not likely to be replaced, and which, although we can't know that yet, would never bake right again.

4.

It was not night, not even when the darkness came
—WS Merwin

When we speak of art giving witness, we usually mean that we are attempting to give form, address or visibility to things that are often inexpressible such as the effects of terror, pain, destruction, and erasure. In this way, the idea of witness, of testimony, is seldom if ever linked to things that are wholesome in our cultures. We give testimony it seems to unveil the hidden, to restore the wished away, the instinct towards the erasure of shame.

To give witness is to create a common body of remembrance, one we can all share in, but beyond that, one that can and must necessarily offer us some kind of catharsis. This is what art strives to do. To build this body out of shared fears, and triumphs, and desires, nostalgia as it were, for something that maybe never existed. This is both the triumph of and the problem with art. It cannot speak of essential truths (if there is even such a thing), or even relative truths for that matter. It can only speak in approximation, because that is what allows everyone into the conversation. This is something writers and artists have always known because the truth of course is that we can never feel each others' pain, but only approach it by relating it in degrees to our own. That this trade in a mutual loss bridges the distance between self and other. We are, it seems, an intrinsically selfish species. In this way, I think, the common body of art, despite its protestations to the unsentimental, depends so fundamentally on this shared trade between love and loss.

The problems art faces then in giving witness are multiple. Here is short and by no way exhaustive list:

> To create a common body of remembrance or experience is to be thwarted or colored by our nostalgia, by our pain and by our worldview, at every turn.

> How do we as artists evoke an event without limiting ourselves to the literal?

> What happens when the event cleaves a space so large in the collective mind that art seems not only inadequate but also almost offensive as a form of address?

> How can artists work within and without binaries to create a kind of ambiguity and yet simultaneous specificity?

How do we create an empathetic yet reciprocal relationship between the art and the trauma/event?

Every true artist knows that art is a weak vehicle for addressing trauma in all its magnitude and yet it is the most durable, the most reliable one we have. In this way the witness of art transcends mere testimony, mere accounting, mere reportage, to define a space that allows for surrender and resistance to occur at once.

That witness works at all is in itself a small miracle. A miracle of what, you might ask? In the oblique way that much truth happens, this is in fact a kind of love. I mean this in the sense that James Baldwin did, the idea that any kind of honest interaction between people requires the relinquishing of parts of the self to each other. Witness is an act of love, not in the sense of the sentimental although that is certainly part of it. What I mean by love is the act of seeing. Why is seeing an act of love? It is perhaps the only true act of love. Seeing slows the world down, bringing it into focus, even for a moment, the object/subject of sight, imbuing it with worth and value, while also actively resisting its erasure. But more than that, seeing requires not turning away from difficulty to the safety of comfort. In a sense the need for safety seems to be at the heart of America's problems – that we will often give up our morality, our very humanity in exchange for that safety. Sometimes it is the safety of race, or nation or even of lack.

Witness works first by seeing and then by lingering. The seeing as I said slows everything down, and the layering creates a thickness, a mass that sits in our consciousness without threat, even if it does reek of menace. And this in turn allows us to approach by degrees, the violence of the event and the damage it leaves behind. The distance between the seeing and the mass is the impossibility of expression and this is conversely and paradoxically the very power of witness.

When we have large-scale tragedy, such as 9/11, Katrina or Haiti, it seems that the work of witness becomes easier. This I know is open to argument—many writers and artists felt silenced by the magnitude of the Jewish Holocaust for instance. But I think that I am referring to a different kind of ease, not the artistic impetus towards witness, but rather the reception of witness.

For as much as we resist it and don't like to think of this, art, in all its forms, includes an audience, a spectator, and a consumer. That fact often determines how we approach witness through art, but that is a somewhat different conversation. For now, it is enough to know that this complicated relationship is part of the process. As Ansel Adams says, there are always two people in every picture: the photographer and the viewer.

Let me however, return to the question of magnitude. Witness in the face of large communal tragedy is easier because we all feel connected to it at some level, we all have some collective stake in the event and witness here allows us to renew our common bonds through catharsis primarily because of a shared loss, or anger or even hate.

The difficulty of witness really begins when the event cannot muster this level of collective tragedy. When the event is about a singular life, even in the midst of that collective. A woman who dies of cancer, a child who dies in a car accident or an unknown woman raped in a war in the distant Congo – all require that in giving witness to it, the artist foregrounds the individual while also trying to create the sense of a larger tragedy, even by its absence within the work, an epic grandeur that can give everyone a stake in this singular life.

My own personal experience tells me that violence disrupts our balance, create a feeling of vertigo, the sense that everything clear about our morality, our ethics and about our worldview is spinning out of orbit so fast we can barely keep up. For most of us, art is the only way to arrest the speed of disintegration, to step back and get a hold of the fragments. Like when you break a vase and take a step back. We see at once the detail of pieces and the whole vase. Slowly we bend, pick up the first piece and consider it. This is witness.

This is to say that it is not the spectacle of the violence that we seek to show as artists, but its erasure of everything, including itself. For the artist, this erasure is created by a direct avoidance of detail or by a saturation of detail. Either of these effaces our ability to fully grasp and thus limit the tragedy through an easy comprehension. There then results a dynamic interaction between the thing itself, the very fact of it, the very materiality of it the event and its trace, its evocative power, its emotional depth, its ability to create expansiveness, to serve both as fact and symbol. In this way the singular life can bear witness to a tragedy larger than itself. This is my stubborn belief, my stubborn hope.

5.

Every time I ask growing writers why they write, they have well rehearsed answers like the following: I want to give voice to the voiceless. I want to speak for all those who cannot speak for themselves. I want to tell my story. I have a story to tell. I want to change things. I want to change the world. And on and on. My favorite one, because it is the closest to the truth I've heard on a first answer was: because I can.

None of these are the reasons why we write. These are the reasons we have come up with to justify why we write. To rationalize, to carve out a space for ourselves, to say we deserve to, we want to, we should be able to.

This is an understandable impulse because many of us live in worlds where writing is not allowed, where the idea of it, the privilege of it, is impossible to just accept either because of gender, or race, or class, or the expectations of others – the reasons are multiple; but the answers we give are answers to imaginary questions. When we give answers like the one above, what we are hearing are the following questions: Who told you that you could write? How dare you be so selfish? And who is going to look after the kids? And what makes you think this is any more than a pipe dream?

The problem is, we have forgotten the central question: why do you write? Why? This is the crux of craft. Until you know why you write, you often will never know what your moral and ethical dilemmas really are, you will never know how to shape characters and stories that live outside of your own neurosis.

While not every writer can phrase the exact reason, they can approximate the shape of the wound, because, yes, we are talking about wounds. These wounds are often nothing more than the narratives we have built up over the years around an imagined or real hurt. But having a wound is not the same as being wounded. The former shapes the desire of expression while the latter merely creates silence.

All writing, and in fact, it has been argued, all art, comes from an existential wound. These wounds themselves are not always dramatic, or caused by a big trauma, but they produce a seed, a trauma deep enough for us to grow the bacteria of narrative until after a while, the wound has no relation to the cause. Wounds are also never to be confused for suffering. The false suffering, to borrow a phrase from Jung, which is associated with art, is not the subject here.

For writers what matters is how to use this infection as the driving force, the very ash of our work. It doesn't matter what form the writing itself takes— Harlequin Romance, Detective Story or that genre that is in so much self-denial, literary fiction. What matters is that the knowledge of the infection allows the work to shift away from selfish interior gazing into a world that it is bigger than itself. It is the vulnerability that allows us to even contemplate the world and so the wound is what lends the work its direction, its outward thrust.

6.

> *There, in the aftermath, was the voice of a man — once the sweet, screwed-up boy...*
> - Eliza Grisworld (Sapphic Fragment)

We are in a car driving down a narrow tarred road. It is hot, very hot, and the dry dust of the harmattan season is blowing in the window. Nauseous and frightened I am on the front bench seat of an old car, the kind with a hand gearshift sandwiched between my father and mother.

My father is angry that I am sitting there, and every time he changes gear, he brings the metal rod of it down on my head with stinging blows that soon begin to draw sniffles and exacerbate my motion sickness.

It is 1970 and my first day back in Nigeria from London. I last saw my father in 1968 before we fled from the war, and I was three, and have no memory of him. We have been traveling all day, arriving in Lagos and being held in the airport in a hanger for hours while my mother is interrogated by an angry Army captain for being a Biafran supporter during the war. Finally we are released and fly in a tin can of a plane that still has bullet holes in the wings. So many holes that my brothers joked that we wouldn't need flaps, and that if we crashed into water we would be fine because we were flying in a sieve.

Finally we arrive at Enugu and meet my father who has been drinking while he waited. He is in a foul mood because he has been waiting. He is angry when I hide behind my mother and won't hug him.

Now in the car, he is shouting at me: Why are you such a sissy? Toughen up, this is Africa. Each word is wrenched out in a different gear, which hits my head in punctuation.

Finally I begin to retch and my mother opens the picnic hamper she had brought from England, especially for family trips like this, bought in Harrods at great expense, and pulls out a napkin and holds it to my mouth as I fill it.

My father screams angrily and comes to a rolling halt, and my mother opens the window and throws out the napkin with a look of infinite sadness. I watch the napkin fall into the underbrush, and my guilt unfurls.

7.

"They say it's the iron in the blood that resists transformation"
—Maureen Seaton

The problem of course is that witness cannot save lives directly, or even alter the course of current events necessarily; all artists know this. What we have is that we can create a shift in perspective, collectively or singularly, that can if not alter, at least dent, the current worldview. With enough blows, we hope that it can be hammered into something malleable yet beautiful. In my experience, this is important because worldview is everything.

Think if you will of Chekov's play, Uncle Vanya. This play ends in much the same way as it begins. It goes through the exploration of loss, of tragedy, of misery, yet in the end it all cycles back. No grand change has happened, no great revelation occurs. And so we ask, what is the point? And that perhaps is precisely the point—that we have to ask. Perhaps this is the most powerful act of rebellion there is, or can be. Think if you will of the idea of God, I mean here the idea that many of us either hold or grew up with: an omnipotent, omniscient, all loving being who has mapped out the best life for us all. And yet we pray. We ask him/her/it to daily change things for us, to alter the world in our favor. Is this act of prayer not then blasphemy? Is it not the questioning of God's order? I offer this not as a point of belief, but to demonstrate the real power of witness, which lies in the power of questioning, however self defeating the question may be. The very act of the question, what is the point, signals that the revolution has begun.

In the United States we are part of a culture that is obsessed on the one hand with the idea of truth telling, with the idea that there is a truth, and that this truth is found in fact and non-fiction, and that this truth once found will be our philosopher's stone; while on the other hand we are experts at denial, erasure, masters of deception, of lying, of mythmaking. So much so that the pursuit of truth, much like our inane pursuit of happiness, becomes the greatest barrier to it.

And this is where the wound and knowing it is important.

True writing, being a writer, is the struggle to wring meaning, to wring value to redeem even the most unredeemable thing, to find transformation in even the most heinous moments, to prove, through a very complex sophisticated telling, that every life can and does and in fact must have value. There is nothing else.

It doesn't matter what the cause of the trauma is, what the dimensions of it, what the pain of it is and how deep it runs, what the facts are, and who did it to us and when, we all write to seduce the world into seeing us as we would like to see ourselves. We are trying to revise the grand narratives of our lives; we are refugees from the world that most people have no choice but to live in, with all their being. We make it possible not only for ourselves, but to others who don't know how to sing, to make a song that makes living bearable. That is all. And yet what a privilege, what a burden, so we must step out of our own way, and yet, paradoxically, to do so, we must stand naked and, to paraphrase Martin Espada, be startled by the bedraggled image we see in the too brightly lit bathroom mirrors of the gas stations of our crossroads.

If we can at least agree on this, then we can perhaps begin to understand that all craft starts here, with a simple question, which most of us can never answer, but must: why do you write, really?

Second Wedding
Cristina García

My father cuts the fat off chicken thighs
    for my mother's arroz con pollo
while my husband-to-be sits
     wide-eyed   listening
to tales of our forebearers
                     in the mountains of Galicia
crooks who used to fatten sick cows
then sell them to unsuspecting peasants.

My beloved is from the honest heart-
    land   never stole so much as a pack
of gum.   What is he getting himself
in to?   Not the telling but the
                      pride
in the telling   how pulling a fast
one makes you smarter
               than anyone else.

Elias
Cristina García

He testified: half his life
in facilities

One of two
      only two
           of thousands
                released
Boys gone wrong
    told: worthless
    told: born bad
    told: can't change

What does forever mean
    when you're sixteen

Bazaar
Cristina García

Swallowing a monarch butterfly
sparks lifelong public eloquence.
Eating iguanas bestows cunning, the wisdom
to let predators amble past.
In ancient China, warriors ate the hearts
of their enemies for courage, to savor
the bitter ferocity of victory.
I've read poetry to my dog since he was a pup
but he still doesn't sing.
Must everything transferred be theft?
Energy doesn't disappear,
but recycles ad infinitum,
like reincarnation without the moral:
investment banker this life, cricket the next.
When that cricket is crushed by a passing
dung cart, where does its life force go?
The universe is the mother of all swindlers,
swapping watches for songs, songs for iguanas.

Raised by Crows
Rajiv Mohabir

before flying south, the koyal lays her egg
to be reared in a foreign language.
the koyal thrusts the eggs from the neat crow's nests
onto the unforgiving earth. their albumen and yolk
puddle on the ground. the young, owned by surrogates,
cannot find a reflection of themselves
in their new homes. this is simply the way it is
until the fledgling is pushed out
of the twigs and string, woven into a new web of difference.
i arrive to new york in summer too,
searching my face in the opaque reflections of the windows in the east village,
wielding an adulterous english, saying *neemakharam*
for *matricide*, instead of *to bite back the salting hand*
of indenture under the east india company,
i say *slavery*. here in this matted world of silks
and fast food i feathered into a beast my mother doesn't understand
why the child's body is so dark yet
speaks in pale ghostly shades not of a mother's tongue?
or why the linguistic sign is an arbiter
of the familial. i return to guyana-in-queens during the summer,
singing: *o jhulo jhulo kanhai palana* at the diwali-mela.
she buys us jamun and sapadilla
but the vendors don't recognize anything
but the skin of the *anya-vapa*, that bird raised by crows,
nurtured on a half-digested vocabulary
placed onto its tongue by Her Majesty's greed and sugar lust.
now in this creole city, they call us *coolie*,
which echoes the name of this fragile thing of feathers.
our names have become as the koyal's song
wafting from the tree line without hope

for a discernable point of origin.

Cover Scent
Rajiv Mohabir

beaver castoreum under the nails
rubbed raw the hunter's hand

(he is lain on the trap too)

grated on steel and
deflated musk gland to draw the other

waiting in the bracken shadow,
of a jagged forest-line.

today the odium of salt and pheromones.

to erase himself he rubs the ashes
from a burnt wand of fleabane

on his dusk arms and forest chest—

*

against the sum, he holds
a picture of himself he wishes to erase:

outside the other boy's house
an eastern cottontail hides three kits.

he lies naked with another boy in a clearing
of palmettos and sand pines,

the first time they touch each other
was with rabbit skinned gloves.

Body
(an excerpt from *Leaving India*)
Minal Hajratwala

To assimilate means to give up not only your history but
your body, to try to adopt an alien appearance because your
own is not good enough, to fear naming yourself lest name
be twisted into label . . .

—Adrienne Rich

Deep in the marrow of every story is a silence. Having struggled, all these
pages, to be transparent, not to overwhelm the stories of others with my own,
now it is my turn to emerge, solid. And I hardly know where to begin. I have
practiced the art of submergence—invisibility, assimilation—all my life. To
metamorphose, now, from neutral narrator to embodied character, self, seems
a great act of exposure. Vulnerability, guilt, freedom, sympathy: Which thread
shall I pull first? How shall I unravel or construct, from all of my memories
and aches, one true pattern, one set of possibilities—one spine?

I might have been named Gita, Saroj, or Sudha. I might have had trouble
in school, been raised under the shadow of Mars, and brought good luck to my
house. The telegram my father sent from San Francisco to Fiji at my birth was
un-mystical:
BABY GIRL BORN 742 PM MONDAY JULY 12TH STOP
BHANU AND MINAL IN GOOD HEALTH LETTER
FOLLOWS BHUPENDRA

It was 1971. My grandmother in Fiji forwarded the vital information—
date, time, time zone—to her astrologer in India. He wrote my horoscope,
which predicted all of the above. Based on an ancient calculus, the stars said
my name should start with G or S. My grandmother sent a gift for "Gita."

But I had already been named, as my parents reminded her: *meen*
meaning "fish," *al* meaning "like." *Minal*, she who is like a fish. They were
college-educated, beyond superstition; they had named me for a friend of my
mother's, just because they liked the sound of the name. They declined to read
the trajectory of my life ahead of time: lucky and unlucky years, characteristics
of a compatible mate, probable paths of education, marriage, and health. Nor
did they perform the sixth-night ceremony, when a pencil and paper are placed
under the baby's crib, for the goddess of destiny to write.

And so I was raised free of predestination.

But not entirely.

My parents believed in destiny, even as they doubted the importance of ritual in shaping it; and the telegram my father received that day—the job offer from the south of the planet—was a kind of proof. With or without a written horoscope, I entered the world with a lucky footprint.

Within six months I was an emigrant, collecting the first international stamp on my passport. I slept all the way from San Francisco to New Zealand in an airline bassinet, aided by a lick of whiskey.

In the normal manner, I progressed from howling to cooing to, eventually, words. In New Zealand I believed we had our own special language, a delightful singsong made up by my parents. It was a code we could use in the public park, where we fed our stale bread-ends from the week to the ducks, or in the grocery store to discuss the funny-looking woman nearby, say, or complain about prices that were too high. No one could decipher our secrets. We used it just for fun, too: My mother said it was time to *inter-pinter* the laundry, to move it from washer to dryer. A bumpy road was so *gaaber-goober*, she complained. She could double any word or name to humorous effect, or for emphasis: Minal Binal, TV BV, bowling phowling.

It was only when we visited India, when I was four years old, that I understood there was a world of other people who spoke the same funny way. Gujarati was a lilting, rhyming language, and with a child's knack I absorbed it completely in the six weeks of our visit. By the time we left India, I had forgotten all of my English.

. . .

I never thought of myself as an immigrant until I began writing this book. Because I was born in San Francisco and now live in San Francisco, my mind skipped over the years of disruption in between; I believed I was only the child of immigrants, the so-called second generation. But the truth is, I have lived through multiple migrations, shifts from one world to another; and these geographic shifts were mirrored and amplified into emotional, mental, and even sexual ones. Each time I cross a border, I feel the push and pull in my body, a cacophony of competing desires. And always there are choices to make: what to assimilate, what to reject. Is it true that we are always, as migrants, and the children of migrants, attempting to choose what my parents call "the best of both worlds"? Or is it possible to transcend—no, not transcend, but enter into—the dualism, the splitting, the uncertain interstices between the worlds? Is it possible to integrate, even heal, the trauma of crossing; of many crossings?

Back home in New Zealand, my Kiwi babysitter was forced to learn a few basic words in Gujarati for a few weeks, until my tongue acclimated again. *Water, hungry, yes, no.* Eventually I would become adept, like all children raised with more than one language, at code-switching, knowing instinctively when to use Gujarati and when to use English. Meanwhile Mrs. Maclean acquired *pani, bhukh, haa, naa*. She fed me Jell-O and a soft-boiled egg for lunch every weekday while my parents were at work. She was our next-door neighbor, and my mother also traded recipes with her—rotli for trifles, curries for brandy snaps. Her daughters, Philippa and Vicki, became my best friends. We were partners in spitting watermelon seeds, hunting for golf balls on the nearby course, and taking swim lessons at the Y. We watched television, and I developed a secret crush on Adam West as Batman. I called their grandmother Gram, and had no memory of my own.

Five years old, I walked unchaperoned—the streets were that safe—every day to and from Maori Hill Elementary School, which, despite being named for the indigenous people of New Zealand, was populated by a couple of hundred white children, one Maori boy, and me. My teachers had innocent, storybook names: Mrs. Lion, Mrs. Stringer, Miss Babe. Once I lost a 24-karat gold earring on the way to school; a neighbor's son found and returned it. And when one of my kindergarten classmates asked his mother, *Why don't Minal's hands ever get clean?* and she reported this to my mother, they simply laughed: Kids say the darnedest things.

I remember our years in New Zealand as happy ones. Traveling back, I have felt a nostalgia for its green hills and cool southern fog, an unaccountable joy, even a sense of home—the original landscape that my body remembers. But when I was six years old, I began peeling the skin from my lips, obsessively, till they bled. My parents tried everything: scolding, spanking, a trip to the pediatrician. I remember the bitter taste of iodine on my fingers, the night mittens; but none of it worked.

I believe that as children we know things, in an almost prescient way, as animals understand earthquakes; that we absorb mysterious signals, the unspoken anxieties of adults, and the plans that are being hatched around us. Did I sense that my parents were planning to shift continents again, and that they were (although they did not say so, perhaps not even to themselves) afraid? Did I take this fear, worry, and uncertainty into my own small body? When I was seven years old, the world changed.

My parents had decided to move back to the United States. When they broke the news, they tried to sweeten the deal: in America they would buy me one new doll every month, for a whole year. Like legions before me, I was seduced by the New World's promise of wealth beyond imagination.

After touching down in Los Angeles, we toured Disneyland and I picked up a Mickey Mouse cap with ears and my name embroidered in yellow script. This rite of passage was followed by a series of moves whose reasons I understood, vaguely, as being connected to my father's work. Of Gainesville, Florida, I remember the terror of roaches, which I had never seen before. In Iowa City, where we lived for a year, our lives seemed brushed by a glamour that only America could offer. One of my classmates was the son of a minor television star. My best friends were redheaded twins whose father had spent time in India and given them Indian names; when I went to their house for a sleepover, I saw with amazement that they each read a book at the dinner table. The twins borrowed my Indian outfits, and my mother choreographed a Gujarati folk dance at our school's winter show. Christmas was, for the first time, storybook white, and important. My parents bought a plastic tree and gifts, to help us fit in. I sang Christmas carols in my second-grade classroom, where we stood for the Pledge of Allegiance every morning and had *The Hobbit* read aloud to us every afternoon. I learned to ice-skate, to sled, to transform deep drifts of snow into roly-poly men and hollow angels.

By the time my father found a permanent position in Michigan, we all had migration fatigue. With each move, I had had to start over: friends, neighborhoods, teachers, schoolyard lingo.

Looking through old class photos, I can't play the *Which one am I?* game with current friends or lovers. Every picture has only one brown girl. Here she is with babyish pigtails, here with a sixth grader's version of a sophisticated braid; here with eyeglasses, now braces; embarrassing shadow of mustache; eyeliner and lipstick; straight teeth, feathered hair, contact lenses. Which one am I? The answer is clear, yet I hardly recognize myself. I was a foreigner to everyone around me, and therefore to myself as well.

And was this queer feeling a part of my destiny, a quirk of history, or some mixture of both? Was it the rich soil in which a certain sense of being different would later take root? Was it a predictor of how I would choose to live my life?

Paper Walls
Jo Reyes-Boitel

one finger is damaged in making a phone call
and another still able to point out
the bad word used in place of please

how one hand can reach another's room
palm against the walls   some hands aren't as telepathic
feel no trigger of heat during the pacing of floorboards
the cadence of vibrations toward outer walls

damaged the tendons of the palm
the structure of the house
when a country on the other side of the world collapses

Far Flung Heart
Jo Reyes-Boitel

1.
Manuela's had her arm
amputated

she still chases the kids
around the front yard and into the ocean.

Normita's medicine keeps
getting stronger, her body

at ease with barbiturates
in place of vitamins.

2.
My mother says she didn't come by boat
but by plane, leaving and landing on cement.

A Cuban will say their life is told in their feet
whether they will be *simpático*
or a villain.

Just before leaving
she should have touched a little ocean
as protection by La Virgen de Cobre.

Her landing would have been softer.

3.
Tio Candy is so fat he's shiny
and his nephew, Hector, working himself
mad in this country, has just bought a house.

On any given day Hector will say
Candido has wasted money on women
and all the whiskey sleeping in his belly.

And Candido, arm outstretched in a toast, will hum
¡Que me mata una mujer!

Dark Mother
Jo Reyes-Boitel

arms extended
luminous dark   the night sky
stars   markers for those pains
healed into brilliance

humid air surrounding her
radiance of waters
welcoming yemaya

yemaya, mother of fishes,
yemaya, rejoicing in oya

oya   our first and last breath
her arms forming the center of our lives
the hurricane of the world outside
oya   sheltering

Lessons
an excerpt from *We the Animals*
Justin Torres

1. WE WANTED MORE

We wanted more. We knocked the butt ends of our forks against the table, tapped our spoons against our empty bowls; we were hungry. We wanted more volume, more riots. We turned up the knob on the TV until our ears ached with the shouts of angry men. We wanted more music on the radio; we wanted beats, we wanted rock. We wanted muscles on our skinny arms. We had bird bones, hollow and light, and we wanted more density, more weight. We were six snatching hands, six stomping feet; we were brothers, boys, three little kings locked in a feud for more.

When it was cold, we fought over blankets until the cloth tore down the middle. When it was really cold, when our breath came out in frosty clouds, Manny crawled into bed with Joel and me.

'Body heat,' he said.

'Body heat,' we agreed.

We wanted more flesh, more blood, more warmth.

When we fought, we fought with weapons – boots and garage tools, snapping pliers – we grabbed at whatever was nearest and we hurled it through the air; we wanted more broken dishes, more shattered glass. We wanted more crashes.

And when our Paps came home, we got spankings. Our little round butt cheeks were tore up: red, raw, leather-whipped. We knew there was something on the other side of pain, on the other side of the sting. Prickly heat radiated upward from our thighs and backsides, fire consumed our brains, but we knew that there was something more, some place our Paps was taking us with all this. We knew, because he was meticulous, because he was precise, because he took his time.

And when our father was gone, we wanted to be fathers. We hunted animals. We drudged through the muck of the creek, chasing down bullfrogs and water snakes. We plucked the baby robins from their nest. We liked to feel the beat of tiny hearts, the struggle of tiny wings. We brought their tiny animal faces close to ours.

'Who's your daddy?' we said, then we laughed and tossed them into a shoebox.

Always more, always hungrily scratching for more. But there were times, quiet moments, when our mother was sleeping, when she hadn't slept in two days, and any noise, any stair creak, any shut door, any stifled laugh, any voice at all, might wake her – those still, crystal mornings, when we wanted to protect her, this confused goose of a woman, this stumbler, this gusher, with her backaches and headaches and her tired, tired ways, this uprooted Brooklyn creature, this tough talker, always with tears when she tells us she loves us, her mixed-up love, her needy love, her warmth – on those mornings, when sunlight found the cracks in our blinds, and laid itself down in crisp strips on our carpet, those quiet mornings, when we'd fixed ourselves oatmeal, and sprawled on to our stomachs with crayons and paper, with glass marbles that we were careful not to rattle, when our mother was sleeping, when the air did not smell like sweat or breath or mould, when the air was still and light, those mornings, when silence was our secret game and our gift and our sole accomplishment – we wanted less: less weight, less work, less noise, less father, less muscles and skin and hair. We wanted nothing, just this, just this.

2. HERITAGE

When we got home from school Paps was in the kitchen, cooking and listening to music and feeling fine. He whiffed the steam coming off a pot, then clapped his hands together and rubbed them briskly. His eyes were wet and sparkled with giddy life. He turned up the volume on the stereo and it was mambo, it was Tito Puente.

'Watch out,' he said, and spun, with grace, on one slippered foot, his bathrobe twirling out around him. In his fist was a glistening, greasy metal spatula, which he pumped in the air to the beat of the bongo drums.

My brothers and I, the three of us, stood in the entrance to the kitchen, laughing, eager to join in, but waiting for our cue. He staked staccato steps across the linoleum to where we stood and whipped Joel and Manny on to the dance floor, grabbing their wimpy arms and jerking them behind him. Me he took by the hands and slid between his legs and I popped up on the other side of him. Then we wiggled around the kitchen, following behind him in a line, like baby geese. We rolled our tiny clenched fists in front of us and snapped our hips to the trumpet blasts.

There were hot things on the stove, pork chops frying in their own fat, and Spanish rice foaming up and rattling its lid. The air was thick with steam and spice and noise, and the one little window above the sink was fogged over.

Paps turned the stereo even louder, so loud that if I screamed no one would have heard me, so loud that my brothers felt very far away and hard to get to, even though they were right there in front of me. Then Paps grabbed a can of beer from the fridge and our eyes followed the path of the can to his lips. We took in the empties stacked up on the counter behind him, then we looked at each other. Manny rolled his eyes and kept dancing, and so we got in line and kept dancing too, except now Manny was the Papa Goose, it was him we were following.

'Now shake it like you're rich,' Paps shouted, his powerful voice booming out over the music. We danced on tiptoes, sticking up our noses and poking the air above us with our pinkies.

'You ain't rich,' Papi said, 'Now shake it like you're poor.'

We got low on our knees, clenched our fists and stretched our arms out on our sides; we shook our shoulders and threw our heads back, wild and loose and free.

'You ain't poor neither. Now shake it like you're white.'

We moved like robots, stiff and angled, not even smiling. Joel was the most convincing, I'd see him practising in his room sometimes.

'You ain't white,' Paps shouted. 'Now shake it like a Puerto Rican.'

There was a pause as we gathered ourselves. Then we mamboed as best we could, trying to be smooth and serious and to feel the beat in our feet and beyond the beat to feel the rhythm. Paps watched us for a while, leaning against the counter and taking long draws from his beer.

'Mutts,' he said. 'You ain't white and you ain't Puerto Rican. Watch how a purebred dances, watch how we dance in the ghetto.' Every word was shouted over the music, so it was hard to tell if he was mad or just making fun.

He danced and we tried to see what separated him from us. He pursed his lips and kept one hand on his stomach. His elbow was bent, his back was straight, but somehow there was looseness and freedom and confidence in every move. I tried to watch his feet but something about the way they twisted and stepped over each other, something about the line of his torso, kept pulling my eyes up to his face, to his broad nose and dark, half-shut eyes and his pursed lips, which snarled and smiled both.

'This is your heritage,' he said, as if from this dance we could know about his own childhood, about the flavour and grit of tenement buildings in Spanish Harlem, and projects in Red Hook, and dance halls, and city parks, and about his own Papi, how he beat him, how he taught him to dance, as if we could hear Spanish in his movements, as if Puerto Rico was a man in a bathrobe, grabbing another beer from the fridge and raising it to drink, his head back, still dancing, still stepping and snapping perfectly in time.

3. THE LAKE

One unbearable night, in the middle of a heatwave, Paps drove us all to the lake. Ma and I didn't know how to swim, so she grabbed on to Papi's back and I grabbed on to hers and he took us on a little tour, spreading his arms before him and kicking his legs underneath us, our own legs trailing through the water, relaxed and still, our toes curled backward.

Every once in a while Ma would point out some happening for me to look at, a duck touching down on to the water, his head pulled back on his neck, beating his wings before him, or a water bug with spindly legs that dimpled the lake's surface.

'Not so far,' she would say to Papi, but he'd push on, smooth and slow, and the shore behind would stretch and thin and curve, until it was a wooded crescent impossibly dark and remote.

In the middle of the lake the water was blacker and cooler, and Paps swam right into a clump of slimy tar-black leaves. Ma and I tried to splash the leaves away from us, but we had to keep one arm holding on, so they ended up curling around in our jetty and sticking to our ribs and thighs like leeches. Paps lifted a fistful into the air and the leaf clump melted through the cracks in his fingers and disintegrated into speckles in the water and cigarette-sized fish appeared and nibbled at the leaf bits.

'We've come too far,' Ma said. 'Take us back.'

'Soon,' Papi said.

Ma started talking about how unnatural it was that Paps knew how to swim. She said that no one swam in Brooklyn. The most water she ever saw in one place was when one of the men from the block would open up the johnny pump, and water would rush and pour forth. She said that she never jumped through the spray like the other kids – too hard and mean and shocking – but instead she liked to stand further down, where the sidewalk met the street, and let the water pool around her ankles.

'I had already been married and pushed out three boys before I ever stepped into anything deeper than a puddle,' she said.

Papi didn't say when or where he had learned to swim, but he generally made it his business to learn everything that had to do with survival. He had all the muscles and the will, and he was on his way to becoming indestructible.

'I guess it's opposite with you, isn't it?' Ma called back to me. 'You grew up with all these lakes and rivers, and you got two brothers that swim like a couple of goldfish in a bowl – how come you don't swim?'

She asked the question as if she was meeting me for the first time, as if the circumstances of my life, my fumbling, terrifying attempts at the deep end, the one time at the public pool, when I had been dragged out by the high-school lifeguard and had puked up pool water on to the grass, 700 eyes on me, the din of screams and splashes and whistles momentarily silenced as everyone stopped to ponder my bony weakness, to stare and stare, waiting for me to cry, which I did – as if it had only just now occurred to Ma how odd it was that I was here, clinging to her and Paps, and not with my brothers who had run into the water, dunked each other's heads down, tried to drown each other, then ran back out and disappeared into the trees.

Of course, it was impossible for me to answer her, to tell the truth, to say I was scared. The only one who ever got to say that in our family was Ma, and most of the time she wasn't even scared, just too lazy to go down into the crawlspace herself, or else she said it to make Paps smile, to get him to tickle and tease her or pull her close, to let him know she was only really scared of being without him. But me, I would have rather let go and slipped quietly down to the lake's black bottom than to admit fear to either one of them.

But I didn't have to say anything, because Paps answered for me.

'He's going to learn,' he said. 'You're both going to learn,' and no one spoke after that for a long time. I watched the moon break into shards of light across the lake, I watched dark birds circle and caw, the wind lifted the tree branches, the pine trees tipped; I felt the lake get colder, and I smelled the dead leaves.

Later, after the incident, Paps drove us home. He sat behind the wheel, still shirtless, his back and neck and even his face a cross-hatch of scratches, some only deep red lines and broken skin, some already scabbing, and some still glistening with fresh blood, and I too was all scratched up – for she had panicked, and when he slipped away she had clawed on top of me – later, Paps said, 'How else do you expect to learn?'

And Ma, who had nearly drowned me, who had screamed and cried and dug her nails down into me, who had been more frenzied and wild than I had ever known her to be – Ma, who was so boiling angry that she had made Manny sit up front with Paps and she had taken the middle back, wrapping her arms around us – Ma replied by reaching across me and opening the door as we sped along. I looked down and saw the pavement rushing and blurring beneath, the shoulder dropping away into a gravel pit. Ma held open that door and asked, 'What? You want me to teach him how to fly? Should I teach him how to fly?'

Then Paps had to pull over and calm her down. The three of us boys jumped out and walked to the edge and took out our dicks and pissed down into the ditch.

'She really clawed you up like that?' Manny asked.

'She tried to climb on to my head.'

'What kind of…' he started to say, but didn't finish. Instead, he picked up a rock and hurled it out away from him as far as he could.

From the car, we heard the noises of their arguing, we heard Ma saying over and over, 'You let me go. You let me go,' and we watched the big trailers haul past, rumbling the car and the ground underneath our feet.

Manny laughed. He said, 'Shit, I thought she was gonna throw you out of the car.'

And Joel laughed too. He said, 'Shit. I thought you were gonna fly.'

When we finally returned to the car, Ma was up front again, and Paps drove with one hand on the back of her neck. He waited until the perfect moment, until we'd settled into silence and peace and we were thinking ahead, to the beds waiting for us at home, and then he turned his head to the side, glancing at me over his shoulder, and asked, all curious and friendly, 'So, how'd you like your first flying lesson?' And the whole car erupted in laughter; all was okay again.

But the incident itself remained, and at night, in bed, I remembered how Paps had slipped away from us, how he looked on as we flailed and struggled, how I needed to escape Ma's clutch and grip, how I let myself slide down and down, and when I opened my eyes what I discovered there: black-green murkiness, an underwater world, terror. I sank down for a long time, disoriented and writhing, and then suddenly I was swimming – kicking my legs and spreading my arms just like Paps showed me, and rising up to the light and exploding into air, and then that first breath, sucking air all the way down into my lungs, and when I looked up the sky had never been so vaulted, so sparkling and magnificent. I remembered the urgency in my parents' voices, Ma wrapped around Papi once again, and both of them calling my name. I swam towards their bobbing mass and there under the stars, I was wanted. They had never been so happy to see me, they had never looked at me with such intensity and hope, they had never before spoken my name so softly.

I remembered how Ma burst into tears and Paps celebrated, shouting as if he was a mad scientist and I a marvel of his creation:

'He's alive!'

'He's alive!'

'He's alive!'

Starfoods, NYC, 2:45am
Mai Perkins

friday night Freedom
revival of New Jack Swing
hip hop's sanctuary
the house of House
and *in* I jump,
hips first—
past cliques of eyeballs and attitudes
anchored in the *boom* of the jam.
    I don't skim turbulence
searching thresholds for scooting in
but rather *lively up* my own
by way of uninhibited
rip-roar—

Karavas, West 4th @ Cornelia Street, NYC
Mai Perkins

"Why not wear a kimono to the West African dance class?" – Anon (lover of life)

The only place
you're likely to find a couple
of Japanese lads, in the middle
of a Greek bar, break
dancing to the *guajira-son,*
"Guantanamera"
is hidden deep in the heart
of The Village—

I find my bliss
within this urbane mélange: an old song
arranged new.

Aiyah!
Sasha Hom

Mom talks about death like it's a long walk to the supermarket.

"When I go, you can have my engagement ring. It's platinum. But you might have to cut off my finger if my knuckles haven't shrunk."

"When I go, cremate me. But wait three days. Otherwise the body can still feel pain."

"Go where?" I always ask, trying to make her name it.

But Mom just laughs at me.

I am in the fourth grade when Poh-Poh gets murdered. I go to Malcolm X Elementary school with five-hundred other kids who run forever across the concrete. Empty hallways, clanging radiators, blood stains and bubble gum. Shibu Inu stabbed Rottweiller with a knife after assembly last week.

"Life is hell and hell is school," Mom says.

During recess we chase leaves, throw rocks and break each other's pencils. We are surrounded by a mile of cyclone fencing. There is only one tree inside the yard. We stand beneath it with our necks tilted towards the sky, waiting faithfully for the leaves to fall so we can smash them between our palms.

I am in Mrs. Jones' class. She is wide as a desk and suffocates us in her breasts whenever she hugs us. She smells of lemons. During class she yells at the kids who throw paper and take the Lord's name in vain. When she makes us read aloud from World History, I sit under my desk. I suck on the ends of chicken bones saved from last night's dinner, smuggled inside my sleeve, and I read Prince Caspian, Ozma of Oz, and The Lord of the Rings. I read any book that comes in a series.

I walk home from the bus stop looking down at my feet.

Step on a crack, break your mother's back.

Step on a line, break your mother's spine.

My real mother is dead. She is spineless. Amoebic. Mom says she was probably unwed and, in Korea, if you have a baby out of wedlock, your family will disown you, like she was disowned for dating a Japanese in college. Her father, my Gung-Gung, disowned her because the Japanese killed his mother and baby brother back in China.

At Malcolm X I find out that I am not white. The girls' bathroom is damp and cold. I am tap dancing and holding my crotch. Laying tiny squares of stiff paper onto the seat as I try not to pee in my pants. They slip one by one into the bowl.

Two girls walk into the bathroom. "You know white people just sit on the toilet seats?"

"Nuh uh?"

"Yep, they just sit they white butts down."

"No way. That's nasty."

"Uh huh."

They flush, then walk away, and I sit finally on the patch worked paper covering the seat, peeing with relief into the bowl.

Chi-neese, Japa-neese, Knees, look at these.

I am not Chinese, even though my parents are. I am not Japanese either. But Gung-Gung says it doesn't matter, the Japanese hated my people too.

I was born in Korea, when the tiger was chasing a rabbit, torn in half like the moon. She left me on a river stone, a park bench, a door step, a front lawn. Three days old squinting at the sun.

At school, I am the kid who thinks she's a dog. I wear my keys with bells around my neck to sound like one, and carry my dog book with me so I can identify all the breeds. I get lice. Mom picks the nits out of my head. I pull the gray hairs out of hers while we watch TV. Chitty Chitty Bang Bang. The Price is Right. Petticoat Junction. Mom laughs at us and says we are monkeys. Dad comes out of the bathroom with his pants around his knees cussing at Mom for not replacing the toilet paper. Mom calls him a baboon and we laugh.

On the playground, there is a wooden bench between tanbark and concrete. I sit behind it and drill a hole with the key that hangs around my neck. When it is deep enough, I will put my key inside it and it will turn. A door will appear like a portal, taking me to my real home where they are waiting, seated around a kitchen table with a cup of cocoa, the kind with the marshmallows that dissolve.

Mom believes in portals, alien abductions and the truth found in the lines of your palm. She went searching for other worlds on Mt. Shasta, but left me at home with Dad with a list of meals I could make us: Hungry Man Fried Chicken Dinner; Spam and rice; bok choy with oyster sauce, egg and rice; Mac 'n Cheese with rice.

She never found the portal. "It's okay," she said standing in the doorway with her crystals. "I'll get there when its my time."

During Science, I sit inside the cupboard. The door is closed. It is dark. Nobody noticed me before. Now Mrs. Jones pulls me out into the hallway and talks about her daughter who drowned. She says, "I know what it's like to lose someone like that. You can talk to me." But she is wrong. Poh-Poh did not drown in a lake, she was shot in her basement closet.

Mom says psychics are cheaper than therapists. They can look at the stars and see backwards. "No use wasting your time when you're being charged by the hour," she says. Mom shows me her coupon: World Class Psychic! 99.9% Accuracy rate! 20% Discount When You Bring In This Ad! She throws me a dress over the backseat of the VW Van. The car's horn is missing a screw. It beeps and beeps and beeps at unpredictable moments and intervals. I do not want to wear the dress. Mom pulls my sweatshirt off, my favorite one with the hole over the eye of the St. Bernard. I start to whine. "If you cry, I'll burn it."

"The Goddess is Alive and Magic is Afoot," says a framed bumper sticker over the psychic's mantel. Petey is a Budgie flapping her mouth at my mother. We are sitting in her dark living room. Petey's legs, folded beneath her. My mother hugging her purse like a pillow. There is a glass coffee table with a few dirty dishes shoved beneath it.

"How can I be of assistance to you today?" asks Petey.

Mom brushes the hair from her face, a habit like smiling at herself in any reflection. "My mother was murdered and I want to make sure she has made it okay. That she isn't stuck somewhere. I mean, it was so sudden and I just want to do something to help her and if she hasn't already made it..."

"What do you think?" asks Petey. "Do you think she is at rest?"

Not Heaven. Not hell. Not rest. Not under. Ground. Gone home.

"No." Mom says. "That's why I'm here."

Poh-Poh prefers ghosts to TV "Because they talk back." In the mornings, she hocks loogies into the sink. Stares out the windows in the hills, looks out over the bay at the boats. Poh-Poh was an orphan like me. Her mother died shortly after she was born and her father left her with the neighbors while he went back to China to look for a new wife. He is still sailing on the seas.

"She is lost," says Petey. "She has a very difficult journey. A lot to learn, there is..."

On Fridays I spend the night with Poh-Poh. On those Mah Jong nights, Poh-Poh feeds me ham hock jouk in ceramic bowls. She uses the bottoms of the bowls to sharpen knives. At night she puts a face cloth between me and the sink, so my nighty doesn't get wet as I brush my teeth. In the mornings when she puts on her make up she says she is putting on her face. At night, she takes it off.

"Aiyah!" Poh-Poh says chattering in Chinese. "The Mah Jong Ladies." She holds open her front door and hides the Quan Yin statue behind it, as Daisy, Pearl and, May file in. Poh-Poh is wearing her lucky jewelry.

Mom is a believer in karma, but Poh-Poh is a believer in luck. The only times Mom yells, Aiyah, is when I leave footprints on the walls while trying to kill flies. She pays me a penny a fly. Poh-Poh pays a nickel a snail.

At bedtime on Mah Jong nights, I have to go to bed with my snoring grandfather. Even though Gung-Gung snores I can still hear ivory bones clacking across the card table.

"Aiyah!"

"Aiyah!" I listen for her laugh from the bedroom.

"Aiyah!" Head thrown back, mouth open wide, teeth exposed for all to see.

"Aiyah!" Gung-Gung, pointing at the evening news screaming. "See, always Bok we. Can't trust hak we. Only Chi-Nese!"

"Aiyah!" Mah Jong pieces singing across the table.

Back home it would be college students next door having parties, Mom screaming out her bedroom window, "Shut the fuck up or I'll call the police!" Mom and Dad fighting and cussing. "Asshole. Bitch." Doors slamming shut. Then Mom in bed with me talking about running away to the circus. She will ride the elephants in sequins and feathers, so beautiful beneath the spotlight. I will be a clown and the cows can chase me.

I wait for the smell of sleep. Oil of Olay and apricots. Heavy eyes. I dream and listen.

Caverns like classrooms. Flooding. A high moon tide. Drowning mice. Smashing starfish against stone. Storm drains and creeks. The rats dog paddling for the shore. Open sky.

"Let's chant for her. We'll form a circle and hold hands," says Petey. "If I can have a moment of silence I can see if I can establish communication with her."

Mom is just like Poh-Poh sometimes. Superstitious. Overzealous whenever there's a sale on meat, and an unreliable narrator.

I am inspecting Petey's dirty dishes under the glass coffee table: a bowl with dried cereal stuck to the sides and a shallow white puddle in the bottom; a cup with pink lip marks on the rim and something dried and brown inside; a spoon, a fork, and an empty crumpled package of Sweet and Low.

Petey is inspecting me.

"Is she okay?" she asks my mother as she points at me. "How old is she again?"

No one answers Petey's question. She's psychic. She should know.

"Okay." Petey sighs and puts her arms down. Shakes them before folding them into her lap. In the distance, a car alarm goes off. A dog is barking. There is dirt beneath my fingernails. Gung-Gung is the one to gouge the dirt out with a toothpick whenever I come over to visit.

Petey repeats herself. "Okay. Okay. I see her in a dark hallway. She is confused. Okay. I think you're right. She's still confused. Funny, I see your father there with her, it's as if he's trying to help her die. Okay. He feels guilt about her death. His higher consciousness knows that it was supposed to be him who passed first, but she decided to take his place instead. Oh. Wait. She says she got tired of waiting. Okay. What was her name again?"

Mom's nose is running, but her eyes are dry. She says she spent her whole childhood crying and it was a waste of time. "Her name is Doris."

"Doris, Doris. Okay. The front door is ruptured. The hallway."

On her open palm, Quan Yin holds tangerines with the stems and leaves intact, an offering for any old crazy who walks through her door. At the top of the stairs to her basement a wind up monkey is clanging cymbals and spinning around and around in circles. In the basement closet, all the stuffed animals are turning brown. We all fall down, like a marionette whose strings have just been cut.

"Okay, so chanting!" Petey says. "She's reluctant to leave. This is all Karmic, you know."

Her hallway is empty.

"Go to the White Light! Go to the White light!" Petey says.

She is watching TV.

"Go to the white light. Go to the white light."

She is offering a bowl of jouk, kicking monkey down the stairs. Playing MJ with the ladies.

"Go to the white light. Go to the white light. Go to the..."

The phone rings and Petey abruptly stops.

"Excuse me," she says. She walks down the hall and picks up her phone. We can hear her talking quietly in the other room. Mom stares at the timer, her eyes narrowed and her shoulders hunched. Her hair is a little matted in the back. There is no eyeliner over her right eye so her face appears half finished.

Poh-Poh before the window, staring at all of the lights. A city of little houses filled with people. A man in a paddleboat returning for her from across seas.

Do our parents return for us in death?

Mom starts to yell down the hallway as Petey walks towards us. "I hope you're not charging us for the time . . ."

Petey stops suddenly, cocks her head up. "Oh my," she says. "The telephone has brought her down to earth. She's ready now. She's ready to go. What a sense of humor your mother has." Then she looks at me and asks, "Can't you hear her laughter?"

Funeral for Confusion
Hari Alluri

though he didn't cheat,
lolo never lost at cards.
he survived two wars.

in form, lola survived him.
on her deathcot, tobacco

wrinkled lips crowing
beside me in tagalog,
the closest language

she knows to english: *you are
just like my husband.* charming,

charmed, i once rolled
a perfect dice game. anything,
alive or else, will

answer if you feel to ask.
not blood, by marriage,

my dead uncle prisms
toward being reborn my child.
after we kill him,

he comes by in raven form,
whispering truths, those truths
my lolo never got

to lullaby. *there's that voice,*
he says, *by blood or marriage,*

older and wiser than you.
sometimes you even
catch it inventing

spirits. under its drunken
tutelage, i touch my head

with dirt, nod as if
i understand, afraid to
hear what else it knows.

there must be somewhere
bodies go inside themselves to rest

Piece by Piece Until Dark
Amalia B. Bueno

She straps the burden on her back.
Her long black braids coil and loop
over chests, under arms, wrapped twice,
thrice, tied snug at their hip bones.
She has tricked death's due, bargained just
one more life for herself, like Prometheus
who stole fire and now the sister on her back
her dead twin, who must pay the price.
The precious cargo she pulls in penance
like a crucifix, a faceless feather-blackened Christ
whose heels mark the forward path red.
The ravens have come, the crows follow.
They smell her sin, they relish her sister's liver.
The thick blood and moist veins are delicious
bites torn loose from the in-between place,
piece by piece until dark.
The liver on her back is pecked away
piece by piece for a meal, dislodged
piece by piece, a single lesson in humility
swallowed piece by piece. The fading sun
reminds the sisters to endure until dark.
Her burden is lightened piecemeal
with temporary respite until dawn
only to start again every morning
piece by piece until dark.

Apo Baket
Amalia B. Bueno

She makes her own cigars, smoothing
The dry leaves like leather, rolling a sweet
Pungent sheet into a not too tight spiral
Then knots its thickness with black thread.

She trims, twists and snips the ends clean, tucks her
Secret stash into a wooden drawer of her ancient
Singer sewing machine, her hidden treasure sticks
To share with visiting friends and neighbors.

Apo Baket smells like the homemade coconut oil.
She awakens from its solid white sleep. She scoops
A dollop onto her warm palms, then massages it
Into thick hair falling on shoulders down to hips.

Oiled and coiled, round and round, she forms
The classic Filipino grandma hairdo, a gray bun
Against the nape of her neck, held hostage
To her tortoise shell comb, the translucent golds
And browns passing for sunshine and earth.

In the narrow halls of Apo Baket's home she walks
hunched and soundless on black velvet slippers,
its gem-splashed embroidery shiny with beads.
Like a snake turning her head side to side
She slinks up on us with her mean, squinting eyes

Ready to pounce, never missing a single detail
Of proof we were up to no good.

She takes her whiskey straight, swigging Seagram's
From a bottle kept safe in the gun metal gray dresser
keeping company with other medicines,
Tiger Balm and White Flower for her aching bones.

Dr. Ramos asks if she's been taking the pills
He prescribes. He also tells her she smokes too much,
Drinks too much, and to please, for her gout's sake
Please, stop eating tomatoes, patani, dinuguan and shellfish.

She hisses at the kind doctor, asking what kind of Filipina
Can live without tomatoes, mongo beans and blood,
Then spits out a stream of phrases—lateg mo,
I am too old, leche, I cannot change now, puneta—
her cussing worse than a longshoreman.

It was at Cousin Bino's house when I first saw her
Pluck out a good-sized bisukul, a freshwater
Black snail floating in a soup of tomatoes and onions.
She held the snail up between her thumb and pointer,

Tapped its back end with a spoon quickly, just once,
Crushing the shell at its most fragile point
Then sucked out the meat from the front with such gusto
I felt sorry for the snail, all of its body gone so suddenly.

Apo Baket outlives her only son, wearing black

For 365 days, becoming harder, more bitter
Striking out and recoiling at loved ones.
She outlives her husband and decides
Not to leave her house for one year.

She outlives her friends, then her neighbors
And relatives one by one. I remember her sadness,
Her open palm revealing shriveled fingers pressed against
Her forehead, her eyes scanning the street for visitors.

I watch from inside the screen door, her profile puffing
That familiar Filipino toscani, her cheeks sucking air,
The tabako's fiery end inside her mouth, a habit of survival
To withhold glowing red light from reaching wartime Japanese.

She nods to passerbys at dusk, her quiet exhale
A solemn recognition. Resigned, she spits
Now and then into a plastic wastebasket
Lined with shredded newspaper by her feet.

Her calm breath relaxes her face, shadowed
In the twilight beneath the bittersweet.
The cigar smoke curls and twists above her
Disappearing with the memories of loved ones,

Bending and sliding like the wisps
Of her long past, unwinding away from her
While the white trails move up, and leaves
Toward the rafters of the darkened porch.

Before Night Descends
Amalia B. Bueno

In Cebu a man in a dark blue suit hides Kali's blade.

He has just missed The Kissing, a strange time when

the solemn lantern maker waltzes with the dictator,

when the rainbow goddess wept and raised twenty-five chickens

and a pig for a bride, when America is in the heart.

On bridgeable shores a man named Ben reaches

for the Andalusian dawn and thinks of killing time

in a warm place. He knows Pinoy poetics

will soon be returning a borrowed tongue,

taken since ancient times to 1940.

Meanwhile, a woman leans forward

to catch the strains of a furious lullaby

that sounds like my American kundiman

wrapped in a star entangled banner. She sees

five faces of exile placed within the eye of the fish

floating, flippin' by a brown river, white ocean.

She embraces the arctic archipelago

and, flinging her wild American self,

is afraid of screaming monkeys who belong

to only one tribe. No one explains to her

why the matadora's zero gravity

leavens the bread of salt or why the gangster

of love—famous as a dogeater—

escapes danger and beauty as he

emerges from the dream jungle.

Colonial legacies and post-colonial trajectories

encourage cockfighting stories

in the hilarious world of Nestor D, who

gladly flees when the elephants dance.

The animals are not home, but here.

At dusk, Nestor reads the forbidden book

and I ask him to catch me a firefly

released by the woman who had two navels.

I ask Gagamba, the spider man why we are poor

and why we are hungry, but to no avail. He is one

of the pretenders of Villa Magdalena in inner city Ermita.

My brother, my executioner, he keeps heroes in the attic.

From Africa to America I have come to terms

with the voices of Pinay women overseas

who are primed for life, these women on fire!

In our image against the unbending cane

they copy the witch's dance while rolling their r's,

summoning prime time apparitions, and patiently

awaiting the evolution of a sigh. In a field of mirrors

during the southern harvest they are woman enough.

At the drive-in volcano they conjure seasons

by the bay, give life to the oracles, foment

revolution in the hall of cracked mirrors.

This is the umbrella country, baby.

Here, the gods we worship live next door.

Twice blessed with sugar and salt

in the company of strangers, you are given

the lowest blue flame before nothing.

You lovely people in the homeland, where

a visitor can have book of her own,

can come full circle with reproductions

of the empty flagpole. The anchored angel

makes things fall away from the seven card stud

with seven manangs wild; lays down

the Jupiter effect on ginseng; lands its wings

on the mayor of the roses. But it is

the 55 Jose Garcia Villa poems, not

the mananaggal, that terrorizes Manila.

This is no time for crying

because let me tell you

it is a strange time indeed

when mothers like elephants

are going home to a landscape, that great

Philippine jungle energy café—

before the night descends.

Peter BACHO Cebu, Dark Blue Suit; Michelle BAUTISTA Kali's Blade; Merlinda BOBIS The Kissing, The Solemn Lantern Maker; Raymond BONNER Waltzing with a Dictator, The Marcoses and the Making of American Policy; Cecilia Manguerra BRAINARD When the Rainbow Goddess Wept; Evangeline Canonizado BUELL Twenty-Five Chickens and a Pig for a Bride; Carlos BULOSAN America is in the Heart; Luis CABALQUITO Bridgeable Shores Selected Poems 1969-2001; Nick CARBO Andalusian Dawn, Pinoy Poetics, Returning a Borrowed Tongue; Benjamin J. CAYETANO Ben, A Memoir; Jose Y. DALISAY Killing Time in a Warm Place; Asuncion DAVID-MARAMBA Early Philippine Literature from Ancient Times to 1940; Milinda DE JESUS Pinay Power Theorizing the Filipina/American Experience; Oliver DE LA PAZ Furious Lullaby; Sharon DELMENDO The Star Entangled Banner 100 Years of America in the Philippines; Agusto Fauni ESPIRITU Five Faces of Exile; Luis H. FRANCIA Brown River White Ocean, Eye of the Fish, Flippin', The Arctic Archipelago; M. Evalina GALANG Her Wild American Self, Screaming Monkeys, One Tribe; Eric GAMALINDA Zero Gravity; Sarah GAMBITO Matadora; N.V.M. GONZALES The Bread of Salt; Jessica HAGEDORN Danger and Beauty, Dogeaters, Dream Jungle, The Gangster of Love; Eva-Lotta HEDMAN Philippine Politics and Society in the Twentieth Century, Colonial Legacies, Post-Colonial Trajectories; Antonio A. HIDALGO The Hilarious World of Nestor D; Tess Uriza HOLTHE

When the Elephants Dance; Luisa A. IGLORIA Not Home, But Here;
Abe IGNACIO The Forbidden Book, the Philippine-American War in
Political Cartoons; Freda JAYME Catch Me a Firefly; Nick JOAQUIN The
Woman Who Had Two Navels; F. Sionil JOSE Dusk, Ermita, My Brother
My Executioner, The Pretenders, Gagamba The Spider Man, Why We Are
Poor Termites in the Sala Heroes in the Attic, Why We Are Hungry Rats
in the Kitchen Carabaos in the Closet, Ermita; Lorna KALAW-TIROL
From Africa to America Voices of Filipino Women Overseas, Primed for
Life, Women on Fire; Stanley KARNOW In Our Image America's Empire
in the Philippines; Melinda Tria KERKVLIET Unbending Cane: Pablo
Malapit, A Filipino Labor Leader in Hawaii; Marra LANOT Witch's
Dance; R. Zamora LINMARK Rolling the R's, Prime Time Apparitions, The
Evolution of a Sigh; Edwin LOZADA Field of Mirrors; Renato MADRID
Southern Harvest; Carmen Guerrero NAKPIL Woman Enough and
Other Essays; Aimee NEZHUKUMATATHIL At the Drive-In Volcano;
Oscar PENARANDA Seasons by the Bay; Pati Navalta POBLETE The
Oracles; Fred POOLE Revolution in the Philippines: The United States
in the Hall of Cracked Mirrors; Bino REALUYO The Umbrella Country,
The Gods We Worship Live Next Door; Patrick ROSAL My American
Kundiman; Ninotchka ROSCA Twice Blessed, Sugar and Salt; Bienvenido
N. SANTOS You Lovely People; Michelle Cruz SKINNER In the Company
of Strangers; Lara STAPLETON The Lowest Blue Flame Before Nothing;
Leny Mendoza STROBEL A Book of Her Own, Coming Full Circle;
Eileen R. TABIOS Reproductions of the Empty Flagpole, The Anchored
Angel; Neferti X. M. TADIAR Things Fall Away, Philippine Historical
Experience and the Makings of Globalization; Helen TORIBIO Seven
Card Stud with Seven Manangs Wild; Katrina TUVERA The Jupiter Effect;
Marianne VILLANUEVA Ginseng and Other Tales from Manila, Mayor
of the Roses, Going Home to a Landscape; Jose Garcia VILLA 55 Poems;
Allison WYNNE No Time for Crying; Alfred A. YUSON Great Philipppine
Jungle Engergy Café, Mothers Like Elephants Selected Poems; Jessica
ZAFRA Manananggal Terrorizes Manila and Other Stories; Jovita Rodas
ZIMMERMAN Before the Night Descends.

Notes on Captain Ahab's Workshop
Before the Poet is Harpooned*
for Martín Espada
Cynthia Dewi Oka

1. There is no White Whale, just endless curbs and girls growing into silver scales. Their hair blackens the sand.

2. The facilitators – trained by Captain Ahab himself – brought sacks of head, blood rimmed binoculars, and inflation. They sharked the streets for little boys and coral reef. An entire section of the beach had been cordoned off for their daily cornrow prostrations. They promised star spangled cloth for whosoever sights the White Whale.

3. The *Call Me Ishmael Award* and *The White Whale Review* publish poems in English only.

4. An island oracle sent her shadow to follow the Herman Melville cruise ship. On deck, the gods of golf put their wands aside to sip coconut juice and observe sunburn noses hollowing out her breasts, steeped in saltwater and roped by the tail-ends of light.

5. Hell is an ocean of cheekbones and torn gamelan sheets. Many fell overboard trying to catch a glimpse of the White Whale's avatar. Floating coffins smell of sandalwood, ferrying prized body parts to libraries, museums and calendar manufacturers across an equatorial flood. Inside, eyes choke on wild winds.

6. The facilitators extracted ore from our memories as insurance for the replacement of legs, in case we lost them during free-write activities.

7. Some of us died imagining Captain Ahab's sacrificial pet. The rest danced an eternal conjugation and found ourselves in sound breaks looping, collapsing into winter blackouts, bus rides piling anvils in our skulls and bread dryer than a quilt of rough hands. Poems come to stand in the place of our spines.

8. The harpoon is made of White Whale ribs.

*response to "Rules for Captain Ahab's Provincetown Poetry Workshop," in *The Republic of Poetry* (2006).

Poem for Prisoner #46664
Cynthia Dewi Oka

In the dimness before the night shift, half-dressed
on a spit-stained bed, I cut my finger on the page describing
the milk you left to sour on the window ledge;

a small obeisance to the human part that wants, needs
to say, "I prefer this, not that," as you stroll silently through
someone else's furniture, planting bombs in apartheid

then risking all of it for a taste of the man who is still sweat,
hurt, a galaxy of longing – the man and not the lion.
The baby sucks my breast dry and in the void,

dogs bark. I think of the choices fathers and husbands make
in places where their families live hunted, hungry,
rabid with fear; where the rich and government are

synonymous with natural disasters – *nothing you can do
about 'em but buckle down and mourn the dead* – I think
of the ways men disappear, into wages, drink, sometimes if

they fight, into symbols. Then our memories of them must be
less important than their sacrifice. I think about the choices
mothers and wives have, to birth and to bury, to be left

behind, to piece lives out of split threads and absences,
to follow, to burn. Every time I stand in my bones and feel
lost, a stranger; every time I shield my face in the dark

I know it is because my ancestors chose to run. To leave
no trace on the windowsills we passed through. Madiba,
if it were not for you, this cut reddening the words

in the dumb light, I might have never learned to say, *Fear,
I am not a lamb on your altar. You do not own me. This here
I touch with my body, I make holy with language;*

this here, everything, this we who will not be moved.

Madame Lemoine
MJ Fievre

HOW PRETTY IS Port-au-Prince on Saturdays, the streets still askew but drained of the crowds. No masses of people rubbing against each other. Port-au-Prince is not tremulous today with busloads of school children. Only the shoe-shine men huddle in front of the bakery, which smells sweetly of *pen rale*, French bread, and beef patties behind its closed doors. Hands slap knees when laughter erupts—volcanic, stretching the cheeks under straw hats. Soon the Epicerie de Lourdes will let the children wander in for *bonbon lanmidon* cookies and mints shaped like small boulders. Young men scrub the pavement with Mistolin, *ça fait la joie de mes narines*. Someone wakens the drunk, slumped like laundry. In some front yards, clothes hang suspended from the lines.

Behind the wheel of his Audi, Papa doesn't miss a bit of the city's awakening, turning his head this way and then that way. The vendors of *fresko* slushies are out now—grenadine is my favorite. Never mind the flies and the mosquitoes. *Mikwòb pa touye ayisyen*. A girl at my school says the ice comes from the morgue down the street. Never mind this girl. *Sa je pa wè kè pa tounen*. What you don't know doesn't slap you in the face.

"Look," I say. "It's one of those mad men."

Port-au-Prince has a lot of crazies parading in ragged military garb, their faces mud-smeared, more bone than flesh, their eyes bottomless, their hair stiffened with dirt and lice—a bonnet of ridicule. Women sitting behind their big pots of *fasomur* feed them because the good word says, "For I was hungry and you gave me something to eat."

When I get out of the car in front of the school, a tall man trotting by knocks my leg with his briefcase; he doesn't even notice and bustles on. A lone *taptap* idles at the light.

"I don't understand," Papa says, "why you can't be well-behaved. Why do you have to speak your mind all the time and get Saturday detentions with Madame Lemoine? You could be watching cartoons right now on Télévision Radio-Canada. What is that show you like again? The one you enjoy so much that you gave up Saturday ballet lessons on account of not missing it. Ah, I remember: *Félix et Ciboulette*."

An old woman sits in front of the school, selling bananas ripe and green, tangerines and mangoes. I don't know where she spends the night. She doesn't ask you to buy a fruit, nor do her eyes condemn your wealth.

"*Félix et Ciboulette*? That was years ago," I tell Papa, waving good bye. "I'm a bit old for kiddy shows, Papa."

What I don't say is that I like Saturday detentions. I like the Latin *déclinaisons* that Madame Lemoine makes us study during the session. An hour into the detention she forgets how badly I've misbehaved. I'm allowed to sit close to her desk so she can tell me about her own childhood teachers. About the one with the birthmark across the nose, who tied a student's left hand behind her back, forcing the right hand to trace the loops and curves of cursive writing.

"Be good," Papa says.

MADAME ANETTE DUNCAN Lemoine. Seventy years old. Always carries an umbrella. Wears her hair big and orderly; keeps her nails clean and well-manicured. Her clothes, both sober and elegant, smell of Fab laundry detergent. Her head unbowed, her cheekbones high, she sits behind a desk stacked with Geology quizzes and French *rédactions*. She's been teaching Philosophy and Chemistry for more than thirty years, and has probably been manning Saturday detentions for that long too. She is feared by most students because she is strict and stern.

This is not the Madame Lemoine *I* know, though—lost in laughter and exciting stories about summer vacations in Les Provinces, cooking recipes from Carrefour and Bwadchèn, and anecdotes about the days of Papa Doc and later Baby Doc. She knows about our history, about the Pompons Blancs and the Pompons Rouges, and the sordid details of the hanging of Queen Anacaona. She tells me about Mother's Day in the old days, about the flowery brooches sold in front of the Sacré-Coeur before and after mass, about the customary *liqueur rose* and *ponmkèt* pound cake consumed at lunch time. As she reminisces about her younger years, her hands help her do the talking. From time to time, she interrupts the flow of words to ask, "How's that *déclinaison* going?" But she knows she'll spare me from reciting *a-a-a-ae-ae-a/ ae-ae-a-arum-is-is* because she likes an audience and would rather speak about Old Port-au-Prince than trust me into silence and Latin.

As she tells me these stories, I cannot help feeling like the center of the universe.

I haven't fooled her—she knows I'm choosing to be here. On Saturday mornings, I don't mind leaving my bed full of plotted dreams when the sky sits awake above the city, when shoe shine-men carry their world in a box slung across their shoulders, ringing their bells. Yes, the first time, I deserved the punishment for calling the English teacher an ignoramus. However, after some quality time with Madame Lemoine, I've learned to orchestrate my misbehaviors so I can end up in her detention room. I know which teachers have a short temper and just how much to speak my mind to get a "Saturday" without La Direction creating a permanent file about me.

The other girl, Valérie, has a permanent file. She sits in the back of the room, away from us, her ears waxy, her shoelaces tucked under the tongues of her shoes. Uninterested. Uninteresting.

I share some stories with Madame Lemoine too. I don't tell her about the knife, but I tell her about Jean, my old neighborhood's crazy. In Christ-Roi, Jean always looks at his shadow, puzzled, and walks with a stagger, his skin bruised and crusted with dirt. I was visiting the neighbors one day but it was nap time and the whole house was asleep. I got bored. Leaning over the railing of my neighbor's balcony, I yelled, "Jean, oh, Jean! Over here! Look over here!" Well, the first rock hit the *choublak* hibiscus flowers growing in Madame Ville's giant brass pot. The other one Jean threw at me landed on the roof. When Jean finally left, Madame Ville brought out a belt. She made me kneel on the cold marble floor and extend my palms. When the punishment ended, I was sent home hot with shame for what I did.

FROM TIME TO TIME police sirens howl outside, and I can see the piles of garbage catch fire and smoke hug the sky.

Madame Lemoine likes me. She likes my prose notebook, the doodles I trace around my poems as if they were memories of her own adolescence. I used to think I was the only one who stayed outside of my dreams, an intruder looking in my own sleep as people act out scenes in stories, but Madame Lemoine says it's the same for her—she's an outsider in her own dreams. I glimpse a smile on her face when I thumb my nose at the other kid and laugh. She tells me about the children in her neighborhood, the uncultured teenagers she worries about. The neighborhood of Bois-Verna, she says, saunters badly forth—rotten pilings, cocaine, quick sex. Some mad kid killed the neighborhood cat with an umbrella. The *zenglendos*—the bandits—if they don't shoot you with a gun, they'll cut you with a knife. "Those are the real crazies," she says. "Not your harmless hobo. These are criminally insane."

She says once that maybe I love stories too much.

When Papa picks me up, the sun is still shining. The shoeshine men have set up a table in front of Epiccrie de Lourdes and are now playing dominoes, their faces frowning, but a smile only inches away.

It's impossible to imagine that Saturday mornings will come to this city vacant of Madame Lemoine.

And when I'll hear, years later, about the cords that tied her to a chair inside her home in Bois-Verna, about the gag, about the strangulation, my fingers will touch reality's face, my own face dirty with tears. The hands of clocks will have spun to make me older then. I'll stand before the smudged bathroom mirror, toothbrush in hand, and I'll see myself as I am now—a thirteen-year-old kid with a Latin book sprawled on her desk, displaying the wrong page. And Madame Lemoine still alive, telling the story of Remus and Romulus. Her words will rise like a dream chorus in my head. I'll be left with a store of memories—the scent of her herbal rinse, for one—and a wave of longing will sweep through my body. Yet the face will already begin to tatter, fading, going out.

I'll think of rain clouds rising over the city, the afternoon giving way to cold rain and beaten down grass.

Tal
Mat Johnson

She sits, he leaves. She twirls the spoon in the coffee I've ordered for her. I don't know if she's too young to drink coffee, if seventeen is too young for that, and don't think of it till I see her with the coffee and it doesn't look right. She sits where her grandfather vacated; he left in search of Amish apple dumplings at the other end of the Reading Terminal Market. They're delicious; he insisted they were delicious, and he insisted that he will buy me one as well, and bring it back to this diner table.

Women have an XX chromosome, men XY. My X chromosome is a gift from my mother who was beautiful and funny and I miss every hour, and that X is the greatest genetic gift I have to offer. It's a gift that goes straight back to Africa, I'm sure. My mom's X chromosome met up with whichever X chromosome Cindy Karp had to offer and beat it into submission. This girl looks more like my mother's daughter than mine. She's even darker than I am, the genes that gave me the palest of tans on her looks like a two week Caribbean vacation. Her hair chemically treated and combed straight enough to be European curly. She's been passing for white and not even knowing it.

"So, I'm a black. That's just fucking great. A black. That's just what I need right now."

"You're not 'a black.' You're black. It's a good thing, nowadays. You can be president." I grin for her. Her smile back is quick and fraudulent. She's trying to act composed and mature and she's not old enough to know how to pull off the illusion like the rest of us.

"Jesus, I thought you would be Israeli or something. I hate rap music. You know, I was the best dancer at Akiba, since like third grade. Guess that's explained."

"I can't dance, sorry."

"Maybe it skips a generation. God, school. He told you to tell me to go back to school, didn't he? He told you to tell me to get back in high school, finish up and go to a good college. That's why he's doing this to me, because it's easy to get into college for blacks. Don't they get scholarships or something? That's what this about."

My daughter is a racist, I think. I adjust that to, my daughter is mildly racist, but I can't do it. My daughter is casually racist, I settle on. She's casually racist. "You dropped out of high school?"

"I'm an artist, too. I'm going to art school anyway. I just need my GRE and a strong portfolio. He doesn't understand that. I could go to The Art Institute, or Philadelphia College of Art, or even Pratt. I'm going nuts in his house. You've met Irv, you have to see what he's like. I'm not going to graduate, like any minute. I'm almost eighteen. I want to get out of the house now. Tell him to let me go, and I'll leave you alone. You can go back to not being a dad." I want to protest this, but my mind doesn't have the words my mouth needs, so I choke on nothing for a bit till I raise my water glass.

"I'll take the year off, backpack in Europe, just build my portfolio," she keeps going. "That's what matters. Ol' Irv doesn't understand that. I'm sure as hell not going back to Akiba Hebrew Academy. Look at you. Look at us. I don't even know if I'm even Jewish anymore."

"You're definitely still Jewish." Where is her old man? I ask myself, then realize this is the same question Irving Karp has been asking himself of me for 17 years.

"Oh right. The whole Jewish Vagina Clause. I guess that fact hasn't changed." When she says "Jewish vagina" I think of her mother's literal one before I can catch myself. I'm so damn pale, my blushing looks like the lighting of a Christmas tree. She sees this, and then her face goes red as well.

"I didn't know about you until a week ago, okay? Irv saw that you were coming to town, finally decided to tell me. I didn't know you were a black till today."

"Okay, look, it's not 'a black.' It's never 'a black,' okay? Just 'black.' Or African American."

"You don't look very African, but whatever," my newfound daughter rolls her eyes at me, twirls her straw. "God, I guess I'm going to have to start using hot sauce on all my food now."

"No, you don't. You can't possibly believe that," I say, kind of laughing, hoping she'll start laughing with me. She doesn't. "Hey, I didn't know you existed at all. But I'm glad, okay? I'm really glad." I tell her. I just say it. I don't say it because I mean it. But when I hear it out there I can tell it's true. My father's gone, Anwen's gone, but here is new family. Seventeen, but new to me.

"I saw your illustrations, online. Some of it's okay," Tal shrugs. I want to tell her about her other grandfather, about my father, about how she just missed him, but don't. I want to tell her that my mother died when I was ten years-old, too, but it's too morbid. Instead, I find myself saying, "You should go back to school. Your grandfather is right about that." It's a safe thing, an easy thing to latch on to, probably the only fatherly advice I'm qualified to give.

"I am so not going back to Akiba. Especially not now."

"Then you'll go somewhere else. It's important. I'll help you. Let me do that for you. For your future. Whatever you decide to do once you get your diploma, that's up to you. But you need to have the choices available to make—"

"You want to help me, want me to go back to school? Want us to be daughter and daddy? Fine. Just get me the hell out of here, and you got a deal. Take me back to Wales with you, that would be awesome. I could got to school there. Or just send me to boarding school. Send me some place like Phillips Exeter. I have the grades. That's it, Exeter. Send me there. Irv will go for that."

"Exeter? That's, that's a lot of loot. And it's so white," I catch myself saying.

"But I'm white," she says, and I look hurt. I must look hurt, because she leans over the table and adds, "I'm as white as you look." Then my new daughter pulls back again, twirling her brown cloud with a nail bitten finger.

Red Polish
jewel bush

A barefoot Laylah tiptoes over a broken whiskey bottle minding its business on the kitchen floor. Shards of glass glitter in the a.m. light. She pours herself a bowl of Sugar Smacks, lifts the chain off the front door and sits on the cool step, damp with morning dew. She shovels spoonfuls of sweet cereal into her mouth savoring every crunch.

The occasional zoom of 18-wheelers passing by rattles her little wooden house along Highway 71; a two-lane stretch of Louisiana corn, sugarcane and soy fields.

A post office. A general store. A church.

Two filling stations. Railroad tracks. A caution light.

Houses sparse and spare.

Laylah watches the cars and big trucks speed away from LeBeau. Moving on to something better.

Laylah's father stumbles onto the gray, cement porch, holding a can of Budweiser with an unlit cigarette dangling from the corner of his mouth. "What you doing out here by yourself?"

Laylah holds her red plastic spoon up, "Want some breakfast, daddy?"

Laylah's father grumbles about losing forty dollars to Man Brown from the plant in a game of dominos and then scolds Laylah for leaving the front door wide open.

"Ok, daddy." Laylah turns the Rainbow Brite bowl up to her mouth and slurps down the sugary liquid. She wipes away her milk moustache with the back of her right hand and heads back inside.

Laylah finds her father plopped down in front of the TV on their sofa that pulls you to the ground when you take a seat. She places her empty dish next to a half a dozen plastic cups of brown booze with cigarettes extinguished in them and ashtrays over run with what she knew weren't cigarettes.

"Daddy, I love you." Laylah throws her arms around her father's thick neck remembering the days before her mother made her go to church, when she would spend Sunday mornings with him drinking Miller Lite ponies and walking around with her shirt off. Like him.

Laylah's father fetches a black lighter from the pocket of his cut off jean shorts and lights his smoke.

"I told your momma six is too young to be wearing red on your nails." Laylah's father stares at the chipping nail polish and takes a deep drag of his Kool Filter Kings. "I should wake her up and tell her about this shit, but then again your momma don't listen to a damn thing I say anyway."

Laylah tucks her brown slender fingers into her mouth like a pocket. "It's not your fault." Laylah's father palms her wavy sandy-colored hair.

Her hair had been combed the night before, but you couldn't tell by looking at it now. Her nervous slumber unraveled her neat plaits, parted in four. She had tossed and turned to avoid sleeping positions her cousins warned would allow the witch to ride her back or the devil to pinch her toes. She had tossed and turned because the ruckus from her father's Bourré game -- where the liquor flowed, where drunk adults bitched about being bumped on jobs and where fist fights erupted over next to nothing -- had kept her up.

"You're getting older, Laylah. You ain't a little girl no more." Laylah's father manages a smile of sorts.

Laylah chews at the remainder of the cherry Wet 'n Wild polish she begged her mother to purchase from the TG&Y in Opelousas, the day they went into town.

"Laylah," Her father stares straight ahead, "I don't want you to be one of them fast-tailed girls. Not you, Laylah."

Laylah chews harder. And faster. Tiny chips of paint pile up in her stomach, and even speckle her teeth. The bitter taste makes her nauseous.

"Do you understand, Laylah?"

"Yes, daddy."

"You don't want to be *that* kind of girl. Don't want you to get a reputation. Know Butch Range's little girl, Valencia?"

"Yes, daddy."

"She about your age." Laylah's father swallows hard to push out the rest, "They caught her at the church bizarre, behind the gym with some boys from down Palmetto Road."

Laylah stops biting her nails. *Caught her doing what?* Her father looks into her green eyes -- what folks "call cat" eyes -- long enough to make them both uncomfortable. Laylah fights back tears. Crying doesn't feel like the right thing to do.

"Do you understand what I'm saying, Laylah? Girls don't need to be playing with boys like that."

Laylah chews harder. Her cuticles are now jagged and raw and on the brink of bleeding. She doesn't know what *that* is but *that* must be bad. She wonders if *that* is anything like what her 11-year-old cousin Lenny did in the barn not that long ago. Lenny stopped when she started to cry. He made her pinky swear not to tell anyone. Not even her best friend Joy, who she had been friends with since Head Start and who she always sat next to on bus 14 on the way to Palmetto Elementary.

This was bigger than the time the two passed around a wrinkled loose leaf paper with bad words scribbled on it and drawings of naked women and men having sex. When Mrs. Jackson found the note on the classroom floor, near Joy's desk, Joy said it was all Laylah's idea even though she was the one who stole the drawing from her older brother, Marvin's room. Laylah lost recess for a month. She didn't rat because she was so glad the principal never called her father.

"Yes, daddy."

Laylah's father sits up and smashes the butt of his smoke into the overflowing ashtray. Ashes and roaches from smoked joints spill onto the wasteland of a coffee table, an ode to the night before.

"Get your fingers out of your mouth." Laylah's father swats her hands. "You're getting too old to be sitting around here sucking on your fingers."

Laylah dries her damp digits on her white flowered gown.

"Yes, daddy."

moonside kalakuta
Sevé Torres

"music is the weapon of the future" - Fela Kuti

in the night his body became a drum
the republic was quiet save the pour
of plantation rum there was a clink on
the wooden bar tables and the lights flickered
the swirl at the bottom of the glass tilted
up meeting   Fela
humming   Fela
whisper Fela

saxophone tracing the arch of a neck
as it sways into his wisdom
unravels knotted logic out of thick air

in pain tables become drums
the clank off metal lids struck by
truth moves on song tongues
echoes deep wails into reed

words that dance off nervous bodies
here risk is beneath the sweat of dancing people

long into the night his words
curve into the silence between
feet and batons meeting flesh

Fela rides belief
in the long horn pull
doubled to draw breath
men cannot beat
the music out of him

> *Come, dance with us*
> *We're making music over here.*

Sure You Can Ask Me about Hip Hop
after Diane Burns
Alan King

What's my street name?

No, I never was gunned down several times.

Yes, my name is Alan.

No, I never dove for cover behind parked cars during a drive-by.

My life never flashed before me like a hologram.

Oh? You think I look like 50 Cent?

My rap sheet exists only in the minds of those who shutter

when I ask for directions, or say, "excuse me," when they block the sidewalks.

No, I never had a record deal.

I did get invited to read at a poetry festival in San Francisco.

No, I'm not a studio gangster, brainstorming street beef scenarios

with an agent, or rhyming in the booth about imaginary riches.

I did write a poem once about mouth-shaped orchids

and their aromatic kisses.

I never took anyone's life, or made a shook one

give mouth-to-barrel resuscitation to a loaded weapon.

I did almost cry the day my niece was born.

Huh?

No, my battle scars came from climbing trees and playing with fire.

Oh? You think I look like Olajuwon?

No, I never had a dream of ballin' in the NBA.

I dream all the time about my first collection

winning the National Book Award.

I've never knuckled up with guys who hid switchblades under their tongue,

or was ever knocked unconscious, left lying on a club floor.

Never bought a hoodie—wait—I did buy a hoodie once.

But I never bought rolling paper, or reefer.

Never bought blunts, used box cutters or brass knuckles.

Never bought anything beginning with the letter "B" except books, Blistex,
and a bible, oh yeah, and blow pops.

I never inhaled marijuana gunshots blown from Death's lips.

Never wrote a love song to a firearm.

I did write a love poem for an aunt I lost to cancer.

Yes, my presence intimidates.

But that wasn't me handcuffed, sitting on the curb,

while police searched my car.

Oh, you rap, too?

That nice, huh?

Oh, you got tattoos?

That street, huh?

Wait! I think I know you.

Didn't I see you in the movie *Jackass*?

Dreams of Comic Book Women
after Lyrae Van Clief-Stefanon
Alan King

Give me everything I can touch:
What's round: What speeds
the blood: What raises the drawbridge:
What will fit on my tongue:
A hunger rising like thought bubbles.

The colors of the dreams are bright,
even at 16, waking to the promise of Betty and Veronica.
I wanted to be Archie,
caught between glossy mouths
like strawberry shortcakes.

Storm's battle suit swallowed her body
the way a boy gobbles a chocolate bar.

I'm dreaming of sweet things: the tempting glaze of a strudel,
the moist center of an apple croissant; or waking to Madame Hydra,
Catwoman and Mystique mistaking me for icing,
a melting popsicle, ice cream running down a waffle cone;
waking away from the hard, inedible edges of this life.

Give me the assassin, Elektra, in her Twizzler-colored suit
hanging as if someone attempted to rip it off her.
Let my appetite for sweet things keep me dreaming through the wars
and unemployment. Let me go on like Ulysses' men, dazed
and wandering—
no one dreaming of home.

Bloom
Alan King

When my doctor saw
a lump on my groin
and said, *It might be cancerous*,
what I took for granted
taunted me: mom laughing
at dad's jokes, her callaloo
with crab legs, my 3-year-old
niece's explorations starting with
Uncle, what's that?

Wasn't I too young,
too green for Death to pick me?
The thought of meeting Him so soon
made my life a smorgasbord
of untasted desires.

I wanted to bathe
on a Bali beach, backpack through
a Costa Rican rainforest, nibble on
a Moroccan vender's
steamed lamb tangine.

I wanted a wife so fine
her hairpin curves
send my heart skidding.

I was a tree surgeon
snipping at fungus on bark.
What bloomed made me
a mushroom in a field of daisies.

My mind became a house
I tried to get in order:
what I didn't know about myself
were unlabeled boxes
waiting to be hoisted

into a delivery van

along with everything else
I ran my hands along,
as if explanations
were in the hard edges
of perishable things.

Oversoul
Mitchell S. Jackson

1.

EVENING CALL and we skip the pig iron and pool tables in favor of strolling the track and circuit a few laps appraising the yard. Since it's one of those dreary summer days we get here where the rain ain't an if but a when, it's looking mighty scarce. Only the diehards out on the pile, laying a soundtrack of grunting and yelling, while meantime a couple of dudes who wished to God they owned a decent jumper play four on four on the gravelly asphalt they call a court.

"Good fortune," he says.

"So that," I say, "is what it's called?"

"No, *that*," he says, "is what it is."

"But to you and who?" I say.

"To me, me, and me," he says. "Who ain't never had none. Who else you need?"

My celly's a lifer on the wrong side of half his life and, most days, especially the ones he's juiced off his world famous Pruno, you can't tell him—it's just my luck I'm always linked with a bootleg philosopher—he ain't Nietzsche, Heidegger, Harold Bloom. But best you mind the venom; the man is also built like a steroid robot with fists big as demolition balls and a teardrop (one he earned back when I was a wee bit) inked under an eye, which means when he speaks, fools—including me—listen.

"All bullshit aside, youngin, only a few finished, but the ones that did, ain't been seen back behind the walls. Now, I don't profess knowin what he do," he says, "rumored a whole lot of talkin and scribblin and whatnot, but whatever it is, it seem to work. So if I was you…"

He stops short when a flabby guard moseys over and stands Gestapo-ish nearby.

"I don't mind the company, but if these folks gon let you fast track, you best get on it. Believe me when I tell you, you ain't built for no long stretch."

My robot-built celly proceeds to turn what should be a friendly shoulder tap into a fucking hematoma. Throbs later, when they sound the horn for the end of yard, the iron-pumpers make a fracas of re-racking the weights.

2.

Cap lopes in and the room freezes in moon-shaped rows of metal fold-ups, a handful of us—me included—with eyes wide as bottle caps and lips damn-near sutured. He takes his seat by the portable board, empties a duffel of books and notes, and sifts through them a moment without a word or eye for any of us. Then he lurches to his feet, shifts what must be fossilized bones, clears his slack gullet, glances from face to face-to-face-to-face, and waits what must be a Julian light year before he says this: "My friends, the world ain't set up for guys like us to win, but that's all the more reason to win." His voice is deep, metallic, severe—a baritone so coarse there must be spikes in his throat. "And if you aren't about winning," Cap says, "then you should leave now. This program is not the place for chickenshits."

It's worth mentioning that nobody leaves, that don't nobody utter a word.

Here might be why: on top of nursing our oh-so-coveted good time, some of us are here because we heard the legend, and the legend is, spectacles on or not, this man can see right through your diaphanous-ass curtain to your guarded lockbox, see what's in that lockbox, then tell you not only that he spied it, but minus any hype whatsoever, how it might produce whatever you need, which, for the bulk of us, at least the ones with an inkling of sense, is an outbound ticket that lasts for all time.

With all the grand stories I heard, a nigger was half-expecting a real live in-the-flesh giant, but no sir, the truth is the man ain't all that physically big. Matterfact, he's intimidating about none, and probably wasn't an ounce more imposing when they began calling him Captain, or Cap—way back when he beat the biggest case the state had ever seen, those salad days of his when, as the myth has it, he was worth more scrilla than a blue-chip stock; no—I'm thinking he couldn't have been but average-sized at best for the span of years a few decades back that he managed over and over the abracadabra-alakazam. And peep, this millennia Cap's a welterweight, stooped to what's likely an inch or so shy of his apex, with paper-white longish hair raked backwards, and a face etched in intricate grooves.

But check it, though, the man's weathered mug is one thing, but his digs are a whole other situation: a pressed cream shirt buttoned to his throat, a pair of army green cargo pants that look half as old as anybody I know, and boots tied tight enough to make the average motherfucker's foot fall right off. He inches along the rows jacking arms and querying names, and it don't take no 3-D glasses to see the deference they pay, respect from nefarious dudes with tattoos on their necks and knuckles, with gully-wide gashes on their cheeks, from the musclebound old head who runs the Commissary Mafia, all of us forfeiting afternoon yard.

Anybody's guess why, when he finally reaches me, the name I give him is the one that no one, and I mean nobody, hears out my mouth unless I'm under oath. Not only that, but the hope is that the man feels my strength, faith, resolve, feels the pledge lodged close by my padlocked lockbox, and the man must have a handshake message in mind himself, cause there ain't sign the first of him letting me loose. "You! You!" he says. "You serious or wasting my time? I'm gonna die. And you're gonna die. And tell me who has a moment to waste?" He says this and hovers stock-still, not that big in life but bigger than life—exponential. He peers into me with eyes that could douse my greatest fear or immolate my fondest dreams, which is why right this second there's a rock band rehearsing in my chest, a flood in my pits, and for reasons unbeknown to me, I'm overcome with the urge to confess my life. To admit how it's one thing to *be* an ex-con, but another thing entire to *feel* convicted. How every stint feels less of time away and more of time at home. How most days all I ever see are emblems of what I could've been.

Plus, here's the stone-cold ignore-it-and-that's-your-sweet-ass truth: either I've had all I can stand or I'll never, not this year, not this decade, not this eon, get enough.

But me, I don't mention any of this. And why? What are you, a priest? Why my nuts! It's nobody's business why.

The room is swathed in jaundiced light and reeks of disinfectant that could knock you dead. For a time, every tiny breath, shift, murmur, creak, cough, sniff could measure on Richter. Then it all softens to ambient noise, and Cap glides amid the pseudo-quiet to a post in the center of it all. He grabs a branch of chalk and scrawls the word NARRATIVE, on the board in leviathan script. "My friends, everyone has a sob story," he says. "But guess what, no one gives a goddamn about your sob stories," he says. "What the world attends, if it attends at all, is who you are now, and what you do with the moment at hand."

You don't have to be no psychic to know the most jaded of us will, no matter the prodding, refuse to treat this man with the utmost gravitas—AKA a silly mistake that most days I'd be content to sit and watch pursued. But for only God might know why, I'm struck with the urge to warn this handful of screwface ne'er-do-wells how we can never *ever* be sure when we've laid eyes on the shepherd of our last—not penultimate or semi-final, but last, as in absolute—chance of saving our oversoul.

3.

THE CHAPEL ain't exactly packed but ain't exactly empty, either. Us graduates occupy the rows nearest the rickety lectern, and sitting behind the lectern in velvet-padded wooden chairs: the superintendent and his masculine-faced female assistant, the scowling lieutenant, the chaplain, and Cap. Cap lets his anthracite-eyes go the distance, maybe to the handful of family members (females mostly, but my girl ain't one of them) or the reporter, the only one present, stooped over his notes, or maybe further to where a duo of squat guards police the exits like them joints are the golden gates of third heaven.

Wouldn't nobody I know consider the ceremony's set up anywhere near lavish, and you'd think the meagerness alone would mean I'm cooler than cool, that my pulse is ticking off at a steady pace, but no such luck; my eyes are caught in twitching fits and this heart of mine may as well be a twittering bird. No lie, it's on the fritz to the point where, if I was another type of dude, I'd nudge the super-sized blockhead who's been locked near a decade for arson and ask if he too feels as though he's swallowed stars. But as I said, that's if I was another type of dude, and let me be the first to tell you, program or not, places like this seldom let us be who we could.

You just don't know what I'd give to have a sense of time whiling away instead of this clock doing a number on my insides right up until the time the chaplain leads us in a prayer so moving even the born-again Muslim among us strikes a supplicant pose.

The superintendent bops up afterwards, flashing a smile—homeboy's teeth are damn-near citrine—that's 9/10 fake, and taps the mic, and recites the most tarnished speech you ever heard about opportunity and life change and second chances, some drag don't nobody believe, if anybody believes, but him. When he's done, he gives Cap a cursory intro, relishes a few camera flashes, and struts back to his seat.

Cap, never afraid of the limelight, matterfact, always in lust of the limelight, makes a production of getting upright and shambling into view. He stops beside the lectern and peers at the crowd and glances from face-to-face-to-face-to-face to my face and clears his throat in a gnarled, wrinkled fist.

"All around us the noise," Cap says, in a pitch that might be magic. "There's the babble of today's news, the clatter of all acts prior, the clamor of expectations. The extent to which one finds oneself in accommodations such as these is equal to the extent one is unable to sever one's self from the roar. Over the past months, these men have discovered they were once ignorant former subjects of the world's boom, boom, boom, boom, have determined that, as it is for us all, the only way to be free is to position one's self as discrete from the din of phenomena." Cap raises a hand, whoops up what must be a chunk of lung, recomposes. "It is only then can one forge a life governed not by what's prior, but what's at hand. Only then can one truly live anew." The man of the moment edges from one side of the altar to the other and cast those stone-colored eyes into the gray distance. "This life I speak of, the life for which these men are now destined, exists as a form of quiet," he says, and gimps off the altar and onto the floor.

He comes to a stop a centimeter from our pew.

"I want each of you to know that when you leave these walls, you will not be abandoned," he says. "That I will never desert you," he says, and ebbs along our row, pausing across from each of us for what feels like the better part of the rest of my life. "My friends, I say this to you with the full measure of what life to me is left: outside, if ever you need, come find me," he says. "In Cap you can trust. In Cap you can surely trust."

He shambles back to the pulpit and stands, lucid as ever, not that big in life but grander than life—colossal. "Friends, family, chaplain, superintendent, when these men you see before you have left the confines of these walls, they will do so not as graduates of a program, but as philosophers of a new way of being."

When it's over, Cap banters with the superintendent, and my word, you never seen so many smiles and taps and nods, never seen a handshake that could end a world war. As I said, nobody from my fam is here, and since, ceremony or not, I ain't at all in the mood for bantering with these dudes' significant others, I don't budge. Instead, I peep Cap dickering among the crowd, watch him hobble over and sit beside me and sift through pocket scraps and turn so we're face to face. "It's tough out there," he says, and lets the silence linger pulses too long. "But tough is what you want. Easy is for half-asses and dimwits, of which you, my friend, are neither."

The room verges on a hush. The guards round us up well ahead of when they should.

4.

YOU CAN lose yourself in increments: this many and that many month-stretches at a time. One morning you slug out of a tiny bunk in some building bordered by razor wire, and your twenties, where the fuck are they? A few sets later, half your thirties—vamoosed, left your sorry-self in a nasty communal bathroom plucking stubborn gray hairs out your chin while mourning the immutable fact your once-superior hairline has begun a full-fledged recession.

What's worse is you lost all of this and what's left of what's left to covet is reaching a few days till last wake up.

Here's how it goes when you touch down. There's the festivities and visits from the people you ain't seen since the last time you were home or maybe a time or two for a distracted weekend visit during the first few months—try and get somebody to see you after that—of your set. How it goes if you come home to a short stash is, if you're lucky, you get kicks from a female or fam or homeboys, the ones that not only say they want to see you back on your feet, but confirm they're beyond fatmouthing by tossing your impecunious ass a few bucks. Those first days, weeks, back in the free world, you see all of mankind's progress in the blink of an eye. When you left we'd just invented the wheel, but now, now we're flying spaceships. Unless you're a sucker, home sweet home equals an abundance of has-beens ready to pay homage to your new (but let's keep it real, most times temporary) swoll biceps with a shot of refurbished pussy. But sooner or later, after you inhale those early, emancipated breaths, inevitably sooner rather than later, you end up gaping into the maw of the real, live, wide, apathetic, show-me-what-you-gonna-do-this-time cosmos—a position that clarifies options for even the most imbecilic of niggers.

Be who you were.

Be who you thought you could be.

Be somebody brand-new altogether.

5.

WELCOME BACK is what the sign says, and you'd think this brand new me was popping the fam's just-came-home cherry with today's turnout: my mama, my sis and baby bro, my twins (walking now), my fine-fine woman, all convened on the porch cheering and carrying on while I lug my luggage, a state-issued trash bag, up our rickety front steps. A trillion pats on shoulders built from a consistent season on the pile, plus yet another faithful push and pull up regime, so many encouraging words all I can hear is a hella-loud drone.

Uncle Sip is in the backyard stooped over a billowing grill, wielding a long spatula, a semi-empty brew sitting on a side table with the meat. Somebody—no doubt one of my young geek nephews—has rigged our giant home speakers so they reach the patchy, hillocked lawn. There's an old soulful voice wailing across them, so you know one of the grown folks has gangstered deejaying duties. My oldest Unc two-steps and nods his unkempt salt-and-pepper natural and keeps right on warbling along to the chorus till he sees me eyeing him from the porch. "What's it is, Nephew?" he says. "What it is, what it ain't, and what it shall be?"

"Unc," I say. "You know."

My response I mean literally. Unc's the only one in the whole fam who's logged more time in the system than me. One of those old heads who—when you're facing new charges—can quote your prospective sentence under the new *and* old guidelines, who's probably spent most of his adult years (probation, parole, house arrest, judge-ordered community service, mandatory out-patient drug programming, city-funded intervention: Clean Slate, Fresh Start, Second Chance…) on some form of paper. But Unc's illustrious law-breaking/rehab history's another story. Shit, I got more than enough trouble keeping up with my own.

The rest of the stage: see fold-up tables scattered around the yard, see the bushes trimmed to neat shapes, see here and there adults (and a few sneaky youngsters) circumventing potholes with Styrofoam cups in hand. See a dominoes game at a shaded corner table where one of my oil-tongued cousins harangues some dudes who don't at all look familiar except they resemble in dress and bearing the old heads who parley in the neighborhood, preaching advice they didn't have the brains to follow themselves.

While I preside over the scene, my woman taps my arm and motions me to follow.

My word, from the front *and* back my baby girl is a cham-P-ion! But the cool part is, her physicality ain't even the half. Yeah, ask any old old head and he'll warn against bestowing an abundance of faith on a woman, any woman, while you're gone, which is sage advice for sure, but maybe once in a millennia you have a shot at finding an extra-special one, the kind who'll stay down an entire set, by which I mean will keep a few bucks on your books, pay you consistent visits, and send enough naked flicks to keep your balls from swelling to the size of melons. And if it's true there's something rare about a female who can do that once, imagine how sublime one is that manages any more than that.

And you, you, you, fair-minded listeners, will you please, and I mean plceeeeeaaaze, hold up on the hasty judgments. Yes, it's true, while I was gone, she might've gave away the goods, but it's also equally if not more true that my heart couldn't stand an investigation.

With the hope that the light of my life is luring me upstairs for a shot of level-ten cranium, plus a skinny-dip in her nexus—the welcome home combo of my star-spent dreams—I hustle behind her.

My woman don't so much as flash a tooth when I tell her how much I missed her, when I ask where she was my last weeks down.

"There's no easy way to say this…" she says, and lets the next moment open up and suck me down.

And peoples, peoples, listen: to hell with what you, them, anyone says. There are times when it pays to be tough as steel. There are times when, no matter, we can't fake an armored heart.

AS IF things couldn't get worse, my P.O. pays a pop-up visit. My P.O.'s an Indian, excuse me, Native American, from some tribe in Northern Washington whose name I can't remember for nothing. You'd think with how bad his people have had it, he'd commiserate or at least show an atom of empathy, but hell nah, homeboy treats me like a direct descendent of Lewis and Clark. Look at this raggedy sucker squeezed in my Pop's (R.I.P.) favorite reclining chair, with his feet kicked up and a notebook in his lap. "Thought I'd drop by," he says, and flashes that supercilious I-own-your-discount-life smirk.

"Drop by on my first day home?" I say, as a question and complaint all in one. "Want to make sure you get off on the right foot," he says. "Despite what you may think, I'm a good guy, have even cut a few loose early. And let me tell you, I'd love to see you finally off my load."

"That's the plan," I say.

"Well, make sure this time your plan includes a job," he says, and scribbles notes.

"Sure thing," I say.

"Great," he says. "How about we see you in my office with pay stubs soon." My trillion-pound P.O.—no lie, the fool must've swallowed a tribe of Apaches—waddles for the door, his long ponytail swooshing across the mountain-sized sweat patch printed in the back of his shirt, his shoe soles worn to the shape of an avalanche.

Chief Loves to Violate turns to me, his thick neck first, then the rest of him. "Looks like you're having quite the party," he says. "But if I were you, I'd steer far clear of any intoxicants. You of all people should know how those piss tests can just pop up."

6.

A FEW DAYS after the festivities, I hit the mall with my kickstart funds—scrilla the old me might've used to cop a sack—stuffed in a pocket and buy a white shirt and a blue shirt and a pair of khakis and a pair of polyester blend slacks and a new tie and some hard-soled shoes, and the next day I scour the city in search of HELP WANTED signs and, with worry I hope is at least semi-veiled, enter corner stores and grocery stores and liquor stores and car lots and car washes and pawn shops and restaurants and blood banks and gas stations and warehouses and dry cleaners to fill out application after application, hoping somebody with some authority or compassion or both will hazard a call to the number I listed, which, truthbetold, is my mama's home phone—a line she guards the way a Rottweiler or Doberman protects its owner—praying at least one fucking living human being will ring me for an interview, but since they don't, I'm left a whole morning gawking at a contraption (a prehistoric rotary joint) I've tried more than once to coax alive by ESP; unsuccessful as shit till near noon when I dress and, since a nigger's license is suspended till the day *after* judgment, slug out to catch the light rail or the bus or, if I'm lucky, to bum a ride or, if I'm less fortunate, to trek infinite blocks on foot to a whole new set of places taunting my soon-to-be-destitute self with virtually unavailable options, conceding my poor chances but filling out apps against the odds—every time wishing like crazy I had a

whole other history to list—before trudging home to pick at leftovers, count
my steady-dwindling funds, stab at sleep, and do it all over again, repeating
the same script for so many mornings it takes on the feeling of a life sentence,
repeating the same script so many mornings that one morning I backtrack to
the mall where I copped my as-yet-unworn interview clothes, to ask security,
stock boys, salesmen, managers, anybody with a name tag or a black or white
button-down shirt for an opening, any opening at all, though there ain't no
signs asking for HELP in view, questions that harvest a steady succession
of NO's, and since a nigger can only stand but so many public setbacks, for
the next who knows how long, I spend hours upon hours at the employment
office searching listings that appear so far outside my realm of possibility as
to be excerpts of science fiction, reading the fantasy paragraphs till I'm good
and debased, then trudging home to eat, watch another eon of depressing
news, count the last of my last few bucks, and on the bleakest nights, lay on
the flattened twin mattress in the room above my mama's head with the tepid
hope my eyes stay the fuck closed forever, but since my wishes materialize
about never, early the next AM, an anonymous force tugs me out of bed and
sends me slugging downstairs to post by a phone that, if it rings at all, is a
creditor or telemarketer, but since it sometimes requires more heart to give up
than it does to go on, with a gloom I pray is camouflaged, I shamble out of the
house and into the jagged teeth of another day.

7.

 BUT EVENTUALLY…outfitted in my brand-new interview threads,
I trek to an address on Swan Island, where I approach this guard in a small
wooden booth who directs me to a huge building at the far end of the lot.
Inside, I'm all but overcome by the horde of eager faces vying for a job that,
to be true, a man with any standing in the world wouldn't use to wipe his ass.
So many of us competing for this minimum-earner only a certified fool would
admit to anything that'd make him even infinitesimally less attractive. But
since, as I said, I'm working on a new me, when I get to the question about a
felony, I write, "Will discuss in interview" in my neatest script.

 A guy dressed in a faded denim shirt and wrinkled Dockers stomps out
and calls my name and, for reasons I wouldn't admit to another man, my legs
are brittle twigs, sticks barely strong enough to carry me to a sparse office: a
desk and a couple of chairs against unadorned walls. The guy—one of those
suckers who's probably settled for an innominate, redundant, riskless life—tells
me to pull up a seat and proceeds to stand on the other side of a wide desk and
stare a black hole through my skull.

 "Well," he says, "I have to be honest. Your work history's a bit spotty."

 "It's been a rough couple," I say. "But I'm hoping things take a turn."

"That right?" he says, scanning the sheet. "So, what's this you need to discuss?"

8.

THE NEXT morning, after picking over food that I ain't spent—as my mama confirms more and more—a dollar on, my attitude is fuck-staring-at-the-phone, so I rummage through my lockbox for names and numbers and make call after call after call till someone produces what might be Cap's home line, but with my luck, might not.

"Well, well, my friend," Cap says. "This is quite the surprise."

He tells me that he can't chat long, but gives me a few seconds to vent before breaking it off. He recites his address and tells me the best time to stop by tomorrow. In this moment, to be sure, my relief couldn't translate to words.

Cap's huge Victorian is in a neighborhood me and my boys used to burglarize like crazy, which is why it don't take much to find his address, to locate a porch stacked with books, logs, and metal junk. I climb the steps without clue the first of what to say and ring a bell that makes the sound of a gong.

You can hear the sound of multiple bolts unbolting, and hinges long overdue for lube. "Well, don't just stand there," Cap says, and leads me into a shabby front room where he points to an upholstered couch before reminding me he has to leave soon.

"What's the trouble?" he says.

"It's all bad," I say. "Between that and worse."

"So I see," he says. "Well, here's the word: Nookie."

"What?" I say.

"Nookie," he says. "You getting some?"

"Are you serious?" I say. "You're not serious."

"My friend, let me tell you. The right woman's a salve for almost any harm," he says, and fastens a shirt button and cuffs his sleeves. "You've got the felled look of a man who's getting less than he should. Or less than none. Go out and score and have a look."

"Huh?" I say. "See what?"

"C'mon," he says.

"That's it!" I say.

"And if not," he says. He strains to his feet and motions me to follow. "Well, I'd love to keep chatting, " he says, "but as I said..."

"Wait," I say. "What about what you told us inside? The narratives. The noise."

"My friend," he says. "You didn't *really* fall for that? Don't tell me you *really* bought all that crap. Jesus, can't a man make a god-for-living living."

"No," I say. "No."

The man pushes the door wide, stands awash in the brightest light I've ever seen. "Listen, pal, don't be chickenshit. We're all up to our eyes in it. Not just you. There's no big secret. Just decide."

"Decide what?" I say.

"'The choice of most consequence," he says. "Whether we save our soul or save ourselves."

9.

MY UNCLE SIP is in a Northeast tavern, posted by the bar, a half-guzzled brew beside him, yapping to some dude who, by the face, could've been an apostle. When I tap his shoulder, Unc swivels hella, hella slow. Judging by his glassy, rose-tinted sclera and the fact he smells as if he's bathed in his drink of choice, he's faded beyond his average percentile. "Nephew," he slurs. "What is it, a blizzard?"

"Try a motherfuckin snow storm," I say.

"Well, pull up a seat and let me get you somethin to set your mind right," he says. "Hold up, is you still on that paper? When they got you reportin next?"

The most I can manage is tossing my head side to side.

"Well I'll be gotdamned Nephew, maybe you should go virgin. Can't play it too safe these days."

"Right now," I say. "Man oh man, Unc, about right now!"

Unc warns against going any such route "just yet," and claims, as luck would have it, he's got an old patna that might could help us hustle up a couple coins.

The bartender shuffles over and Unc orders a pair of stiff ones. A bulb dies and the jukebox begins to moan.

What I say to Unc is this bet not be no drag, that I hope to God it ain't no drag.

"Aw naw, Nephew," he says. "This here's legit, a real live one. You know old Unc know one of those on sight."

The drinks arrive and they're iceless and clear and filled to the lip..Unc pinky-stirs his double shot, pats his pruned ultra-sheened fro, flaunts a grand gold-capped smile, lifts his low ball to the heights, and suggests we toast, as he says, "to the future." But me, I look beyond old dude, down my drink in a gulp, bang the glass on the counter, and with the ass-end of my kickstart funds, order another round.

Interior Security Regulations

(Rohwer, Arkansas 1942)
Mia Malhotra

instructions to all living persons japanese in the following ancestry area aliens will be evacuated pursuant to non-alien ancestry noon this dated 12 o'clock p.w.t. saturday commanding executive order no. 33 headquarters may 3, 1942 no persons will be permitted living no japanese will change residence area after 12 o'clock noon p.w.t. saturday may 9, 1942 without obtaining permission commanding general southern california sector civil control station located permits will be granted such only for purpose the uniting members family emergency grave in cases evacuees must carry property following them on departure for assembly go to civil control station between hours the 8AM the 5PM bedding (no mattress) linens for members each of family articles toilet for members each of family will be packaged marked plainly with name and owner numbered in accordance

*

1. Female evacuees shall not enter the barracks of male evacuees.

2. Male evacuees shall enter the barracks of female evacuees when ordered by a Caucasian who is head.

3. All evacuees shall obey. They shall give possessions without reserve.

4. He will control and supervise meetings by his physical presence and enter all evacuee quarters day or night.

5. Parents are required to instruct their children in these regulations and the necessity for obedience.

6. Spoken language of a contraband nature will be confiscated without compensation.

7. Songs of praise or worship shall not be sung.

8. There will be no evacuees. Any such persons will not be tolerated.

9. Destruction will be witnessed by a member of staff.

10. This will show what was destroyed, listing quantity and brand.

*

An alien of enemy nationality shall not travel or make trips or move.

Lights shall remain off throughout hours of darkness. The child crying in Block 9 must not fear the dark (night too has children, nurses them with wet, cracked nipples   tells them hush)

wind rushes in through the widening seam in the wall. Rough boards nailed against light   desert   sand

Disturbances are prohibited. The woman in Block 9 must not cry out, back raked by stiff sheaves of corn, mattress ticking, the sliver & prick of boards

the husband lowers himself   roots into the body. Someone shifts on the other side of the sheet   hung across the room, a tight screen

She learns to pray this way, teeth clenched, back taut   air hissing through lips *our father who art in heaven thy kingdomcome thywillbedone—*

she's in the body now. It's dark.

The barrack's quiet, husband curled in sleep. Woman's face pushed against the wall into the black crack of night & beyond that

more black   desert. Wire. *Tools may be used as weapons, including knives with blades placed in mess halls.*

Sleep widens like a jaw, yawns   black   *lights shall remain off*

shall not travel shall not make trips stretches prickly across the woman's face arms   neck taut in the dark. No child, no woman   *shall not move*

Dissection
Roopa Ramamoorthi

"One Frog is Green, and one of them is spotty
They bear one common name
And yet they vary, and talking modulate their voice diversely"
Thus is your croaking catalogued
in hymn 103 of the Rig Veda
written two thousand five hundred years ago

Some call you Indian bullfrog
with eyes that bulge like soap bubbles
I've heard you herald
the first rain of monsoon
as precious for a forgotten farmer
as a priest's prayer

In 12th grade science I studied you
Rana tigrina with the tiger spots
Family Ranidae, Phylum Chordata
You came chloroformed
With bare hands
I pinned you on my wax tray
and took a scalpel
made the first incision on your ventral side
close to where your hind legs join your body
cut and cleared skin and muscle
to expose your stomach, spleen and pancreas
your burgundy liver and tiny heart
I was grossed out by your yellow fat
scrutinized your intestine and wondered
if your system was really just a miniature of mine

your digestive system came easily
but the arteries and veins were another story
I pried and poked and ruptured
to excavate your bloody intricacies

I did not stop to think of your story
Your father mounting your mother
A tadpole hatching from an egg
that escaped being eaten
developing lungs, shedding tail
metamorphosing into a full blown frog

No, I had my board exam to think of
you were only a digestive system to me—10 easy points
not a living, beating, breathing body

that I had to kill to study
the story of a sacred coupling
calling for a mate

Those were the days
when I was old enough to know of a kissed frog
who became a prince
but too young to know
a kissed prince
can also become a frog
that cannot be dissected.

Twinning
Faith Adiele

The world in which we live has its double and counterpart in the realm of spirits.
Indeed the human being is only one half (and the weaker half at that) of a person.
A man lives here and his *chi* [spirit double] there.
—Chinua Achebe, *Morning Yet on Creation Day*

Until I was born, I was a twin.

At least that's how the OB palpating my mother's abdomen was preparing to explain the length of her uterus, the fact that a short girl was carrying so high. Holly, a pony-tailed college sophomore with cheeks as rosy-plump as any baby's, shifted on the sticky vinyl and chuckled. My father Magnus was also short.

"Only five-foot-four," Holly told the doctor, at this point in the pregnancy savvy enough not to look anyone in the eye. "He's a graduate student from Nigeria."

"A Negro?" the doctor blurted, not quite sure which was more surprising — that this babyfaced girl with her odd, Nordic vowels was admitting to miscegenation, or the fundal height of the fetus.

My mother nodded. She was used to this part. It had started eighteen months ago, eyes either widening or narrowing at Washington State University's sole interracial couple. Holly and Maggie were, in fact, the only interracial couple they knew. This among ten thousand students.

But strangers weren't the problem. Just a few months ago she'd lain down on the living room floor of her father's house and resolved never to get up. Holly recalled the rough scratch of carpet against her cheek.

The rug, sculpted gray wall-to-wall, swirled in dizzy circles beneath her, nubby to the touch, as she'd reviewed her situation: home for the summer and knocked up. A white girl with a black fetus. A nineteen-year-old college student, the first in her family of immigrants to have made it past high school.

Her college career (her ticket out of a future of annual pregnancies and a laconic farmer husband) was officially over. That morning her father had stopped her tuition payment. "Tell your daughter," he'd roared to his wife, my grandmother, "that I will throw her out of this house, *outoftheGoddamnedfamilyitself!*"

Holly felt a bit like those tragic letters in *True Confessions* magazine. In junior high she and her best friend had squealed over lurid accounts of the perils awaiting the modern girl. *Dear True Confessions,* the reader letters always began, *I never thought I would be writing to you.* So many girls despairing across America! Giggling, Holly and Rita hefted their rootbeers and read in unison: "But I am desperate and have nowhere else to turn!" But now, what would her own letter say?

Dear True Confessions, I don't remember much, just a few images: Pappa shouting, ears and throat purple; Michael-Vaino slamming his door, all adolescent angst at such a sister; Aiti hurrying soft whispers from room to room; Täti Rauha twittering-nervous in the background; Uncle John, glued to the television screen, secretly relishing Pappa's discomfort, I'm sure. And me down on the floor, the quiet one for once. Can you imagine?

Back at the clinic, the doctor had stopped palpating for limbs and pressed instead his stethoscope against her tight skin. He glanced at the stalled clock above the two metal folding chairs, away from the green examination table that bled stuffing through several gashes, then announced: "Twins, perhaps!"

And Holly, who would spend her pregnancy as she had spent most of her life, a book like a shield before her, lowered her latest paperback, and finally looking at him, gasped.

It was the winter of 1962, and White journalist John Howard Griffin's account of medically darkening his skin in order to masquerade as a "Negro" through the segregated South was climbing the best-seller charts. "Humph," my mother scoffed, pursing those tulip lips, petals plump. "It took a White man to tell White America the truth of Black America!"

Griffin himself scoffed at how White Liberals sought him out, based on his few weeks of Blackness, rather than listen to actual residents of Black America. The irony was not lost on Holly, the daughter of newly-middle-class Americans busy disowning her because of the dark fetus lengthening inside her.

My mother read about White bus drivers who drove Griffin miles out of his way, about the constant threats of violence from unfriendly Whites and the sexual demands from the seemingly-friendly, about the difficulty of finding a job that wasn't menial, a place to pee, a safe bed in which to rest.

Her breath rasped, asthmatic, irregular, through the cold examination room. She read, fear stirring an already-cramped belly, about the two countries Griffin inhabited, returning to Whiteness when he thought that he would lose either his mind or his life. After his story was published, his effigy was hanged in the center of his hometown—a half-black, half-white dummy with a yellow streak painted down its back. Holly herself had never seen an interracial baby.

The doctor eyed the tower of charts rising from the gray metal folding table and shook his head: Neither had he. All he could say was that it was uncommonly long in the womb, the number of knobs he could grip indeterminate, the fetal heart sounds muddied.

My mother's eyes, not nearly as blue as the rest of her family's and so droopy behind thick black frames that they could fool you into thinking her sleepy or passive, blinked a code of distress. Her birth defect, an orange stain on the right iris, pulsed in and out of view beneath the sweep of lashes like a swelling clot of blood. *There—gone. There—gone.* She had no idea how she was going to feed this long baby on its way to becoming two. How to feed two babies.

"Ask your family," the doctor advised with a click of his pen. He assumed that the family was speaking of the pregnancy. Was speaking, period. His hand flew across her chart. There was little else he could do; the electronic fetal monitor, which would in just a few years bring ultrasound technology to hospitals, was just being invented. "See if a predisposition for twins runs in the family."

My mother stopped blinking and considered the sobering possibility that her family was still involved. That her mother's knot of tight-lipped Finns and her father's bando of blustery Swedes clustered across the Pacific Northwest had anything to do with the number of children in her womb. She shook her head, ponytail whipping from side to side. Better to ask Maggie, the short, thirty-year-old graduate student from Nigeria who loved to talk, who loved children, who came from a country of families, a country where a father could never tell his child, "You are dead to me; I no longer have a child."

My father Magnus was sturdy and dark as teak, with a generous mouth and the brown eyes Holly craved in a sea of Nordic blue. The problem was that they had broken up over the summer and he was now in eastern Canada, nearly three thousand miles away.

"Twins," Holly finally responded, a raspy whisper. The book slid out of her fingers and tumbled to the scuffed linoleum floor where it lay splayed, spine cracked. *The shocking true tale!* the cover screamed in lurid, swamp green letters. The silhouette of a man hunched its shoulders against the assault of White America, face hidden in shadow beneath the title: *Black Like Me.*

Afterwards, Holly speed-waddled back to the room and dashed off two letters, one to Maggie, one to her aunt. She knew that her mother and Täti Rauha met twice a day in one of their sunny, pastel kitchens. There they huddled in floral housedresses, sipping colored water made from anemic tea bags they used and re-used, pressing them into the hollows of teaspoons with their thumbs and winding the strings till they formed tiny brown bricks.

Their barrel-chested husbands, the non-Finns, were always accidentally dislodging these weightless fossils of teatime, which dropped from cupboards and tumbled off the backs of stoves like locusts. "Just use a new bag, *forchrissake!*" they blustered, jamming down their work caps and stomping their work boots. "The war's over!"

But the war was never over—after 600 years of lording it over Finland, Sweden was used to getting his way—so the sisters nestled closer, tightly-coiled pin curls and swirls of cinnamon pulla wilting above teacups. They whispered a steady stream of New World Finnish and plotted siphoning funds from household accounts.

Whenever a scrap of voice curled around the wall, the husband—Holly's Swedish father or Irish uncle—shifted uneasily before the television news and called out, "Hey, what are you two doing in there?"

The hook-nosed sisters would stop for a second, blue eyes narrowed, and drop their voices to the mere memory of sound. As if anyone could possibly understand their hybrid Finnglish, a language designed for two speakers—the third, a brother, lost.

"Your tytär wrote to ask, have we any kaksoset in the family?" Täti Rauha mouthed, and Holly's mother's beauty queen eyes widened. "Kaksoset? Two babies?" She leapt up, dipped into the hallway and returned hefting the family album, which she dumped onto the yolk-bright Formica. "What shall she do?"

Together they tipped open the embossed leather cover. There were no twins on their side, the Finns. But, *look*—two sets of stillborn kaksoset on the Swedish side, the four births quick notations on the heavy back pages.

Up in Spokane, Holly ripped open the lemon-colored envelope veined with Täti Rauha's curly script. "C'mon, c'mon!" Scraps of paper fluttered over the mountain of her belly like the autumn leaves the day she left home. Sunnyside, the town in southeastern Washington she had fled at seventeen and been exiled from at nineteen, was a dry indentation of earth cupped in a ring of purple hills so matte they looked like a painted backdrop for one of the TV Westerns she and Michael-Vaino grew up watching. True to the promise of the town's name, the sun shone oppressively 360 days a year, never a rainy day for reading indoors, always blue sky and an adult commanding: *Go outside and get some fresh air!*

As a child Holly crouched behind bales of green hay and pulled up her shirt. After retrieving the paperback flattened against her belly, she glared at the landscape. The Rattlesnake Hills, winding north, held Seattle's rain at bay. The Horse Heaven Hills arched south, holding her in. The child Holly read deeply, fully, the way the non-asthmatic breathe, the way the men tumbled into sleep after harvest, boots half off. Eventually she even forgot to give the occasional holler or whoop, so that her parents could tell themselves she was really playing this time.

Now nineteen-year-old Holly gathered the contents of Täti Rauha's envelope. There was a note gossiping about the other department store clerks, the "girls" as her aunt called the fifty-year-old widows and divorcees; a letter from her mother reporting on the two sets of dead Hanson twins and how the farm cats were surviving winter; and a money order that Holly would cash at the drugstore in town, fully intending to buy useful things like larger panties but somehow losing focus mid-aisle and returning with *The Challenge of Abundance* and two books on Cuba.

"Don't worry, dear," one of the few friendly nurses reassured her over the payphone. "Two sets of twins in the previous generation isn't serious." Holly knuckled her glasses up the bridge of her nose, *half* relieved, and the nurse added, "Provided, of course, there are no twins on the father's side!"

While she waited to hear from Maggie, Holly made a list of her belongings. Other girls tucked cigarettes and love letters among their nightgowns, but Holly's drawers swelled with lists and charts and project ideas: Countries she planned to visit, paperbacks to add to her library, French vocabulary to teach the baby (babies?), weekend chores, a historical timeline of the Roman Empire. Of the hundreds, perhaps thousands, of lists my mother has made during her lifetime, this one she can recite from memory.

Discounting things on loan from her parents, the sum total of Holly's 1962 belongings were: (1) a hi-fi stereo and a box of EPs and LPs, (2) a wooden rocking chair, (3) her graduation luggage layered with Capri pants, sweater sets and cotton smocks, (4) her black wool dress with the tiny buttons (more on this later), (5) an empty trousseau chest lined in cedar, (6) a print of Van Gogh's *Starry Night*, and (7) several cartons of books. It was just enough to furnish a single room, she estimated. Would it be enough to raise one lengthy child (or two shorter ones)?

To calm herself, my mother read. Halfway through *The Challenge of Abundance*, in the midst of Theobold's critique of Western consumerism, she recalled that most traditional societies viewed the birth of twins as an abomination. However, if she remembered correctly from her Anthro course and conversations with Magnus, one of Nigeria's tribes rejoiced. Holly buttoned on her mother's old plaid car coat and headed for her second-favorite spot after the bookstore: the library.

"No idea," the librarian said coldly, jerking her head towards the dusty anthropology stacks and pointedly ignoring Holly's belly.

Handkerchief to nose, my mother discovered that Nigeria's Yoruba led the world in twin births and even had twin gods. My father's people, on the other hand, considered "unusual births" unfortunate. Unusual Igbos included newborns with teeth. The feet being birthed first. Twins.

The shadow fetus shifted in Holly's belly, perhaps willing itself not to separate. Remain whole.

She read that a pregnant mother who fails to perform the necessary Igbo prenatal rites risks dangers, ranging from difficult labor and twinning, to the child being cursed by the gods. "Gods-schmods," Holly muttered, pushing the book away. She certainly wasn't going to honor her father or ancestors, even if she *were* Nigerian and knew the rites. Eventually overcome by old-book-dust, she jammed her tissues and cough drops into her patch pockets and toddled past the librarian's glare.

When the letter arrived from the University of Ottawa, she ripped it open and scanned quickly, mumbling phrases aloud. "Christ Almighty, Maggie!" she cursed the African convention of weaving slowly around an issue, as if conversation were a tribal praise song or Highlife tune with instrumental flourishes and digressive harmonies. "Get to it!"

You have what it takes, began Magnus's usual praise of her fortitude. *If only I could do more,* he agonized. *Keep faith in yourself and God.*

"Yeah, yeah, God schmod," she grumbled. "I'll keep faith myself, thankyouverymuch."

My father's answer to her query closed the letter. *Oh, didn't I ever tell you,* he'd written with characteristic enthusiasm, *I myself am a twin!*

*

"What about *Marassa and Midnight*?" Mom asks.

"Oh." I ponder. "That sounds somewhat familiar."

She laughs. "It should!"

Upon publication of my first memoir, a reporter has emailed a set of questions, including the name of my favorite childhood book. I can remember my *first* books—African fairytales Mom penned and illustrated herself when we were poor. And the rare picture books with mixed-race characters that PBS has filmed us reading to each other. I vaguely recall the chapter books on Great Women and Minorities Throughout History that I studied during our home summer school, I the sole student. I recollect a serious Norse mythology phase. But had there been a single favorite book?

I call my mother, who for years has hoarded my collection of (three thousand) children's books in her garage, part of a misguided strategy for leveraging grandchildren. Now she's simply archivist to my obsessions.

"I can't recall how many times you read *Marassa and Midnight*," she tells me. "You used to sleep with it under your pillow!"

"Seriously? You think I'd remember something that strange!"

When a package arrives a few days later, I'm surprised to unwrap a young adult historical novel set in Haiti. Perhaps it isn't so surprising. I've been raised to admire Haiti, the first black-led republic in the new world, the only nation born of slave revolt, the first country to recognize the sovereignty of my father's homeland when it seceded from Nigeria. (The book was published when I was three years old, the year before my father disappeared to the breakaway republic of Biafra.)

The eponymous Marassa and Midnight were sons of a West African king and had been stolen and enslaved in the New World. One twin became a revolutionary during Haiti's fight for independence. No wonder the book appealed to me! While other girls imagined themselves *The Little Princess*, awaiting rescue from obscurity and restoration to their rightful thrones, I awaited the call to battle.

There were other striking parallels that must have whispered to me from the book's nocturnal rest beneath my pillow. Marassa and Midnight were twins, clearly Yoruba. References to twins and their supernatural powers filled the novel. The boys lived below twin mountain peaks (*The little boy twins had never been in the least afraid of the peaks towering above their own twin peaks*) named Dove and Diamond, same as Midnight's twin hounds. Marassa was taken to France by his owner, while Midnight remained in Haiti until twin revolutions reunited them, the French Revolution paving the way for the Haitian Revolution two years later. The name Marassa refers to the Divine Twin, the twin spirits in both Yoruba and Haitian vodoun who have the power to bring both happiness and disaster, depending on their unstable temperaments.

The text beneath my head, like the landscape of my childhood, was suffused with longing. It articulated my own unspoken predicament: *Twins cannot be separated! Yet it had happened.*

*

The future. If my mother had stayed in the library longer, she could have known some of it. She might have discovered my birthright, the Igbo obsession with twinning, not twins.

Every Igbo has chi, a *spirit double*, who acts as her personal god and determines her fate. Our proverbs are filled with cautionary tales of fools who tried to defy their chi. Chi links us to the Supreme God, Chi-ne-ke (Chineke) or Chi-ukwu (Chukwu), who at the moment of our birth endows us with our own individual portion of the divine.

The resulting human is only half of the whole being. Each individual is twinned, existing in two worlds, her corporeal body walking here on sunlit earth, her spirit double skirting the shadow realm of the spirits.

In March, when the Rattlesnake and Horse Heaven Hills are buttery with yellow wildflowers and the irrigation ditches clogged with velvet-silver pussy willows, I will arrive to this world. Twenty-one inches long, all bright-skinned and dark-eyed. It will be, according to my mother (the only informant), miraculous.

The jittery obstetrician and nurses will wait, collectively forgetting to breathe, for their first biracial baby, and it is I who must slap them to life: *Wake up!*

I will reach with tiny golden fingers for the name Holly has mulled in her head over two months—*I'll keep faith myself*—and swallow, the way Igbo accept ideas, into the belly.

I will arrive with baggage.

I will arrive carrying genetic tribal memory.

I will arrive with work to do in America.

I will be, rosebud mouth working, *open-closed*, hungry. For the ones who accompanied me halfway on the long, hard journey to the New World.

My African chi hesitates on the threshold, one of the few souls with a choice at the Door of No Return. She's a homebody, unadventurous, quiet. She gazes back at the shadow realm. Now there is another one hovering beside us—fylgia, a *Follower*—called up by the naming. She is Nordic, restless, more animal than human. My Black and White doubles regard each other, on this new ground. We wait.

Eventually each whispers, "I will wait for you." Drops my hand. Makes me forgets her name. Pushes me out into the noise and light and blood, alone.

The New Cotton
Nikky Finney

They are just boys
Chain ganged to the side of the road,
Dressed to the nines in sunny orange,
That shade of red that never
Seems to set, familiar color
Of that foreign flower,
The kind you can close your
Eyes in sleep and still see,
But these boys are not flowers
Anymore, no thing that can be
Seen to bloom has been left to bloom,
In this place where a chain around a
Black man's ankle is that state's
Jewel, but if you still own your
Eyes, you know, they are still boys.

They do not yet know how
To bend, someone has not yet
Passed on the secret of how
To save their backs for the rest
Of the journey, someone forgot
To offer the old way of how
To get through the whip
Of their young days in order
To reach the sweet rock of
Their old, they angle
And arc carelessly, not knowing
They are matchsticks of American
History, never squatting down low

In the grass, never bending
At the ankle or thigh.

They are such proud brittle lion
Trees about to break in every
Direction, but free, the weave of
All their fabric wasted
In the constant picking up
Of useless plastic things,
That as I get closer to them,
That as I pass,
Looks white and sticky plump,
Some kind of new cotton
Stuck inside their reaching
Robeson hands.

The Girlfriend's Train
Nikky Finney

"You write like a Black woman who's never been hit before."

I read poetry in Philly
for the first time ever.
She started walking up,
all the way, from in back
of the room.

From against the wall
she came,
big coat, boots,
eyes soft as candles
in two storms blowing.

Something she could not see
from way back there but
could clearly hear in my voice,
something she needed to know
before pouring herself back out
into the icy city night.

She came close to get a good look,
to ask me something she found
in a strange way missing
from my Black woman poetry.

Sidestepping the crowd
ignoring the book signing line,
she stood there waiting

for everyone to go, waiting
like some kind of Representative.

And when it was just the two of us
She stepped into the shoes of her words:
Hey,

You write real soft.
Spell it out kind.
No bullet holes,
No open wounds,
In your words.
How you do that?
Write like you never been hit before?
But I could hardly speak,
all my breath held ransom
by her question.

I looked at her and knew:
There was a train on pause somewhere,
maybe just outside the back door
where she had stood, listening.

A train with boxcars
that she was escorting somewhere,
when she heard about the reading.

A train with boxcars
carrying broken women's bodies,
their carved up legs with bullet riddled
stomachs momentarily on pause
from moving cross country.

Women's bodies;
brown, black and blue,

laying right where coal, cars,
and cattle usually do.

She needed my answer
for herself and for them too.
Hey,

We were just wondering
how you made it through
and we didn't?

I shook my head.
I had never thought about
having never been hit
and what it might have
made me sound like.

You know how many times I been stabbed?

She raised her blouse
all the way above her breasts,
the cuts on her resembling
some kind of grotesque wallpaper.

How many women are there like you?
Then I knew for sure.

She had been sent in from the Philly cold,
by the others on the train,
to listen, stand up close,
to make me out as best she could.

She put my hand overtop hers
asked could we stand up
straight back to straight back,

measure out our differences
right then and there.

She gathered it all up,
wrote down the things she could,
remembering the rest to the trainload
of us waiting out back for answers.
Full to the brim with every age
of woman, every neighborhood
of woman, whose name
had already been forgotten.

The train blew his whistle,
she started to hurry.

I moved towards her
and we stood back to back,
her hand grazing the top
of our heads,
my hand measuring out
our same widths,
each of us recognizing
the brown woman latitudes,
the Black woman longitudes
in the other.

I turned around
held up my shirt
and brought my smooth belly
into her scarred one;
our navels pressing,
marking out some kind of new
Equatorial line.

The Sound of Burning Hair
Nikky Finney

Osage Avenue, Philadelphia, 1985

Dropping a bomb
Is not the same
As throwing it
One can be
A nervous mistake
The other a dead intention
So they knew when they leaned
Their ticking arms
Out their flying doors
That bullets would never be enough
That bullets could tear
And nightsticks
Could render unconsciousness
But what would debone
Tough dark meat
From nimble arrogant quick-healing joints
They knew when they threw it down
That bullets might slice a path
Through some unruly moppy untamed heads
But what would singe
Beyond skin and scalp
Under hair shafts and past regeneration

Fire could
Fire could

So by all means

Let us throw fire
So a jacklegged flame was sent
To do a human being's job
And then they inhaled
Like the humpbacks they are
And drove their regulation
Three thousand feet for cover
Leaving only fire
To lick away
Every thick-haired spirit
Within a Three Mile Island radius

Lives have been torched in a back-alley murder
And strangers doing head counts
Have trampled through our homes
Without first wiping their unsorry souls
Philadelphia is not Hiroshima
But hair on fire
Echoes the same
And straight or nappy minds
Can lift their ears
To any burning bush
And hear rats crawling away

Though fire is out
Though smoke has cleared
Though bullet-embroidered backs are buried now
It is all ways ours to decide

What shall we read to the children tonight
Can we pull it from ourselves
Do we still
See Jane
Can we still say aloud in sacred bedtime story voice

That Dick still shoots a silver toy pistol
Does Spot still run Monarch butterflies
Or do we see Spot
Chasing our Birdie
Trespass running
Up our Black woolly-headed alley
Can we see Birdie
See Birdie run
See Ramona
Screaming for Birdie to keep running
Screaming for John to make it to Afrika

Scream Ramona
Your hair
Is Fire

Hotter Than July
(Remembering Stevie Wonder and East Coast Summers)
Jourdan Keith

Note: In the 1970's cat gut was used to make lacrosse sticks

> The stretch marks across her
> ashy brown skin were like curved earth
> cracked, pushing her dry hip
> against the summer sky for rain

Our confession aching for
the sound of caramel and chocolate skin
the company of eyes that hold the scent
of summer sidewalks steaming in the sprinkler
the pink bubble gum smack and pop of laughter
too loud across the wide open turning of double-dutch lips

> My confession like rain
> I miss the childhood I never knew
> And the one I had

I have been absent since my buffalo face wandered
leaving the hot asphalt plains of grade school
playing jacks on the front steps, hopscotch &
the joy of metal jungle gyms, our bodies thumping
against the concrete

I have been absent since migration forced me across
the groomed turf of white girls at private school
into cat gut cradles & cleats
into a game

I did not know I was playing

Until I became a substitute
for myself
calling out at the last minute

> Her confession
> she'd put her hands
> down a redhead's pants
> groping for her Irish ancestry at Catholic school

They had been caught in the locker room
tongues tangled/tunics above their waists
KOOL menthols and Marlboro Lights mingling on the floor

Selections from *Diary of a Dreamer*
Alberto Ledesma

I used to think my father was a cyborg bracero when I was a kid. He always worked and never seemed to take a sick day off for any reason.

It wasn't until I was in 6th grade that I finally found out that he was human after all.

Mama' woke us up late at night because Papa' had had an accident at work. The machine he had been operating had crushed one of his fingers.

On the way to the hospital mama' worried about papa's health and about how we were going to pay the hospital costs.

The company paid for all the costs before they laid him off and hired another cyborg bracero.

On the Metaphysics of being Undocumented:

JUST BECAUSE YOU ONLY VALUE MY ARMS AND MY BACK IT DOES NOT MEAN THAT I LACK A MIND. WITH WHICH TO REFLECT ON MY CONDITION. THE TRUTH IS THAT I COULD WRITE TOMES ABOUT THE WAYS THAT EXPLOITATION SHARPENS A WORKER'S ABILITY TO SEE HOW SOCIETY REALLY WORKS. BUT THE KIND OF LITERACY I POSSESS IS NOT ONE THAT YOU VALUE; MY VOICE IS NOT ONE YOU CAN HEAR. SOMEDAY IT WILL BE MY CHILDREN WHO WILL TRANSLATE MY EXPERIENCE IN A FASHION YOU WILL FIND HARD TO IGNORE.

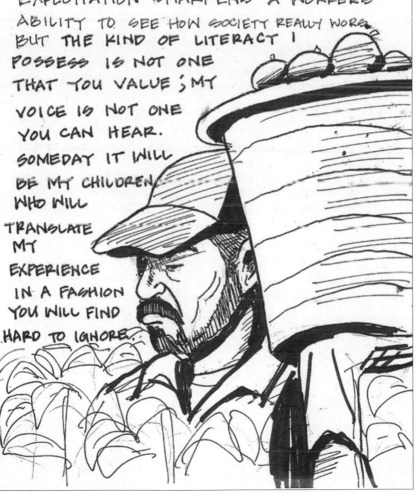

How I Became My Mother's Daughter
Laila Lalami

"Hold still," Milouda said. "It'll only make it worse if you move." She squeezed my earlobe between her thumb and forefinger. The needle was new, unused—she'd shown it to my mother when we arrived in her makeshift salon in the old medina of Casablanca. The sound of Arabic music and bicycle bells filtered through the half-open window from the cobblestone street outside. Taking the needle out of a red box with a French brand name, she said, "Only the best for you, *lalla* Fatima." My mother nodded, unused to the title of respect the clever Milouda had used; she was the kind of woman with whom meat vendors felt comfortable haggling.

A woman sat under a color poster of Olivia Newton-John, waiting to get her hair straightened, and Milouda told her this would only take a minute or two. She turned on the stove and held the needle over the flame until it turned charcoal black. "Wiggle your toes," she ordered.

Instead, I put my arms around my mother's waist, looking for the comfort of her soft belly. I felt the pressure of the needle on my right earlobe and the sharp pain when my skin gave. I bit my lips, forcing my cries back in my throat. I felt pearls of blood forming on my skin, one thick drop landing on my shoulder, next to my tank-top strap. I jerked my head to look at the blood. "Stop!" Milouda cried. "Hold still." My mother put her hand on my shoulder, giving me a small squeeze of encouragement.

Milouda pulled the thread through the hole in my earlobe and made a loop, tying it at the base. I reached for it, eager to feel my first earring, this temporary one that would precede the gold studs my mother had promised me when I agreed to get my ears pierced.

It was over in a minute, as Milouda had promised. Then I heard the ruffled sound of money changing hands. I admired my reflection in the mirror. My mother stood behind me, her hair in a loose bun, her green jellaba clashing with her yellow neckerchief. We grinned at each other.

I reached for her hand. Normally she'd tell me that, at ten years old, I was too old to be holding hands. "Not a baby anymore." But today she let me.

"Let's go show your father," she said. I knew, though, that the real reason she wanted to drop in on my father was because she wanted to surprise him, to see if he was indeed at work even though it was a Saturday. She had started to suspect that he was having an affair.

What I hadn't told my mother was that I already knew my father was having an affair. I knew the other woman. Her name was Beatrice Sauget and she was my French teacher.

I'd always walked to school on my own, but when I sprained my ankle after I fell off my bike, my father started to drop me off at school before going to work. He'd ask Mademoiselle Sauget how I did in class, his hands weighing on my shoulders or stroking my hair, and then he'd kiss me goodbye. After a couple of weeks, my ankle got better, but he still wanted to drive me to school every day. He started to wear cologne that made me sneeze in the car on the way over. He put on suit jackets over the usual button-down shirts he wore at the office. When we'd arrive on the steps of the school he'd cheerfully say "Bonjour," and start chatting away with Mademoiselle Sauget. Their conversations started to get longer; they'd talk about books they'd read, movies they'd seen, places they wanted to go, but he always had a kiss for me before he left.

My mother never suspected Mademoiselle Sauget, who was always friendly to her and told her that I was good at conjugation. My mother couldn't speak French very well and she only nodded at my teacher when she picked me up from school, her eyes shifting quickly to avoid having a longer chat. She seemed so out of place, in her jellaba and her leather slippers, and always, always in a hurry to get home. *Je sais, tu sais, il sait, elle sait,* I repeated as I walked through our house, but she never paid any attention to my recitations.

My father never swore me to secrecy. Perhaps he expected my discretion because he always said that the two of us were so alike. My mother often sat in the living room alone, eating sunflower seeds and watching Egyptian movies on television while the two of us read in the dining room, each of us bent over a comic book—*Tarzan* for him, *Tintin* for me. If it was warm, we went to the beach, while my mother stayed home because she didn't want to wear a bathing suit. He taught me how to swim, played soccer with me, and took me mussel picking on the rocks. I remember once, when my mother offered to put *ghasul* on my hair, I refused. I didn't want my hair to smell of oil and spices for several days, the way hers did. I wanted it to be soft and straight like Mademoiselle's.

"Are you sure?" my mother asked, taking one of my pigtails in her hand and looking closely at my split ends. "It'll make your hair stronger."

"Leave it, Fatima," my father said. "I don't want her looking like a peasant."

I was relieved and thankful and I skipped out of the living room, swinging my pigtails. My mother followed me all the way into the garden. "We can do it on the weekend," she said. "And you can wash your hair on Sunday."

"But I don't want to."

"It won't smell, I promise."

I shook my head no. Her dark, sad features seemed to melt on her face. She heaved a sigh. "You're so stubborn, just like your father." She turned around and headed back inside the house.

When my father dropped me off at school the next day, Mademoiselle Sauget smiled at my father and called him by his first name, Hamid, which even my mother never did. I wanted to correct her, but I didn't. I stood between them, looked up at him as he was explaining something with big, dramatic gestures. I waited for him to put his hand on my shoulder or to stroke my hair. But he never did. He didn't kiss me goodbye. After a few more minutes of hushed conversation, Mademoiselle Sauget came into the classroom, sat on her desk, gave us something to read and looked dreamily out of the window at the florist across the street. Her pearly white skin had turned pink on her cheeks. She dangled her legs under her pleated blue skirt as though she was in a hurry to dance.

At dinner, I sat across from my father and watched quietly as he ate, carefully picking out pieces of the meat *tagine* with his fork and knife. When he finished, he pushed his plate away and got up without saying anything. I was waiting for him to fetch his pipe and go sit on the veranda. I always sat next to him, enjoying the smell of his tobacco, which lingered on my clothes long after he was gone. But that night he said he was going to get some air. As he put his jacket on, my mother asked what he thought about getting my ears pierced. She said I was getting old enough now. I turned to look at him.

He shrugged. He seemed to be somewhere else already.

I pressed him. "Do you think I should get them pierced?" I asked as I tugged at his sleeve.

"It's up to you," he said, and checked his collar in the hallway mirror before leaving.

"Okay," I said to my mother. "I'll go with you."

On the day I became my mother's daughter, we left the hair salon in the medina, and walked hand in hand to the taxi station. I asked for an ice cream. "After we go show your father," my mother said, already waving at a red cab.

"Please, Mama," I said. "Let's go to Les Délices." I dragged her toward the ice cream parlor where I remembered Mademoiselle Sauget said she liked to go. We'd done a class about our favorite foods the week before. Mine, like my father's, was mint tea; hers was strawberry sorbet from the fancy place near school. "Please," I begged. "Let's go now."

My mother smiled, tilted her head. "We can go, if you want," she said, as though she'd given up on the thought of catching my father in the act.

Requiem
Leah Silvieus

Short-lived, uncommon
among the magpies and sparrows

that stunned themselves against
our front window, the escaped parakeet

found us and survived. We bought a cage,
and there her mottled feathers fought

the mesh, churning like a choking
motor. The plastic latch was not enough

to hold her in, and she died, crushed
in the jaws of the housecat,

her wild-winged heart
too much for him to bear.

Migration
Leah Silvieus

You say that you are doing this to spare me,
but I know otherwise. You are flying away

for the winter, as you always do, soaring
toward shores that never see snow.

In your shadow, old pine sweeten
into orange groves; crows kaleidoscope

into flocks of scarlet macaws, flamingoes.
You melt the Great Lakes into firmaments

of starfish. To leave a place, yes, is to understand
we own nothing: some of us are born birds,

others, the trees that hold only their brevity

What We Left Behind
Mūthoni Kiarie

In the beginning, the sandy ground was littered with the things that those who went before us had abandoned: sisal sleeping mats, many with the threads that bound the fibers together loosening as they flopped in the wind; suitcases; water troughs; beaded jewelry; tin cooking utensils; thin cotton dresses, skirts, shirts, and trousers; woven baskets, the kind that carried cassava crops from one home to another, and bigger, more elaborate baskets, the kind that were given to a new bride on her wedding day; rubber-soled sandals, ones for tall men and ones for smaller men, and thinner ones for women, flimsier ones for children, and all black, blacker than the people whose feet they had once adorned. But as the days went by and we continued to walk, there were fewer and fewer of these things, and instead we began to see a scattering of carcasses from animals left to die in the dry desert heat.

The flies rose and settled as we approached, like the large flocks of swallows during harvest season that would dance in synchrony to the wind above our cassava fields. As we walked on, we came upon even more carrion, outnumbering the sparse desert thorn trees. We took to stepping over the rotting flesh, ignoring the ripeness that rose into the air, sticking to us, thick and pungent like the smell of fermented porridge. Vultures too circled, settling in with the flies on the feast that cluttered the landscape.

Uncle had been writing to Mother from Nairobi for months urging her and Father to come away and stay with him. She dismissed his fears, writing back to boast about our bountiful harvests, how well I was doing in school, how quickly Brother was growing, this cousin's successful wedding ceremony and dowry arrangement, Father's prestigious government job, anything good she could think of. She didn't mention the anxious stories I heard her whisper to Father late in the night about the Others who were raiding nearby villages, about this neighbor, that relative who had said something about the government in passing or carelessness and had disappeared shortly after. She said to our father that Uncle was a traitor for leaving this place that was home. She cried sometimes when she read the letters to Brother and me. She and Uncle had been so close, she said. "Can you imagine if your brother abandoned you? Wouldn't you cry too?" she asked me.

The Others came in the light of day without fear of retribution and splayed Father open. When we heard the neighbors screaming and could not tell if it was they or their animals on fire, Brother and I ran into the forest and hid like Mother taught us. When it was quiet, Mother came to get us from beneath the roots of the old trees where we hid, and she brought us back to the house where Father was painting the ground a lush red. She was limping and her dress was torn in front. She tried to pull the pieces together to cover her thighs. Her lip was swollen and looked like if I touched it, the blood would begin to flow and cover my finger. She sent us around to gather the things we would carry: food, water, our clothing, and sleeping mats. Mother grabbed the letters from Uncle and buried them between her breasts underneath the shuka she wore. We left in the night with those that remained from our village: many children, many women, few men.

When we started out, Mother was always crying. At first we cried with her, Brother always asking when Father was coming to join us until Mother shouted at him to stop asking for things that can never be again. I took Brother away then to look in the sand for small grasshoppers and ants that we could take back to Mother to roast. Now we hide in caves, and the rare tree groves we find during the day and we walk swiftly in the night. The rations are almost gone. We have started leaving people behind. They lie weak and unable to get up when it's time to move again. Yesterday, our neighbor's grandmother didn't wake up. Those of us with some strength whisper-sang a funeral song as her daughter wailed softly and covered her face with a cloth.

Mother cannot carry Brother anymore. We stay two nights in one cave even though we know it's not safe. The others in our group move on after the first night. They say they will walk slowly so we can catch up. But Brother cannot walk. His eyes are so wide open, his body so small, and I count his ribs, slipping my fingers between each from one side of his body to the other. He giggles and coughs at the tickling of my finger. Mother is on her haunches by his side, rocking back and forth sometimes, passing her hand over Brother's forehead and kissing it at other times. She pulls aside her shuka and hands me one of Uncle's letters to read aloud. The words are bright and encouraging. They paint a world unimaginable: food and water, a roof that does not let us see the sky, no one to hide from or fear, and no more walking. "Come, sister," Uncle's words plead. "Let me help you." Brother smiles slightly as I read. Mother's tears have dried by the time we trudge away, my hand in hers, Brother's gaze and soft gasps for breath on our backs.

A woman's baby died today. Even though I'm too old, Mother begs the woman and promises her rations for two days if the woman will let me suckle her milk. I climb into the woman's lap, our bones clanging together like faint cowbells as I settle on her thighs. Her arm cradles my head as she pulls out her flat breast, the skin flaxen, and pushes the rough nipple into my mouth. I take it greedily, as instinctively as I would have almost ten years ago, sucking the warm milk. Her eyes look beyond me to the still, small bundle at her side and her tears mingle in my mouth with the sweetness of her milk.

Some in our walking group say we have just three more days to walk. They tell us that we will be welcomed with plates of food and a well so deep and full, no one will tell us how much water to draw. Hold on, they say to each other, taking turns to bear the weight of one another. They carry Mother until they cannot.

Mother made me read her another of Uncle's letters before we left her leaning on a short thorn tree with barely enough leaves and branches to shade her. The stiff pages of the letters scrape my chest underneath my shuka, uncle's words of promise squeezing my heart. What will I say when I see him? I think I will tell him Mother's eyes were closed when we walked away. I think I will say her back was strong and steady as she propped herself on the thorn tree to watch us go. I think he will be happy to hear that.

Prayer for a Pomegranate Heart
Janine Mogannam

For Neda Agha-Soltan, whose name means, "voice." Neda was killed in Tehran during the 2009 Iranian election protests. Her last words were, "I'm burning." the Iranian government prohibited her mourning.

born with a bullet pointed at my heart
dying on the street in the city that i love

clouds of black and green gather around me
as faces blur, voices fade,

bodies form a shield to block the sun
as i am relieved of the burden of blood

my ripened heart splits open
seeds bursting and scattered to sow

they plant themselves into the road
& grow towards me as my soul is uplifted.

but i will thrive
inside the burning that has taken my body

breathe mint and honey into the scald
reclaim my young skin and lungs

my voice will cut through clouds of gunpowder and gas
enter the throats of those who deny my mourning

their tongues will be cut out & replaced
by tongues that sing only my name

& i will rest in sublime serenity
while my eyes haunt them for eternity.

Hands in April
(fairuz)
Janine Mogannam

homemade chorus holds a cross of green palm fronds against her hands
all gathered in a quiet bedroom
now still   the chair a throne   she a princess
softly singing low   just a little longer
her blood slowing   rubbing skin   time nearly out

remembering these hands that set love simmering   hands working proud
until elastic skin   thick blood   pulled palms still
the light *fairuz*   turquoise   as grandmother shrinks away
these rose palms   lemon hands   always moving   skin
an ocean   fallen palms   she: panting   white
before red heart skips & stops

her song *fairuz*   her voice a bird
her sunday   her english   making proud   a life across oceans
sixty-seven years   she rests now
with ivory soap   red lipstick   blue music escorting her home
her love scratching memory   never forgotten
sugared lemon hands now sing   .   go sweetly

Leaking Bodies
Rae Paris

You find L. hunched over his wine glass at the bar, a dimly-lit Spanish place in the Mission that reminds you of vampires. Shove the newspaper in his face. "See," you say, "just like I told you. Dude's taken other people's bodies, drained the fat out of them, injected them with silicone, and preserved them. Now they're leaking plastic and human fat."

"Cool," says L. He doesn't sound impressed.

The front page of the "Arts and Living" section features a woman's flayed body. Her breasts jut out in the way that only silicone-injected breasts drained of human fat can jut. Her back arched, her legs close together, feet pointed down, arms stretched wide, muscles cut and peeled away from the tops of the arms like wings—a skinless dancer flying through the air. *The Bodies are Leaking* runs the headline. A thick, cloudy liquid, says the paper, in puddles on the floor of the gallery. Read this out loud and imagine pools of tears, what it might look like if every inch of a person's body could cry. That would be something—arms crossed, sobbing discreetly from an elbow, catching the tears in your cupped hand. Tell this to L., and when he says crying from an elbow sounds too complicated, remember when you were together L. was more concerned with logistics than poetry, one reason why sex with him was never that great. Say, "Well, where would you cry from?"

"I wouldn't."

"But if you could?"

"My cheek, I guess. If I had to."

"But everyone would see. You can hide your elbow in your other hand." Sit on the barstool next to him, cup your left elbow in your right hand, and rest your chin on your left fist to show him how easy it is. "See," you say. "I could be crying right now and you wouldn't know it."

"Okay," he says. He downs some wine, licks red off his bottom lip.

Remember it's been five months since you last saw him, and over two years since you broke up. Remember *you* broke up with *him*. Remember you're supposed to be friends. Remember how easy it is to fall back into these conversations where there's no point and no one wins and all you want to be is right.

The flayed woman's staring at you both, sort of. Her head leans back and tilts to the side, and her eyes bulge like they might pop so it's hard to tell. Make up a song in your head whose only lyric is *I want to be flayed*.

"Hey," you say. Tap his leg to the rhythm of the song in your head.

"Hey." His eyes stay on the flayed woman.

Remind him it's been five months, the longest the two of you have gone without talking. When he says, "I know," give him a side hug, which he leans into, sort of. Exit the awkward side hug as graceful as a flayed woman.

When you texted him a few days ago, he sounded excited: *Of course*, he wrote, *I'm in2 bodies*, especially leaking ones, which made you laugh out loud, but now you sense something's up. A lot can happen in five months. For the last five months, you've been wondering if moving in with F. was a mistake. For the last five months, your empathy for the battered women at the shelter where you've been volunteering has turned to hate, so much that sometimes you want to punch them. You know better than to say this out loud. At the shelter, you blink a lot and hope the feeling will pass.

The bartender, a hairy White man dressed in black, a silver crucifix stuck in his hairy, pale chest, places a little glass bowl filled with orange goldfish snacks on the bar. He pours you a glass of wine from the fancy looking bottle of red L. has already ordered.

Eat goldfish and ask L. how he's been.

"Fine," he says.

Drink. Watch couples enter the bar and sit at small tables behind you. It's Friday evening. People are happy. A red votive candle sits in the center of each table. The bar you thought felt like a cave is romantic. L. picked the place to meet. Think, *all is not lost*. Add this to the "I Want to be Flayed" song.

You have a little time before you leave for the body exhibit. Drink more. Let L. talk about his PhD program in Anthro. Suck on goldfish. Push the grainy fish to the roof of your mouth. Say, "Wow, that sounds great. Such good work. So interesting." In the mirror that lines the back of the bar, a bottle of whiskey hides part of your face. Blink a lot. Fight the urge to hit both of you for this stupid conversation.

"What about you?" he says. "How's cleaning houses for rich people going?"

What you want to tell him is how lately, you've been thinking in fragments. Objects move, but when you look—nothing. Something is slipping away. Above the bar, two crossed swords hang over a stuffed bull's head. The bull's painted red eyes glower.

"Like roadkill," you say. "I've been feeling like roadkill." You rest your hand on his left thigh. "You know what I mean?"

In the past he would've said yes, or done something, anything other than what he does now, which is give you a vague smile, squeeze your hand, move it away from him, back to your leg. Then, he pats it. "You're just going through a phase," he says in that PhD voice he started using a year ago when he began his Anthro program at Berkeley. "Maybe you should go back to school," he says. "Stop being a maid."

Earlier, on the train ride over, an older Black man had looked you up and down. "My, my, my," he said, spacing out each word as if you were supposed to fall and melt somewhere in between. You started singing the Johnny Gil song in your head. *My, my, my.* My love? My little chicken gizzard? My fuck? Your patted hand sits on your thigh, still and rejected.

"School is for assholes[1]," you say. "I'd rather clean up real shit."

"How's F. doing?" he says.

Pour yourself more wine. You moved in with F. five months ago, right around the time you and L. stopped talking. L.'s looking at you in the bar mirror. The light from the votive candles, a flickering line down the middle of the bar, makes his white skin even paler, almost translucent. You can hear it, the told-you-so inside his question about F., as if he already knows you're going to lie. "F.'s great," you say. "We're great. Really great."

"Good," says L. "I'm glad you two are great."

F. has no idea where you are or who you're with right now. He paints houses for a living, focuses on masking edges, not letting lines bleed into each other. At first, you thought it was love, until you moved in with him and saw it up close—more like control. F. might treat you like the child he wants to have soon, but F. would never pat your hand like you were his little pet. F. is Black and L. is White. This matters in all the kinds of ways people want to say it doesn't.

The candlelight plays more tricks, makes your brown skin wrinkled and dim. This is it, you think, how you'll look in twenty years: over forty, and sitting in some bar, trying to pretend as if you're not trying to hook up with some reject from your past. Shake your head and there you are again. Drink some more.

---

1   She met L. in a beginning Anthro class when they were undergrads. She planned to study history, to get her B.A. and then her doctorate, be the first in her family, but she dropped out of school after a couple of years when she realized everything was fucked and no degree would change that. Of course M. had always known this, but her courses proved it. All the stories, really part of one big story, ended the same: if you weren't rich and White you were screwed. The last straw was in a class where the White professor, an expert in African American history, was giving a lecture on the migration from the South to places like Chicago where work was scarce and living conditions deplorable. He suggested maybe slavery wasn't that bad, at least the slaves knew they'd have food and shelter. For a minute or two, M. couldn't hear or see anything. When her vision and hearing returned she'd left class and went straight to admissions and withdrawn, afraid of what would happen to the rest of her body if she stayed in school.

L. raises his glass. "By the way, congratulate me. I'm getting married."

You're about to throw a handful of goldfish in your mouth. Close your fist and dig your fingernails into your palm. "To *what's-her-name?*"

L. has been dating a Korean woman from South San Francisco, not even a real city. He met her doing fieldwork for his dissertation, something about borderlands, or maybe extended kinships. You can never remember the working title. You blame your inability to remember the woman's name on their on-again off-again relationship. "How's what's-her-name?" you'd ask. It had never bothered L. before, but now he turns, finally looking at you. "You need to remember her name," he says. "She's going to be part of my life forever." He tells you her name again.

You immediately forget.

The restaurant is buzzing louder with people getting drunk. You unclench your fist to crumbled goldfish. Your fingernails have made sharp, smiling dents in your palm. You should feel something: jealousy, love, hate—something—but no, just a hole opening inside another hole, crumbled, dented, but those aren't feelings at all, are they? Look at him. Say, "So that's what you've been doing these past five months?"

"Yep."

"Why didn't you tell me?" you say. "I told you as soon as I moved in with someone."

"Over the phone."

Don't apologize. After you started seeing F. and he started seeing *what's-her-name*, you and L. still slept together every now and then. When you moved in with F. you dumped him for good. That's how things worked between you two. He should be glad he got a phone call.

"It feels really good," says L. "to love someone who loves you back. I want that for you. I really do."

He sounds as if he believes what he's saying. You want to throw something at him. Blink and drink more wine.

"Does this mean we won't be able to talk anymore?" you say. You miss your conversations, which were sometimes better than the sex, which were often better than the sex.

"You moving in with someone didn't keep us from talking, not at first anyway."

Ignore the accusation. Say, "That's different."

"How?"

"I don't let people control me."

"You don't let people in, period."

Remember the conversations you never had: L.'s taste for brown and black girls. Before you, there was that Afro-Peruvian girl, and before that some Filipina woman, and now *what's-her-name*, his native informant. And his mother. When his mother wanted to take the family to New Orleans to a luxury hotel that used to be a plantation, you and L. fought. Remember the way you screamed: "Would you get a mud mask at a concentration camp?" He went on the trip anyway. Later, he confessed that after the Afro-Peruvian girl he hadn't wanted to date another Black girl. He didn't want to have to think about certain things. "But then I met you," he said. It was supposed to be a compliment. Soon after, you dumped him. Some things you never want to explain. With F. you don't have to. Not having to explain matters in all kinds of ways people want to say it doesn't. Money was another thing—he had an allowance. The real truth: you didn't love him enough to deal with any of it. When you were together, he said he loved you, and you believed he believed it, but that didn't mean much. How could anyone really love anyone when there was so much bullshit? How could he love anyone now? He was just trying to replace you with someone less Black. You swirl the wine around in your glass. You could easily be drinking someone's blood.

L.'s busy munching goldfish. He's smiling, tapping his fingers on the edge of the bar to the flamenco music playing softly around you. You remember another reason you broke up: you hate the way he chews.

"Congratulations." Your raise your glass. "I'm happy for you," you say even though you're not.

He raises his glass. "Sure you are."

"Really," you say. "I'm really, really happy for you and…," you stop. L. eyes you. "For you both," you say.

You clink glasses. Imagine all the glasses clinking all around the world. Beginnings or endings? Either way, the sound is the same: hundreds of tiny hearts shattering. You slosh the wine around in your mouth to loosen goldfish lodged in your back teeth. All you feel is drunk.

***

Walk close together after leaving the bar. Let the wine and his announcement convince you your nostalgic. The truth is you began scheming the moment you texted him, but let yourself believe you're innocent. When he asks if you're cold, understand his question is an offering. You've been here before with him, with others. You know what to do. Nod. Let him put his arm around you. "Thanks," you say. Remember moments, like now, when you convinced yourself you wanted to love him. I love you. *Do you love me? Check "yes" or "no."*[2] Most of the battered women at the shelter still believed

2   Once in fourth grade, M. checked "no" and endured the wrath of a short Filipino boy

in love. You don't get it. Love always comes with a footnote. "Never depend on anyone," your mother would say. "What about Jesus?" "Sometimes Jesus has his hands full." When God closes a door somewhere the virgin opens a window. Tell that to the battered women. Sometimes love just comes with a fist. Remember your father—no fists, just a hard absence. L.'s arm around your waist like something you can almost taste.

In the car, reach for the radio at the same time. Your hands fumble together a second longer than needed. Your arm falls on the armrest. His arm drops on top of yours and remains there for the twenty minutes it takes to drive through the city to the body exhibit at the Masonic Center. Don't say a word. Pretend as if none of it's happening. Name it and it disappears.

He parks in a dark corner of the parking garage. In front of you, a concrete wall with faded graffiti you can't read. He makes whorls on your wrist with his thumb. You pick up his hand and gave it a puppy dog kiss. "It's hard not to feel as if we missed something," you say. You want to laugh. The line sounds like something you heard on a soap opera.

L. traces your mouth with his fingers. "We did miss something," he says, which makes you want to laugh even more, but he's serious, and so even when your stomach lets out a massive growl, and you want to giggle because you're a little drunk and hungry you still don't laugh. You smile and think about serious things: dead babies, the pregnant woman who came in last week with half of her face bruised. Think about something else.

You wait, and then you're leaning toward each other. L. presses his mouth to yours. You open your mouth and run your tongue across his bottom lip. The tip of his tongue touches yours. Not just a tongue. An ex's tongue. An engaged tongue. An almost-married tongue. A no-longer-yours tongue. *What's-her-name's* tongue. You thrust your tongue out even more. *Mine.* Climb on top of him. Let him pull you onto his lap. The steering wheel presses into your back. Hands fumble underneath clothes, between legs, negotiate buttons, a zipper. You wore a skirt on purpose, but your tights. Hold on to the headrest, lift up while he pulls them down. First his fingers, one and then three deep. He was never very good at this. You swat his hand away and lower yourself, and then he's inside. Something presses down on the horn. A knee. An elbow. God? *When God closes a door somewhere a virgin opens her legs.* No, you're always getting it wrong. Let his hands grab your waist. Hold on tighter to the back of the headrest. Say, "Yes! Yes!" When he says, "Fuck me," don't laugh. And, then, like a flasher's overcoat, the car door flies open and you tumble out. Pull up your tights. Readjust. Walk towards the exhibit in silence.

---

whose name she refused to remember. He told her "no" first, he said to everyone, and besides, he added, he didn't like Black girls anyway. The short little shit. She pegged him in the head with a four-square ball. M. hates that she remembers him, hates that she remembers all those moments that feel as if someone has run off with a piece of her. Those moments of theft obscure everything else.

***

The sign at the entrance announces the exhibit: *The Universe Within: a Journey into the Wonder that is the Human Body*. You walk through a short hallway and then turn right into a cavernous room filled with bodies, some in glass cases, some free-standing. The room is meat locker cold and stinks of dead things. You cover your nose and try breathing through your mouth.

L. wrinkles his nose and sniffs. "What?" he says. "I don't smell anything?"

His face is a little less flushed than it was a few minutes earlier, but his eyes are wild, moving everywhere.

"You can't smell that? It's awful."

In high school, you dissected fetal pigs—the prickly hairs, the incision down the abdomen. Large metal trashcans with heavy-duty black bags held all the pigs. Your biology partner had asked her to go to prom with him, but you couldn't separate him from the smell of formaldehyde that seeped into everything in the classroom. You told him no. Even now, when you try to recall his face, a gaseous, pimply cloud fills your head. The smell in the exhibit makes it hard to forget you're looking at real dead people.

L. grabs your hand. "You wanted to see this. Let's go."

You hold his sweaty hand. You don't mind pretending as if nothing has happened. You both work better this way.

The exhibit isn't that crowded: couples, artist-types with sketchpads, some families, and a few small tour groups. A fresh faced group of young medical students surround a White man in a white coat who points at the bodies. The young people grip their clipboards and take notes. Their little lab rat heads go up and down. Except for you, and the preserved bodies—all Asian, and the two old security guards—Black and Mexican—everyone in the room is White.

"What's wrong?" says L.

"Nothing."

The bodies are arranged on platforms in various positions to show the workings of muscles, organs, and arteries. The first one: a young boy sitting on a bike, his legs attached to pedals, his hands glued to handlebars. The bike's front license plate says, "Forever." *She's going to be part of my life forever*, L. had said. Maybe. The car episode has made you generous. "You know," you say, "I wouldn't mind meeting her."

L. is bent over a calf muscle, examining the tendons. "Sure," he says.

It'll never happen. You don't mind.

You move through a row of bodies that are standing, sitting, playing basketball. One body, its feet stuck to skis, is sliced down the middle. All of the bodies are skinless. Preserved eyeballs look out from what were once living and breathing Chinese faces.

"It's sort of weird they're all Asian," says L.

F. refused to go to the exhibit when he'd found out some of the bodies were unclaimed, possibly murdered, tortured, or part of an extensive black-market body trade. Even after you told him the guy returned the bodies he thought were stolen, F. still refused, saying it wasn't right. How could you know for sure? You still wanted to see them. You thought you'd find an answer to something. F. told you the only thing you'd find is that it's fucked up.

"I told you he got them from Beijing," you say.

"That's not what I'm talking about," says L. He slips into his PhD voice again. "It's a little creepy. They used to put real people in cages for fairs all the time."

"These aren't real people. They're dead. And they're not in cages."[3] You

---

3   M.'s about to remember something she's worked hard to forget. In an anatomy class in high school, her science teacher was explaining steatopygia to the class. To illustrate, he projected a picture of a naked Black woman onto the screen. The woman stood in profile, her arm at her side, staring at something M. couldn't see. Her nipple and breast pointed forward and her butt jutted behind her. She stood frozen, only half of her body visible. It gave M. the feeling that there was nothing on the other side, just a shadow. No one else seemed disturbed by this, by any of it. Students gasped or laughed at the immensity of the woman's butt. "Is that real?" someone asked. Someone else said it looked like Trina from third period. M. held her breath until the screen was blank again.

Of course, the idiot teacher didn't say the woman's name—Sarah Baartman— didn't say anything about her life, how she was a Khoekhoe woman, a slave, born in the eastern Cape during a time when White settlers were wreaking the usual colonizing havoc—stealing land, enslaving, raping, murdering; didn't say how the animal-like descriptions White travel writers gave to the KhoeK-hoe helped set the stage for enlightened scientists like Linnaeus, the Grand Wizard of race, who classified Khoekhoe as "homo sapiens monstrosus," the same category as feral children; didn't say how these travel writers and scientists were obsessed with Khoekhoe bodies, first with men's testicles—believed to have only one—and then with women's supposed elongated labia and what was seen as excessively large buttocks; didn't say how their fascination of the buttocks—the visible—became a stand-in for what couldn't be seen—the genitalia and sexual depravity it represented; didn't say that because of her perceived abnormalities and sexual appetite, Sarah Baartman was displayed in freak shows in London in 1810 where she was poked and heckled; didn't say anything about the debate going on in London about the prohibition of slavery and how that might have been connected to Sarah's exploitation, to the ever growing need for evidence of racial inferiority; didn't mention anything about the embattled court case brought by abolitionists on Sarah's behalf where, under suspect circumstances which included a questionable contract, a judge determined Sarah was not being held against her will; didn't say anything about how after the court case her owner displayed her outside of London in smaller venues, how her so-called contract"was sold in 1814 to an animal trainer who took her to Paris; didn't say anything about how in 1815, still in Paris, she was prodded for three days by seven White scientists who wanted evidence for their sexual fantasies, how one asshole tried offering her money but Sara said no thanks, refused to let them see between her legs, didn't say what this act of resistance would mean for generations of Black women, how we'd hold onto it; how the image the class was seeing was drawn by Cuvier, one of the asshole scientists who compared Sarah to monkeys; how she died later that same year, how they made a plaster mold of her body, how they took sixteen hours to dissect her, how they preserved her brain and genitalia in glass jars and displayed them along with her skeleton and the plaster mold of her body; how at the time M. saw the picture, Sarah Baart-

cover your nose and mouth and breathe. The stink is getting stronger. "C'mon," you say.

You move toward the glass cases. Some cases only hold body parts: a smoker's lung, a stroke victim's brain, an alcoholic's liver, as if the only thing that matters are the parts that turned against them. Inside one case, lies a body cut into slices like meatloaf. Spaced a few inches apart from each other, the pieces stretch almost ten feet long.

You let go of L.'s hand, put both hands on the case, and lean over it. "Whoa," you say. "Check this out."

One of the guards, a slim Mexican man with curly grey hair, about seventy years old, steps forward and asks you to remove your hands. The guard points to the floor sign: *Please Don't Touch the Glass Case.* "Too many fingerprints," he says.

You lift your hands and say, "Sorry." The guard walks away.

L. laughs. "You're going to get us in trouble."

"Stupid rules." You clasp your hands behind your back and peer over the case. You're amazed at the clean, precise slices, at how orderly and tantalizing it makes the inside of the body appear.

People move around the case pointing, giggling quietly, staring with open mouths, shaking their heads, and avoiding each other's eyes. Everyone whispers, as if they're staring at an open casket. A young White Goth woman

---

man's brain, genitalia, skeleton, and plaster mold were in a basement in the Musée de l'Homme in Paris; didn't say anything about who Sarah might have loved, the children she lost. And of course he couldn't have known that eventually, in 2002, after much pressure and activism, France took eight years—eight years!—to basically say to South Africa (and to other countries), "Okay you can have her back, but the rest of the booty we've plundered is still ours." No. He didn't mention any of this. All he talked about was Sarah's rear end as if it wasn't connected to anything, not even to Sarah herself. But he didn't have to. In the few seconds the slide was projected onto the screen M. got it just by looking at it, how she was seen.

I won't include the image M. saw that day. Pictures of Sara are readily available in some version everywhere. The nude or partially nude images are often flung about, out of context, removed from the story of her life. I've given an abridged version but if you really want to know about her you should read anything and everything by Yvette Abrahams. There's also a helpful book by Clifton Crais and Pamela Scully. The images of Sara, as Yvette Abrahams points out, say nothing about who Ms. Baartman is but rather reveal "the minds of those who made and viewed them." The teacher, of course, didn't talk about this either.

It's because M. is about to remember that she interrupts L. Of course, she doesn't realize this, but she's been doing this her whole life, both running and trying to remember. In fact, the reason she dropped her beginning Anthro class was because the professor began showing slides from Clifford Geertz's work on Balinese cockfighting. The slides of brown people next to enraged fighting cocks triggered a slight loss of hearing that she experienced more intensely later in her college history class. She's tried her best to avoid all situations that might trigger the sudden freezing up of her senses, but she's a Black woman so, of course, that's impossible.

I don't know what would happen if M. could remember this moment or any other forgotten moments, if her choices would be any different. In this story, I haven't allowed her to remember. In that sense, I've failed. At times, it's hard not to feel as complicit as the travel writers. Like all good stories between natives and colonizers this one is far from done.

dressed in black—black ruffled skirt, black lace shirt, black lipstick, her face pierced with silver earrings—approaches the opposite side of the case from M. and places her hands on the edge. "This is so cool!" she says to the guy standing next to her, a thin, pasty boy with dyed black hair brushed over his forehead, his eyes barely visible. "Can you believe they let him get away with this? Look at that! Holy fuck! They sliced him up!"

A mother standing with her daughter nearby presses her lips together in disapproval at the Goth girl's language. The woman pushes her young daughter, who is staring open-mouthed at the Goth woman, away from the table.

"Holy fuck," says the Goth woman. "Holy fucking fuck."

The guard approaches the Goth woman and asks her to please remove her hands and lower her voice. He points to the sign again.

"Lighten up," the Goth woman calls out as he walks away. "It's not a funeral."

The guard turns and puts his finger to his lips.

The Goth woman sticks her tongue out and puts her own finger to her lips. "Shhh, back," she says. When the guard turns away, she runs her fingertips back and forth across the case as if she's playing the piano. The guard turns around again, but she takes her hands off in time and holds them underneath her chin, trying to look serious. She catches you staring, and winks.

"He's just doing his job," says L., loud enough for the Goth woman to hear, and then he walks away.

"You with him?" the Goth woman says.

"Yes," you say, and then you realize how that sounds. "I mean, no, not really. We're just friends. He's getting married. I live with someone."

"Oh," she says, "that. Been there." She looks back down at the sliced body. "Holy fuck," she whispers.

You join L. who has moved to a case that holds a woman's reproductive system. Two boys, no more than ten years old, lean over the case.

"What's a vulva?" one of the boys says.

"Huh?" says his friend.

"A vulva. What's a vulva? Is that the same as vagina?"

The other boy shrugs. The boys turn towards you. You start to answer, but L. pulls you away. The boys wander over to the body of a boy throwing a baseball.

You stand slightly behind L., your chin almost resting on his shoulder.

"Wouldn't you have been happy if someone had told you what a vulva was when you were young?"

L. puts his hands behind him and squeezes your hips. "I liked discovering it on my own."

In front of you is a man's body, his legs apart, his hands on his hips. A shriveled Vienna sausage penis sits between two equally shriveled fig-like testes. The testes hang from two thin fettuccine straps. You remember you're hungry and still a little buzzed.

"It all makes sense," says L.

His mouth is right next to your ear. You want him to stick out his tongue and lick your neck.

"You don't realize how fragile what you're carrying is until you see it like this," he says. "I mean, look at it. Look what's holding it together. It might as well be rubber bands." He moves one hand toward his crotch.

You stare at the penis. Was the exhibit supposed to be this arousing? Was that why people came to see it? Maybe after the exhibit people went home and mauled each other, maybe they imagined thin tubes connecting their life force, fragile muscles, and networks of arteries. You share this with L. He suggests you've had too much wine.

"I think it was the goldfish," you say.

Please Don't Touch the Body. Please Don't Touch the Bodies. Please Don't Touch. Like nuns warning against masturbation, the signs are everywhere. How are you supposed to know the body without touching? Only recently ropes had gone up because people started stealing. When the exhibit was in L.A., two women ran off with a thirteen-week-old fetus. One opened the glass case, and the other dropped the fetus, about four inches long, in her pants pocket. They caught it all on tape, but they didn't catch the women. In San Francisco, ropes went up to prevent stealing but also because the bodies started leaking. Newspapers talked of contamination, poisons. People complained, but you don't see any liquid anywhere.

You walk up to the guard who told the Goth woman to quiet down. "I thought the bodies were leaking," you say.

The guard shakes his head. "They fixed that."

"How?"

He looks around the room, uncomfortable. "They don't leak, and if they do we wipe them off." He scurries away.

"It's still interesting," says L. "Let's go see the fetus."

The woman's front is split open from neck to waist. Her rounded stomach holds the carcass of an eight month old fetus. Perched on either side of the open stomach, the woman's hands look as if they've been interrupted from extracting the fetus. The placard next to the body says "Birth." No other identifying information is given. *When you need to learn, you cannot mourn*, the man who created the exhibit had said in the paper. You tell L. this is why there are no names next to the bodies. "It's supposed to be educational," you say.

L. is silent, still amazed by what he saw a few seconds ago. You try to feel the awe L. felt when examining the penis, but the fetus barely seems human, and the heart, just a hardened mass of chocolate pudding. You're glad the women who ran off with the fetus haven't been caught. You imagine them in a cottage up north, Bodega Bay, Jenner, somewhere near the water, a full-size refrigerator devoted to the fetus, the fetus in a small glass jar on the top shelf in a room with a view. The women must have felt something when they stole it. You haven't felt anything for so long. The sex you just had—already gone.

You do a quick check of security. The guards are on the other side of the room. You tell L. to cover you.

"What?"

"The heart," you say. "I'm not leaving here without feeling something." You put one leg over the rope.

"Don't be stupid," says L.

"I'm not the one who's getting married."

"What does that have to do with anything?"

Everything. Nothing. Stop listening. You stretch out your arm, but you can't reach. You put your other foot over the rope, step onto the platform, and wrap your hand around the heart—smooth and cold. It doesn't feel like much of anything. It feels preserved. That's not a feeling either. *When you need to love you cannot mourn. When you need to mourn you cannot love.* No, that isn't it. You're always getting it wrong.

A voice asks you to please step away from the body. Don't listen. Soft drums, and a high-pitched woman's voice singing in a language you can't understand pour from the speakers in the ceiling. Why didn't you notice the music earlier? New Age tribal bullshit. You would've joked about it with L. You take a deep breath through your nose, swallowing the stink as best you can. Behind you, the guard's hands reach for your waist, but you hold on tight to the heart. A cracking sound, important parts tearing, snapping away, and just like that, the heart is in your hand.

You turn. A small crowd has gathered. Hold the heart up. The crowd stares, not at the heart, but at you, as if they can see inside you.

The other guard, African American, reaches for the heart. "Miss, please," he says. "We have enough trouble."

Shake your head. Move the heart closer to your chest.

The Goth woman raises her fist and shouts, "Right on. No one owns the body." Earrings, like tiny handcuffs, pinch the Goth woman's eyebrows.

"What are you doing?" says L. He looks sad. He puts out his hand for you. Your afraid what will happen once you cross back over the ropes. You miss F. but if he was here, you don't know if you'd take his hand either.

Tomorrow's headline: *Woman Breaks Woman's Heart.*

"Just give it back, lady," the guard pleads. "It's always the women," he tells the crowd.

Soft drums spill over you, a wailing voice on top of the drums. Clutch the heart as if it's your own. Make up your own lyrics. My heart. My little pudding. My little chocolate heart.

Peach Tree Fruit
Sharline Chiang

Science says
it's probably advanced maternal age

I can't stop thinking
it's this tree in me
cursed by some wizard
waving a boney wand in floating
ink smoke
my eggs quivering
opal beings
like the magic beans in James and the Giant Peach
fighting for their lives

If only I could save one
put it on my fingertip
say there
you are

All I need is one

Exhibited
Sharline Chiang

Saartjie Baartman says to Afong Moy:
they shall never again call me Hottentot Venus

Afong Moy: they still call me Afong Moy
before that
Juila Foochee ching chang king

what is your name?
no one knows
my name is also not my name
it made no difference to them
they made me gyrate nude
they made me show my feet
they treated me like an animal
they treated me like a doll
I was a slave, left to die
I was a curio, left to disappear

from memory

Apology Accepted
Gail Dottin

I don't normally cry over the presence of mannequins, but when I saw this one the tears rose.

I am in Panamá. It's the fall of 2008, though there really is no fall here, just moist heat all the time—weighty, greedy clouds hoarding droplets like kids collecting marbles until they are too heavy to hold. Exhausted and defeated, they let go in the air—sheaths of water rushing out for days, sopping, overrunning the land, keeping people housebound and waiting. For the first time as an adult I am living here on my own—not a vacation visit with my parents and family who know this place as home no matter how many decades they have been dug in and planted in the States. Panamá City is where I am making home for now—in El Cangrejo, a cosmopolitan neighborhood of tourists, expats, and natives, of simple stucco homes and new glass condos (some of which I'm told are funded by Nicaraguans wanting a place to hold their money away). I've received a Fulbright Fellowship to come here. My project: researching the builders of the Panamá Canal. But there's more.

It is time for me to have a Panamá address, be in these streets. I have left New York, my city, my admissions counselor job. I'm 41 and have some things I need to live out and see. Mainly, I want to find evidence so that no one can deny who my grandfather was, and what he lived through. I need to align the pieces from various stories my parents told over the years: the complexity and beauty of how are we are both West Indian and Panamanian; why my father was raised on the Canal Zone; what my grandfather did; what he found in Panamá as a new recruit from Barbados at 19. But there are still spaces that need filling in.

His ID photo four years after the end of canal construction and nine years into his canal career reads "Gang# 155, 1918." My grandfather, Reginald McPherson, is a smooth, tight sheet of black, intent eyes; he is twenty-eight years old and no smiles. He worked in a storehouse then as a foreman in Paraíso—moving parts, checking-in supplies and machinery orders. In the early 1900s, as a 50-mile gash of land tore open from the soil of the tangled tropics from the Central American rainforest, about 200,000 West Indian men provided labor. These men, who had whipped machetes through cane on white-owned plantations in the British West Indies, traveled to Panamá and joined Atlantic to Pacific for the better life that was promised to them, a better life envisioned during toil. The majority of the recruits, 60,000 of them, came from Barbados—including my paternal grandfather.

In late May of 1909, the Peerless Steamer brought him to Panamá, five years into the construction. As a young man, he worked various jobs through its completion in 1914, from waiter in a hotel for white tourists coming to visit the muddy and musky endeavor in their crisp linen suits, their eyelet dresses, and parasols, to laborer. Afterward, he became one of the few recruits hired to stay on and work for the canal at that storehouse, where he worked until he retired at 62. My father's doppelganger peers out from the small square of Granddad's disability benefits identification card in 1968, the year I turned one and his fifteenth year in retirement. His face appears fleshier, his features fuller, creases in that once tight skin, low cut wavy hair, thick square eyeglasses.

My father, Vivian McPherson, grew up in La Boca, a tiny grid of a town on the Pacific end of the watercourse, one of the many Caribbean communities of canal workers and their families. He spent his youth there during the 1930s, going to school, playing baseball, swimming, being a boy. He's now in the eleventh year of his own retirement from Manhattan corporate life as an accountant, some of which was spent supervising the finances of a U.S. shipping company that pushed goods through the canal he lived next to, that his father helped to build and run.

My granddad died in Panamá on October 11th 1969, without ever meeting me, his two-year old granddaughter, his son's first child, the only girl. My parents my father, the son of a canal worker, and my mother, also Panamanian-West Indian but raised in the city—saturated our Queens home with the best of their cultures: the story music of Panamá's favorite son, Rubén Blades, from my dad's hi-fi, the rice and peas, *bacalaoitos* (crispy spicy cod fritters) amidst the Mac and Cheez, and roast chicken meals of Mom's dinner-time repertoire. Mom's visits or phone calls with my aunts would alternate between English and my mother's fluent Spanish, the Spanish saved for when they wanted to talk about their kids. Dad spoke some growing up, but having attended American schools on the Canal Zone and being surrounded by English speakers from the British islands and their children, he eventually let it go. Neither of them spoke the language in their own homes as children, only with friends in the city, so it never really occurred to them to teach my younger brother or me. Besides, it was a way of keeping things away from the children. So I studied some in high school and college yet was never taught but a few words and phrases in my house. Still my parents tried to talk to me as a kid, to fill me with tales of both my grandfather (*Abuelito? Would I have called him that?*) and the lives that men like him lived. From early childhood through my teens, I would walk out of the room, leave the dinner table or sullenly roll my eyes and tune them out, sigh and wish out loud for them to "Stop talking about this Panama stuff"—I couldn't have it.

Because it seemed like I always ran crying to my mother's lap. Always ran into the house from playing to find the balm of her hand smoothing my hair. "They're just jealous," she'd soothe. I told myself to believe that every time they'd say it: "White girl; you act like a white girl." I liked to read; so the school bus aide would find Mom when all the neighborhood kids spilled off at my stop to ask her was I always like this, to tell her that as spitballs sailed over my head and other kids were ricocheting with chatter and mischief, I sat quietly reading *Encyclopedia Brown* or some other book all the way home. On those afternoons on Mom's lap after the tears dried, Mom pulled out the Scrabble board and it would become a better day. Lively and wise brown children like me ran around my neighborhood, lived next door, across the street, down the block. I went to school with these children, middle-brown like me, and those lighter or darker. But I had only one brown friend. "White girl," the black kids called me "white girl." Not Oreo, no euphemisms, only clarity. So I couldn't have more difference. I couldn't. I couldn't have Panamá.

But my parents, they tried to tell me about the Gold & Silver; that as the passageway was being constructed by Caribbean workers, the Gold & Silver Policy was erected, dictating the parameters of their agency. Blacks like Granddad were paid in the lesser Panamanian balboa—silver—while the greater American dollar—gold—was doled out to their white American supervisors. In that 1918 photo my grandfather was earning $40 per month on the silver roll working in Paradise and never made more than $109 a month—$0.63 per hour—in his 43-year canal career; his white supervisors started at $87 per month on average along with additional money paid if the worker had a wife plus benefits like vacation pay. My parents tried to tell me that neither the "Silver Men," as they were sometimes known, nor their families were to live, eat, shop, drink water, be buried, be educated, relieve themselves in the same places as Gold Roll whites who had the most ideal living and working conditions, moving into new homes built by black labor and granted access to fine social clubs which were served and scrubbed by black hands.

Though American recruiters had arrived in Barbados promising good work, good pay and new housing, these workers lived in shacks and vermin-infested barracks on the Zone; maybe the lucky ones found a place in the city. There were no new homes built for them until nearly the end of construction. And if granddad or any other Silver Man tried to leave for a bit, say to take money back to their families and rest from the grinding work, they were fired. Signs indicated what hue of metal corresponded to which bathrooms and commissaries and clubhouses—etched into the stone, painted everywhere. Blacks were apprentices beneath pale American supervisors, despite the fact that white turnover was high since they often returned to their U.S. hometowns for less demanding work. Their more experienced black "apprentices" became the underlings of newly arrived Caucasian U.S. superiors. Only in the rarest of occasions would blacks like Granddad be named foremen, and even then, they had white overseers and the title carried no pay increase.

Thick women and dusky-complexioned men looked and sounded like they could be my dad's brothers; my father's friends were not strangers to me. But I never questioned how they knew each other. During my childhood I answered the door in my substantial afro puffs, letting them into our house, where they'd either hug me like a young niece —"What goin' on wit you, Miss?"—or be cordial, but be all about getting to business with Dad when they came to pick up the income taxes my father had prepared for them.

And then there were club meetings. I was always hearing about them. Dad was always getting ready for one or getting a call from somebody about something that had to be discussed at one, going to one or asking Mom to or "Order dis' t'ing for me for club meeting, okay, Olga?" I opened the door to let people in to these meetings in our basement, grew taller, but no more aware of what these gatherings were for. I knew they were a group, El Pacifico, but didn't know more than that. They'd rush in, anxious to get downstairs, say quick hellos to Mom in the kitchen fixing food for afterwards—"Smell good in 'ere, Olga. You cookin' up something good!" I was there when the meetings were over and they dimmed the lights and it became a basement party. I never thought about how these people knew my dad. But slowly I grasped that these weren't friends Dad had made from work or even college, that these meetings, this Club El Pacifico, was their high school alumni association, that they gathered each month to plan fundraisers to send money back to charities or students, that they'd come up together, gone to school together in Panamá on the Pacific side of the canal—thus their name—, that they moved to this country together, that after the talk was done they were moving to the rhythm of their childhood music with their husbands and wives, the Celía Cruz and Beny Moré of the neighborhood get-togethers and dances. Though he is nearing the eighth decade of his life and he's been living in New York for more than fifty years, Dad still has friends he's known since they were in Zone grade schools.

But still I didn't know that the school they all attended was segregated, that Dad and these friends of his had fathers and uncles and grandfathers who worked on the canal. I didn't know that all schools for children of West

Indian labor were solely occupational, created to make them useful labor for the canal. My parents tried to tell me. That even though my dad was born on American land, he was not an American citizen there, forbidden to be such because it would wrench the simplicity of the Gold & Silver system of privileges and payment to have black children of Silver laborers be eligible for Gold advantages. The Gold & Silver was an open secret on the Canal Zone and in D.C. So perseverance was the custom. Neighbors in La Boca, Paraíso, Red Tank, towns for Caribbean labor, were linked together by canal work and island traditions that made the transit and the understanding of how things were.

This black tide being hired for jobs in Panamá, jobs given to outside labor because Americans deemed Panama's citizens lazy, far less industrious than the West Indian, was an abrasion that only chafed and burned more deeply as the States amassed twenty-two military bases in the Canal Zone by the time the canal was placed under Panamanian rule for the first time in 2000. When U.S. canal authorities forced Blacks off the Zone after the construction was completed, former laborers built new communities in Panamá City. "Which was no better," says Mom, a Panamá City kid. "They called blacks *chombos*, niggers." The longer Caribbeans like my grandfather stayed, the more pronounced and vocal the resistance to them being there became. Books like the 1924 diatribe *El Peligro Afroantillano: La Defensa de la Raza* railed against this dangerous West Indian and by the 1940s Panamanian presidential candidates built platforms on how they would handle this Panamá problem.

Mom used to go on, "If you were dark-skinned, you couldn't get a decent job in Panamá." When applying for work, especially in white-collar positions where your face would be seen, like in banking or at a front desk, applicants were to submit the customary résumé and cover letter but also include a photo. When decent work did not come, many people turned to other means.

So for much of his life, during and after his Zone career, my grandfather was a numbers man. I'd heard parents of kids on my block—Southern transplants, Harlem natives—talk about playing the numbers and thought it was some piece of black American culture. So hearing it wasn't new or American, that my grandfather didn't play them but actually had a part in their operation, this I found curious. Dad would say, "My father put on his hat and had his little notebook would take down the bets, collect the money." On Sunday mornings my grandfather got dressed like he was going to work at the storehouse, his pudgy belly revealing his love for food, stressing the buttons of his short-sleeved dress shirt and belted in his slacks. He walked among the coconut trees, door-to-door collecting money from his regulars, through the blocks of La Boca, all named after the Caribbean islands from which their residents hailed—Guadalupe St., Jamaica St., Barbados St. As each bettor opened the apartment door of the wooden two-story buildings, he noted each name and amount in his little book and all the money was given to another man who paid him a percentage. "And when you see 11:00, no lemme see…," he looked up, squinching his eyes to see his father "10:30 because 11:00 he's very busy. He's counting. He would count, the money fall on the floor you think it's not counted. And a woman came by him one day and he busy busy and she went to pick up the money and he would take his foot and…" Dad stomps on imaginary bill. "He already had it counted!"

After he retired in 1953, Granddad, 62 at the time, moved to Rio Abajo, an impoverished district of rooming houses in Panamá City where many former West Indian canal workers lived. He'd been evicted from Canal Zone housing, as he no longer worked for the canal nor had children in school on the Zone. The year his father stopped working, my own father, in his early twenties at the time and with two years of junior college on the Zone, boarded a train from Panamá as a U.S. soldier. The Korean War was stirring and the American government allowed recruits from the Canal Zone for the first time.

My father didn't think about the reality that this had been done before, that his birth in Panamá resulted from the States needing people like him and his father to work for them. Granddad was only a little younger than Dad was when he left Barbados and arrived on the Zone. To my father and many of his friends it was just a way out. Trim and handsome in his uniform, pencil moustache, and right-angle jaw, Dad left to begin to create a life in the States that would allow him to become the retirement fund his father needed and deserved.

After more than four decades on the canal, Reginald McPherson received a monthly pension of $45, an amount arrived at by the canal governors by a formula they devised: a dollar per month for every year you worked, not to be more than $25. In 1954 the checks increased to $45 as fissures were spreading in U.S. segregation law. Still, the Gold & Silver policy remained on the Canal Zone until the 1980s. Mom and Dad spoke about all this, spent Sunday dinners and drives in the car retelling these stories to me, for me. But youth can be a blinding slurry of ignorance and arrogance. I felt like I couldn't afford to let it in. I was invested in being young and American, trying to fit in and irked by their chatter about this old-time Panamá place when I was growing up in New York, the coolest place on earth. Why were they still hanging on to that country? Why were they trying to pull me in?

In 1999, at 31, I came to Panamá with Mom, Dad, a dozen of his La Boca High School alum and their families to celebrate the 50th anniversary of their first graduating class. Sliding through the canal, heat on me like a bodysuit, my hand reached out to touch the bricks of the locks. We stood around the ship, some of us wearing the t-shirts Dad had made for the trip—a dark photo of canal laborers digging, between the words "West Indian Builders" and "Panama Canal Construction 1904-1914." We waited for the gargantuan iron doors to close, for the sea in the locks to elevate us. I discovered that those stories hadn't been completely silenced in me, that slices of my parents' recounted memories slid to the front to my brain, pride, and understanding. Back in New York, I searched the books and documentaries available, looking for black canal lives, never really feeling sated. I found a few written or produced by Caribbean scholars, inhaled them. But for the most part, I got facts about the structure: three locks—Miraflores, Pedro Miguel and Gatún— which lift a ship 85 feet during its transit, considered the 8th wonder of the world.

As a kid, each year February was alit with the 1000-foot TV screen glow of documentaries about the Civil Rights Movement—28 days of slow motion PBS, a school assembly, an ABC Special Presentation revolution celluloid: Freedom Fighters in contrast. Students at lunch counters that didn't look like students to me, not like me—casual but geeky, jeans and high tops—but like grown folks in jackets and ties and Sunday coats and dresses. The "Whites Only" sign over the counter. The cameras panned their faces, determined, until the coffee pot held by a white hand is freed of its contents, scalding the lap of the once silent protestor who leaps in agony. The still, pale masks around them watching. Water fountains marked with the race of throat the water was meant to quench. Portraits of charcoal faces bending over them to moisten beige lips. I put my grandfather at that fountain, under those signs. This Gold & Silver thing, this is what it called up in me. The films and documentaries were public declarations of this unjustness in America. History acknowledged. Where was that voice and vision of what my grandfather endured? And then, when pieces were aligning, I finally began to ask Dad about the discrimination, about how Grandad felt working under these conditions my father tells me, "He didn't talk about all that. He just accepted it." My Dad told me nothing, that after a long workday there was no tirade set free from my grandfather's lips, saved for his entrance into his home. It was just the way things were. I needed to go back to Panamá .

So now I am searching for more. I have studied Spanish for two years, gathered up words and verbs and grammar, put it all into myself to bring here, to this country, to understand. I go to Casco Viejo—the cobblestoned colonial village on Panamá Bay, now gentrified into a warren of boutiques and galleries, real estate offices, and renovated condos in Spanish brick and brightly painted wood, while the neighborhood's poor homesteaders hold on in closet-like quarters. Mom and Dad made it out of Panamá. They were young and able and came to the States in the 1950s, which at the time was certainly not any less prejudiced than the country they left. But there was possibility. My grandfather stayed. His body was tired and there was no savings to begin elsewhere or to go back to Barbados. Maybe if Granddad had lived longer my father might have brought him to New York, once Dad had more under him and secured us. Still, I know my father took care of him, had to. When I ask about the discrimination, he tells me "I sent him money every month! Every month till he died! He couldn't make it otherwise!" So I am here to visit the Interoceanic Museum of the Panamá canal. I want to see if those displaying this history will honor him and name the ugliness for what it was. So often the images I've seen and the words I've heard trumpet the greatness of the American feat, thumping Teddy Roosevelt soundly on the back for his vision. But it's fairly common to find only a passing mention of the labor force that came from the West Indies to build it. "Gold and Silver," "discrimination," and "segregation"—these are words hardly used.

Walking through the museum, I prepare for the nature of the displays: what a colossus of American innovation, the medals given to white workers to boost morale. Then, on my way out, I see it, and the tears form behind my eyes: a simple, brown, male mannequin in the white cotton shirt and dark pants of a canal laborer, a shovel propped in his hand. I took a deep breath and read words on the plaque in front like *"sistema segregacionista" "discriminitorio continua"* and *"segregación se institucionaliza"*. The museum is a Panamanian non-profit which has support from the Smithsonian among other historical preservationists. So these words are the shamed Panamanian and American apology that Granddad died without ever hearing.

I was last in this building in 1999 when it was technically closed, during that trip with my dad and my family and La Boca alumni. The museum, a stop on our city tour, was closed for cleaning that day. But our guide begged our way in, telling the manager that, as descendants of canal builders, it existed for us. At the time there was only one floor, and the canal was in the final months of American ownership. This plaque was not here then. After the canal's changeover to Panamanian rule in 2000 the museum expanded. A former Spanish Colonial hotel from the late 1800s, the bedrooms were refinished with new wood flooring and painted archways and now hold the exhibitions, the history.

The day I meet this mannequin, it is a quiet Tuesday afternoon. The sun is coming through the windows. I stand on the landing overlooking the exhibits below. A docent nearby is talking to his co-worker. I keep looking at him, unconsciously trying to connect. He sees me and we take steps toward each other. Teary and shaking inside, I search and conjugate and try to put together my acceptable but imperfect Spanish, but now even English is failing me. *"Ese hombre, él es mi abuelito. No exactamente, pero mi abuelito trabajaba en el canal. El era de Barbados, trabajo de 19 a 62. Todo de su vida."* I told him my grandfather's story, that he spent his life there, lived under the bias described, that he died before I could know him. The docent listened, nodded, attentive and taking me in, his face softening as I spoke. Still I don't know if he understood why I needed to tell him this. But I'm sure of why I had to be heard.

Vulture
for Angel
Li Yun Alvarado

three feet tall under the grip
of featherless human hands

its instinct, to draw near
the aroma of any impending
end, like the Gods who circle
at the first sign of sacrifice

instinct fails and the beast
wants distance from death

the hands, expert craftsmen,
kill quick, bathing their bodies
in the screams and stench
of the dead, finally released

His Thumb on My Belly
Li Yun Alvarado

To the right of my belly-
button: purple-black

oval print on sun-kissed
flesh. A spirit pinching

while I sleep. Is it
him? A hint? Here,

he whispers. Singed
meat. His thumb on my

belly. Now you know.
And they (some strange

foreign they) say there's comfort
in the knowing. Basements

are forgotten places where moldy
lies cling to dank walls.

On my back: the prickle
sting of inked flesh.

It knows how to burn.
Bruise. Heal. His thumb

on my belly. My aunt

lights candles, piles pennies

in corners, tells tales
of muertitos who pinch

at night. Like him. His
thumb on my belly. His

boys clothed in black
masks called "friendship."

Minions, I call them. When
they faced him, (my thumb

on his belly), not flesh, not lead,
not prayer could stop the blood.

Comadre
for Diana
Li Yun Alvarado

I.

There is no word
for this,

in english.

II.

hijo:

conceived
en ingles.

nombrado
in spanish.

nacido
into both.

madre
madrina

we never
mother

a solas.

Orchard Beach: Section Four
Oscar Bermeo

orchard   northbronx   thickheat   dampsheet
   beachtime   relief
boardwalk   beercans   boombox   bodyrock
   lowtide   dankdusk
jointpull   nightswim   freefloat   campfire
   dimlight   starfade
suresurf   shorebreak   gonebreath   nosleep
        rumtoast   sipup
handhold   armknot   legtwine hiplock
   comeday   hazebreak
heatwave   highjune   dayshade   orchard

I'm Jus Askin
After Huu Thinh's "Asking"
Oscar Bermeo

I ask sidewalk: How does sidewalk live with sidewalk?
— We don't judge who walks here.

I ask fire hydrant: How does fire hydrant live with fire hydrant?
— We keep each other cool.

I ask brick: How does brick live with brick?
— We make it day by day
holding each other up.

I ask city: How does city live with city?
I ask city: How does city live with city?
I ask city: How does city live with city?

Mixipino
Anna Alves

Jules Serrano wonders wants wishes plucks a linen-sleeved vinyl disc from a creaky crate, slides the 33 rpm record out, his fingers caressing the grooves, tiny striations smooth soft never scratched no not scratched until he did the scratching learned the scratches got the skillz to make music from the mess of song and screech and bass and brawn of lyrics and orchestra and gunshots and bravado, all the voices rapping who am I and who are you and fuck tha police and fight the power and Elvis being a hero to most but never meant shit to me mother fucker was racist, simple and plain, mutha fuck him and John Wayne.

His father loved John Wayne. The one thing he knows, which his mother told him. That's a lie. He knows two things. His father was Mexican. And he was gone, ever since Jules was born. Three things he knew then. John Wayne. Mexican. Gone. His mother, Petty short for Petunia, was Pilipina. Too many Ps make you spit so he goes with Filipino instead. He's half Hispanic so he figures he's cool with that. He's down with the brown two times over. So what if he says Hispanic instead of Latino or Chicano like the hard-core guys from San Francisco State—he's thirteen years old and doesn't care. He likes the "Hissss" of Hispanic over the "Lat" and the "Chih."

Jules places the vinyl disc reverent on one of the waiting flat wheels on the turntable altar, reaches back, slides another vinyl disc out of the crate, slips it from its sleeve, sets that one down too, on the other. He yearns to do this right, like his heroes Mixmaster Mike and Q-Bert and the Scratch Piklz, hometown boys from Daly City who blew up the globe with soundscapes. Mixed and scratched all the way to London Bridge, to The Ultimate Competition. Conquered the world so often, they were blessedly retired. But Jules is just a beginner, bought the turntable and records crate last week, secondhand, from his cousin Bong in San Jose, who was moving on to digital and monitor, who no longer wanted to lug around history in heavy crates, nostalgia expired. In the documentary film Scratch, Q-Bert said he always wondered what music would sound like on Mars, and that's what he listened for when he crafted his genius mixes. Reaching beyond turntable and bedroom and home and town, state and country and Earth. Headphones scattering DNA of humans amongst the stars. Jules believes that if everyone learned how to halo the sounds, the world would be a better place. Maybe even better than Mars.

That's why he decided to be a DJ. His best friend Gabby Gonzales from next door—the girl of the snappy serenade, her voice a feisty singsong—says, "It's because you watched Scratch and saw all the Filipinos and now you think it's cool." But, it was the movie La Bamba that did it. Lou Diamond Phillips—Filipino, Mexican, Indian, what?—playing Richie Valens, a Mexican-American rock star, making Latin sounds as American as apple pie. Or rather, making Mexican flan like apple pie. Which meant Philippine leche flan was fair game too. It was the mix it up that got him. He marveled that Lou Diamond could be Mexican in La Bamba then Indian in Young Guns then Filipino in that movie he wrote and directed himself Blind Ambition which no one saw nor liked but he did—saw and liked.

God said, in the beginning was the Word. But he had to say it first, that Word, so it could be heard. Jules is not good with words. When he meets someone, he listens. A voice has its own music, a timbre, a volume. His mother makes melodies, yet bites her words, sharp, cuts off the ends. Her Tagalog lisp softens the sharpness of the English truncating. Once, her sound embarrassed him. Now, he hears mash-up of countries, beats of the States over bass of old Filipinas, no rhyme, just reasons that extend beyond him and his mom and this house and San Francisco, even California. Reasons wrapped up in a series of sounds he would like to isolate and intermingle and intersperse at will, bridge cultures and countries, span oceans and universes. Somewhere in there was Mexico, too, and Jules yearns to find it, digs for salsa and mariachi alongside Tagalog ballads and OPM. Besame Mucho entwines enzymes with Dahil Sayo. Resurrection in the reverb; perhaps in sound, found.

Girls Night Out
Anastacia Tolbert

there we were
proof we spent a portion of our lives growing children
our stretch marks high fiving through designer sweaters
harboring fight the power & nina simone t-shirts
sneaky little gray hairs talking occupy & academic posturing

                                                                              pose

for a cell phone picture
halleluiah i-phone for all the ways you help us communicate
hit send/send it to the people we miss/tell them—everything is good.
all is well. lots to see.

                                                                              pose

our fat asses/size 8 jeans
sharing a roof with women whose
shoe sizes all together equal 10
we must decide quickly
do we suck in our bellies & sit without talking
or do we continue to chat while our bellies teeter over our pants
&
we completely understand there are more pressing issues in the world but…
which do we do
because visible muffin top or invisible muffin top—this we can control
remedy: s l o w l y place our purses & scarves over our bellies.

                                                                              pose

i wonder what they think of us
with our calf stubble
unwoven hair
colorless toes
our eye lashes just boring/just the ones we were born with/black

                                                                              pose

on the other side of the room sits a
japanese rasta with a good camera
his smile
jerk chicken & jasmine tea
gesturing to take our picture
asking to have a piece of our whatever
to run between his lens
let me take your picture

                                                                        pose

we & our big asses & big hair & big feet & sandalwood & recipes
smile a forced |who me| kind of smile
like get in front of the class & say a speech
about thomas edison
or butterflies
or raging volcanos
or pillaged lands
kind of smile

Let's Play House
Tatiana Richards Hanebutte

Fred Crenshaw Jr. was not a good father, but on Friday nights he pretended to be one. Picture him: freshly shorn, sharply dressed, seated at the head of a rent-to-own table.

"I see you rockin' that ponytail again," said Fred.

Sitting across the way was his lovely wife—well, baby's mama—Nanette. Back when things were good, she loved to go all out for him on Friday nights: Makeup on her face. Dresses that showed off her big Alabama legs. Fresh curls in that long, pretty hair that'd had all the boys trying to get her number, once upon a time. These days, no matter what kind of father Fred made himself out to be, Friday nights were a chore for her, a peacekeeping compromise. The best he could hope for was a clean shirt and a splash of lipstick. And that plain ass ponytail.

"Yes, this is a ponytail," she said in response to his frown. "Yes, I'm wearing my hair like this again."

"Why though?" Fred asked. "It ain't like you baldheaded, like these other girls running 'round Greenville."

A giggle—this from their son Omar—his raison d'etre, the only thing he ever did right—who was seated in his place to the right of Fred. Nanette sighed.

"You sure do talk about my hair a lot," she said, focusing on the collards as she scooped them onto her plate. "But if I remember right, you ain't got no problem with a baldheaded girl from time to time. Right?" Fred rolled his eyes while Omar looked from Nanette to Fred, not sure where the conversation had just gone.

"Here we go," he muttered.

"No, don't worry, we ain't going there," she said. "I'm just letting you know that pretty hair takes time, money and energy, and since I don't have none of the above, what you see is what you gone get. Plus," —Fred cringed as she plunked the bowl down onto the table— "I have to be in the mood to wear my hair out. And tonight, I am not in the mood."

"Oh you ain't?" Fred could take this as a warning or a challenge. As usual, he chose the latter. "We'll see," he said.

"See what, Daddy?"

"Stay outta grown folks' business, son," he replied, but when Nanette walked into the kitchen, Fred winked at the boy. Omar grinned in return, his dancing eyes and off-centered smile a reflection of Fred's own.

As he presided over this scene in Nanette's apartment, Fred could imagine Heathcliff Huxtable gazing upon him from a recliner on high, lips pursed in a smile of approval. You're alright, Fred, he would say. Omar certainly thought he was doing a good job: in his eyes, Fred was a king, a man to imitate. He incorporated his father's intentional limp into his second grade walk and on this particular evening had lobbied, without success, for permission to change into a khaki shirt and matching pants when Fred arrived clad thusly.

"Mommy, now can I—"

"No," she said as she returned to her seat.

"But why?" This was the third time tonight she'd told him no.

"I already told you: That ain't appropriate for dinner." She threw an irritated glance in Fred's direction. "Ain't appropriate for nowhere, really. It's something drug dealers wear."

"But that's what Daddy's wearing!"

"Daddy don't live here," Nanette pointed out. "That's why he gets to make up his own rules about everything."

"Well I like his rules. I want to live with Daddy!"

"Oh really?" she said, one eyebrow raised. "You want me to pack up your stuff?"

"No ma'am," he said, picking at his greens. He knew not to give the wrong answer to this question. "But next time, can we have Family Night at Daddy's house? Daddy, can we? Please?"

"Soon as I get it set up," said Fred. "And at my house, everybody gone have to wear a khaki suit to dinner. With a pair of J's." Omar grinned.

"And Mommy too?"

"Especially Mommy." Nanette snorted.

"Look here little boy," she said, her eyes softer than her voice, "Mommy doesn't do Jordans."

"But J's are cool!"

"As for you," she said to Fred as she cut her chicken thigh, "The day you actually have a place to stay is the day I'll buy a khaki outfit, with J's to match."

Fred sighed. He'd made few serious attempts to get an apartment since Nanette kicked him out last year because he was sure she'd take him back. But aside from the odd week here and there (and the occasional family night that turned into family morning), Nanette had been surprisingly resolute about enforcing The Conditions this time. (The conditions of return: 1. Get a job; 2. Keep that job, for more than a month; 3. No more baldheaded girls.) He'd really wanted to move out of his little brother's place, just to show her, but here in Greenville, Alabama, the only way to make serious bread was to build car parts for the Koreans. There were always more broke people than job openings, so the factory only hired folks every now and then. His cousin tried to get him on the last time they had an open spot, but the engine in Fred's car ran hot the day of the interview. When he got there—thirty minutes late—the manager wouldn't even see him.

Things were better last year, when Nanette was still willing to overlook so much stuff. Like that time Fred lied about paying the light bill, and the power got cut off while she sat in the living room with her friends. Or when the repo man showed up to take back the flat-screen TV, which they'd only bought because Fred wanted it so badly. She even let it slide when Fred got fired because he clocked out for his lunch break and never went back.

What she could not ignore, though, were the two women who came through her line at the Wal-Mart.

"These hoes walking 'round here all stuck up thinking they got their man on lock," said the pudgy one. Her friend—a stick figure, with streaks of purple in her ratty weave—nodded in agreement. "She just don't know: while she be ringing up groceries and shit, I be fucking her man. In her bed."

"Not in her own bed, Skeeter!" said the friend.

"Yes, honey. On her green bedspread, in that room with them tacky zebra print curtains." She dropped a box of condoms onto the counter. "How much these is?"

The next day, Nanette put Freddie out.

But petty bitches notwithstanding, Nanette never cancelled their family night ritual, which they started the first Friday after Omar was born. She claimed this was for Omar, but Nanette didn't always stop Freddie when he leaned in to kiss her on the neck. So tonight, as on all Friday nights, they sat together, the three of them around a table, and ate dinner. As a family.

"Daddy, look at my waves!" Omar said, bowing to show off the top of his round head. "I bet they make you seasick!"

"Yep, son," Fred grinned, "I'm so seasick."

"I know you are!" Omar replied. "'Cause I brush my hair a hundred times a night, just like you told me. You better get your lifejacket, Daddy!"

Fred laughed. After seven years (seven!) he still went soft inside and couldn't contain his smile whenever Omar said "Daddy."

Fred had never called his own father Daddy. Just Crenshaw, the same thing everyone else called him. He imagined that at some point in their lives they'd all lived together—Fred, his mother, his little brother Boo, and Crenshaw. But Crenshaw must've left before Freddie was old enough to ask why he wouldn't let them call him Daddy, because Freddie did not have a single memory of them living under the same roof. He did, though, remember the last time Crenshaw came to see them.

"Ya'll clean up now," Mama had said. "Crenshaw's comin t'night."

Never having been a presence in their household, Freddie remembered Crenshaw as an event, his last visit as exciting as each of the ones preceding it. Their little house was caught up in the Crenshaw frenzy of putting away toys and putting on clothes that weren't too small; of killing roaches, of brushing teeth extra hard. Even his mother, stoic as she usually was, impassive as all people who work themselves to death, even she would throw herself into the excitement. That day she ran around their government rental, straightening up everything, including the things that Freddie and Boo had already cleaned. Freddie had known Crenshaw was really coming this time because his mother made sure to stock their leaky refrigerator with a six-pack from the bootlegging man next door. As the time drew nearer, she reminded Boo to clean the wax from his ears and told Freddie not to "throw all that stuff under the bed" while lining her eyes with the remnants of a black kohl pencil. In the middle of all this crazy, she squatted down and gripped Freddie by the shoulders.

"You ready?" she'd asked.

Freddie grinned, seeing his giddiness shining back from her eyes.

"Yes ma'am," he said, nodding hard and smiling with all thirty-two teeth. She had returned his smile and kissed him on the forehead before finding more things to clean.

And when Fred Crenshaw Sr. finally got there, two hours late, the three of them fell silent, each wondering at this unreadable man who had graced their private space with his cool. For Crenshaw was the smoothest man Freddie knew: fresh Jheri curl, shoes bright as the gold edging his front tooth, pants creased sharp enough to cut. He parted his lips in the brightest smile Freddie had ever seen; still, no one knew what to say.

"Come here boy," Crenshaw said suddenly, scooping up Boo and lifting him high, so high that his little brown head tapped the ceiling. Laughter tumbled from everyone's mouth, making everything bright and shiny again. "If you act right, I might even let you drive the Cadillac." Through a gap in the curtains, Freddie stole a glance at the shiny black car.

Crenshaw sat down heavily in the room's nicest chair, a faded pink recliner someone had given them. He pulled Freddie close enough to breathe into his face, close enough to smell the aftershave and sweat.

"You doin good in school, Junior?" No one but Crenshaw called Freddie Junior.

"Yes sir," Freddie said, looking steadily into his father's eyes like Crenshaw had always instructed him to, trying not to blink.

"You been bein' the man of the house like I told you to?"

"Yes sir, Crenshaw," Freddie had answered, sticking his tiny chest out as far as it would go. Though Freddie was proud, Crenshaw's luster had faded just a touch, and he looked at the floor instead of Freddie's eyes, when he said, "Thass good, Junior. Real good."

And it seemed to Freddie that this had been the point when his mama appeared, touching Crenshaw's shoulder with a hand calloused from working a loom at the textile mill, a hand that still managed to feel soft when it caressed the surface of your skin. Crenshaw looked at her with a light in his eye that Freddie would not understand until years later, when he had to tell Nanette why he'd lost his third job in three months, and all she said was, "Baby. My baby." Not every woman can kindle that kind of light in a man's eyes, and bathed in this light from Crenshaw's eye his mother changed—she became soft. Blushing. A woman. As they stood there having an exchange he could not understand, Freddie quietly took Boo's hand and walked to their bedroom.

***

"Good morning."

His mother was leaning against his doorframe, still in her sleeping gown. Still smiling.

"Hey Mama," he said. "You ain't going to work today?"

"No, baby. I called in this morning." Freddie was about to ask why when he remembered.

"Crenshaw!" He sat straight up in the bed. "Is he—"

"Shh!" she smiled. "He's still here. He's 'sleep. Now go on in the kitchen and eat your grits so you can get ready for school."

"Aww, Mama! We still gotta go to school today?"

"Yes, y'all do," she said, kissing him on the forehead before turning to wake his brother. "Come on Boo. Let's go wash you up."

Freddie dragged himself to the kitchen. Stepping onto the cold tile, he stopped short: Crenshaw was not asleep after all.

"Morning, Junior."

"Good morning," he said, surprised by how small the kitchen looked with Crenshaw in it. He squeezed around Crenshaw and sat at the table.

"You getting ready for school?"

"Yes, sir."

"What grade you in now? Third?"

"Fourth."

"Fo'th! That means you 'bout old enough to drive the 'Lac!" Freddie giggle. He ate the rest of his breakfast in silence, stealing glances at Crenshaw between bites.

"Freddie!" called his mama. "Come on wash up and get dressed before that bus gets here!"

"Yes ma'am!" He looked at Crenshaw, unsure of how to exit.

"Gone and do what ya mama said, Junior," he said.

"Yes sir," said Freddie. But he hesitated.

"Something on ya mind, Junior?"

"Umm...no. I mean yes, sir." Freddie inhaled. "You gonna come back tonight?"

"Tonight?"

"Uh-huh. And...and have dinner with us?" Say yes, thought Freddie. Say yes. Freddie knew families were supposed to be together at the end of the day, laughing and talking and eating dinner. He didn't know any people who did this, but he had seen it on TV enough times to know what it was supposed to look like. Maybe if Crenshaw came to dinner tonight he would come again tomorrow and all the the tomorrows after that.

"Have dinner?" Crenshaw smiled. "You want me to?"

"Yes!"

"Alright then," said Crenshaw, smiling as he scooped more grits onto his plate. "I'll be waiting for you when you get off that bus."

But when Freddie got home from school, the Cadillac was gone.

And what was so hard about dinner, Freddie often wondered in the days that followed. He wanted to sit at the table, him facing Boo and Mama facing Crenshaw. Freddie wanted to tell them what happened in school that day, and he wanted Crenshaw to complain about how hard they were working him down at the pulpwood mill. Freddie wanted Mama to rub the back of

Crenshaw's neck while Freddie reached over and said, Could you pass the peas, Daddy. But the Cadillac never did show up outside their door again.

So when Nanette came to him two months after their junior prom, eyes red and nose sore from crying, Freddie was seized with terror that quickly turned into a hope for things he'd never known.

"You gotta stop crying," he had said to her as they sat on the curb outside his mother's apartment. "I promise I'ma take care of y'all. And I'm gone give the baby everything I ain't never had. We'll get our own house, and every night we gone have dinner together."

"I ain't cooking every day," Nanette said, sobbing a little less. Freddie laughed.

"Ok, not every night. But every Friday night, though. Friday night is gonna be Family Night." He could see the three of them sitting around their own little table. Happy. Nanette knew all of this and so continued to have dinner every week with a man who continually broke her heart.

***

After dinner Freddie put Omar to bed. He read him story after story. Another one, Omar kept saying, and who was Freddie to refuse? Especially tonight.

"And the gingerbread boy said, 'I've run away from a little old lady and a little old man, and I can run away from you, I can, I can!' You think he gone outrun 'em?" But Omar had fallen asleep.

Fred walked out of the room to find Nanette standing over the sink washing dishes. She had taken her hair down. Freddie brushed her hair to one side and planted a soft kiss on the back of her neck. She didn't stop him.

When they were finished Fred got up and went to the bathroom. When he came back, he was fully dressed. Nanette sat straight up.

"Where you going?" she asked. "It's 10:30."

"I got somewhere to be," he said, not looking at her.

"Hmph," she said. "Only things open this late are legs and liquor stores."

"That's yo problem," he said, putting his chain back around his neck. "You always think I'm into some shit or doing some dirt. You don't ever give a nigga credit for trying."

"What the hell you trying to do at 10:30 on a Friday night?"

"I'm trying," he said, "to avoid traffic. On the Interstate." Nanette's brow wrinkled.

"What you talking 'bout?"

"I'm fixing to drive to Orlando," said Fred.

"Orlando? For what?"

"You know my cousin Frank? He said it's a lot of jobs down there right now, and he got plenty extra space." Nanette just stared. Any fight that had been in her was gone. "Don't look at me like that. You know it ain't shit for me in Greenville." Nanette let out a hollow laugh.

"It ain't shit for you here? Oh, so I ain't shit? Your son ain't shit?" She tried to blink away the angry tears that threatened to run down her face. Fred walked over to the bed and sat down, pulling her toward him until her head leaned against his chest.

"You know that's not what I meant," he said. She tried to pull away but he wouldn't let her. Held her tight, with his face against her hair. "Y'all the only thing good things I ever did, but I keep fucking up. Hell, you said it tonight: I ain't got no place to stay. No job... I even much had to borrow the gas money from my brother." Somewhere in the walls the air conditioner kicked on, and for awhile the only sound in the room was its steady drone. Then Nanette spoke.

"You can stay here."

"You just saying that."

"I mean, you can't stay forever... But ain't nobody got time to be driving to Orlando for dinner every Friday." Fred smiled a small smile. She smiled back. "See? You don't need to leave Greenville. You can stay." He sighed.

"No I can't. I want to, but I can't." He waited for Nanette to protest again. When she didn't, Fred stood up. "Come on," he said. "Walk me out."

Even this late, the air was warm and sticky; still, Nanette hugged herself as she followed him across her balcony to the top of the stairs. "I'll call you and let you know when I get there," he said, turning around for a final kiss, but she was already heading back inside.

Fred had never understood how a man could just up and leave his family forever, no remorse, no looking back. But as he walked back to his car, where two suitcases lay neatly packed in the trunk, he found it wasn't nearly as hard as he thought. He got into the driver's seat and put his key in the ignition.

***

Omar had learned to dread the morning after family night. He never knew if his father would still be there and sometimes, if he put his ear to the wall as he lay in bed, he could hear his mother crying. So every Saturday he'd close his eyes and cross his fingers before peeking out of the window. If Freddie's car was still there, he'd smile and run into his mother's bedroom and snuggle between them until his mommy made everyone get up to have breakfast. If not… there were always cartoons, he supposed. Eyes closed, he got out of bed and creeped over to the window. He crossed his fingers, took a deep breath, and opened his eyes.

Omar grinned.

Fred had not left, not yet.

Your Life or Hers
Norma Liliana Valdez

the two of us sit in a coffee shop talking of dollars and rents and
people we haven't seen in over a decade (you don't see how I'm
driving my fingernails into the palm of my left hand) Paty's heart
has failed   drug-induced comas split-open chests and this reminds me of the poem I'm writing for our son   you think he's
just going through a phase a phase like the one you went through
when you were his age when you'd see your mother in the plaza
and walk the other way   when you'd try to manipulate her with
your anger because she wouldn't let you have a rooster as a pet   or
a toy you remember how when you were a child you knew that
place you grew up in like your own skin   you knew every rock
used them as markers to get to the river and la peña   you killed
birds with your slingshot played shoot-outs with the other boys
you have stories of childhood pure and innocent   the middle
of eleven children the night before you left for el norte you only
told your mother you were leaving because she asked   you and
three other boys turning into men in Tijuana winter crossing   no
one talks about the deaths in the desert caused by hypothermia
the coyote gave you money to buy a used coat   you waited and
waited until the time came to run and didn't stop running except
for the moment the midnight helicopters hovered above   you hid
in scrub brush   saw a woman being raped   and ran away   *your
life or hers   hombre   your life or hers*   tu niñez perdida   now our
son at ten years old goes hours without talking to me   furrows his
brow   looks long past my gaze and you're sure he's just trying to
manipulate me with his anger because I didn't buy him that video
game   the one with the prostitutes and stolen cars

Daily Horoscope
Norma Liliana Valdez

Daily Horoscope

SCORPIO (Oct 23-Nov 21)

There is a story of a woman who wears golden bells and feathered dresses. Her body will be broken and thrown from the steps of an ancient temple. From her severed thighs currant rivers. She will embody the sublime. She will inhabit the skies. Become moon. You are born dismembered. You are born of muted spices. Mud-tinged velvet, lush between your fingers. Today you will awaken in a cascade of luminescent waters.

Emotions: Re-membered ~ Money: Irrelevant ~ Love: Self
Power numbers: 10, 23, 39, 41, 70

Night Man

Torrie Valentine

I loved a man more
than my own mother,
& he wanted to die,
& all the gods
could not keep him
from trying,
and now this sadness
comes over me like the smoke
from his cigarette use to,
 traveling through light
and space,
settling on everything
around us,
this sadness
it is an ocean
with no bottom,
it is an anchor
made of stone,
it is the metal
on the ship, the bolts,
it is the bough,
it is not the sail,
it is his face
that comes to my dreams.

Jehovah Witness

Torrie Valentine

Someone taped a cross to our door
the day he tried to shoot himself
to blow his life away.

Some smiling girl came
& put it on our door
along with a message
about Jesus.

Do you think he will forgive me?
he asks, now & then,
maybe of himself ,as he slid the bullets
into the chamber.

& what could I tell him?
I who had strung him up
with my own hands,
I who had loved him
into madness.

I who had strung him up
into the only sky I know.

Except tell him what I heard
from a man in passing,
that our lives are our own
to give or to take or to shoot
but they are ours
to do what we will with them.

So yes come & bless this place
yes come and consecrate the wood
& the metal & the cigarette smoke & the booze

yes come with your Jesus & your love

The mans hands are shaking
Yes come & unbind him from the sky
unstring him with your small hands and your big God.

We Are Witness To Their Murders
Monét Cooper

"The ones that don't live to grow old/always die young/at war of ourselves"
—*Raheem Jackson*
"Police said Raheem's death was not related to a spate of shootings between neighbor-
hood gangs. Of the 30 people killed in the District this year, about half are under the
age of 24."   —*The Washington Examiner, April 7, 2011*

sirens of black boys spit shot eleven times into Raheem's shaking

heart cursing

there are no witnesses here

rising in this oven
agreeing in Congress
only babies howl at anyone who will listen
their doughy beginnings knead us into
recalling how we once marveled
at the specters of those who escaped death
merely by pushing their way out
of openings as narrow as these lines
which reminds me of a funeral named Junior My Neighbor
dangerous as chocolate glass sliding down the dirge of his throat
he drinks to unremember
the unwanted khaki of life
detritus kamikazes from his
lips like bullets shedding themselves of a trigger

there were no witnesses there

to tell him each sip stumbles into a clarion sighing
every beautiful thing he lusts after will never be his just

Junior whose liver grows weeds the color of his hands
toothless hollers nipping
themselves around women who would rather be anywhere but in the drink
of his umber words
another ginger thigh swishes past
he slings the worn rubber of his fingers around a mirage
as his spigot opens again
black boys point
rot toward the other's head
two barrels prepare to exhale steel

to no witnesses okay
no witnesses

in Georgia, my daddy's biscuits burn themselves the color of sky before night-
fall as blue as my right ventricle jamming in the caverns of my heart
all this —

and each day we step out of our doors
names crackling across the moat of tar
separating houses as much as lives
Junior and I stretch our waving palms toward the other
holding the air between us like gods

Eulogy
Monét Cooper

your son died today
his cheeks a chorus of flies
floating on cherries lolling inside his tongue

opened his head
molasses fell out with plastic shoe ties
coating the desk with a mist of grease

he broke in half
stomach candies sailing into lines
Jesu Christo Ms. Martinez said to a Skittle

his arm spilled from a sleeve
broke away to rest high over his eye
Amen I told a chair

the internment was completed in a class period
we know you would not want to wait on time
the way it takes a body
folds its organs into compost

plus we call you every week
about a law he has allowed his hands to break
like rulers in Mr. Moreno's Pre-Algebra class

you never return calls
demand a conference
reach for the office door slam it with such force
we know you are here to finally
take his wrongs in your arms tell us
you will help us fix his leaks

now water runs everywhere

Curse
Monét Cooper

Disobedience never felt
like accepting apples from
a banded bowl of yellowing snakes

No,
disobedience smacked
my lips
over independence
bitter as Adam's betrayal

Eve loving him whole
through his mess
of growing stomach
declining hairline
sagging bottom
increasing shortness of temper (and breath)
and endless drivel about
naming creation

But my mom is Lord (master and savioress)
and she heard not the crunch of young adulthood
a breeze of life's growth
in my speech

spit being sucked through teeth
like venom rustling veins to
offer the seduction of fruit

looted
from the
mind of God

She removed herself from the throne
flaming sword slapping leaves over my tongue

I'd been caught
with my mouth dangling
words open as a stripper's yoni

taking syllables
off during
the lunch rush

First Memory
Linda María Rodríguez Guglielmoni

In hill-towns, from San Fernando to Mayagüez,
the same sunrise stirred the feathered lances of cane
down the archipelago's highways.

Omeros
Book Six, Chapter XLIV, i
Derek Walcott

"You know what they say, that your first memory is who you are,"
the manicurist had declared without looking up at her client sitting across the
table from her.

As an answer, the older woman had quietly observed to herself, "It
isn't hard to tell either about you." And Gabriela had worked on, rhythmically
cutting, then layering on her client's nails, the silk strips, translucent as the
pale butterflies that now gathered on the abandoned sugar cane fields in
Puerto Rico.

Gabriela, who had a baby, worked at home in her laundry room at
the back of her rented house. She couldn't afford to buy, so she often moved,
transporting her belongings from place to place, together with her clientele.
She was good at manicures and reconfiguring spaces and making due, and
told her mid-afternoon appointment that her laundry room used to be an
office with an air conditioner and, "The woman that owns this house is… bien
católica. She lives next door and her mother lives in the corner house across
the street. The mother only has that one daughter, who like her abuela, never
goes out. Doesn't have a boyfriend, no, not even un noviecito, tú sabes. It looks
like she's never going to get married, jamás se va a casar, jamás y jamás… so
they lent out the house to the church, for the priest, for *padre Ángel.*"

"¡Qué casualidad! When I was a girl, my first confession… the
priest had that same name… se llamaba Ángel," finally Gabriela's client,
who appeared to be in her late 30's but probably was already in her 40's,
remarked. Then she mused on, "I lost count of how many Ave Marías y Padre
Nuestros I had been told to pray, and for what sins?" And after thinking for
a moment about her sins, she had added in one breath, "My best friend in
kindergarten was a boy, also called Ángel. His mother was a teacher in school
and sometimes my mother would pick us both up after school and we would
play, I don't remember exactly what we played at, but then I didn't see him
anymore until some years later when we met crossing over a highway on one

of those elevated pedestrian things, tú sabes, which usually no one uses, and he was coming from one direction with his mother and I was walking from the other direction with my mother, and when they stopped to chat, he didn't say anything to me, just hid behind his mother's skirt."

And so taking turns, the two women put together a conversation, all the while sitting close to Gabriela's washing machine, a well-used appliance which she kept covered with a large plastic sheet so that the mildew and rust which always seemed to take over everything in the tropics would stay away a little longer. But then, suddenly, it was time for the final nail filing. So Gabriela went quiet and slipped a dust mask over her nose and mouth, and straightening her back, the client draped her hands over the small table that stood between them. At that moment—perhaps to amuse herself or simply because since first grade when she had learned to read in Spanish about la Gata Mota and in English about Jane and her brother Dick and had developed a habit of reading everything from street signs to can labels—the older woman began to glance at the bottles and laundry detergent boxes on the floor. There she found nothing out of the ordinary, just the usual bleach and powdered detergent combination, plus a plastic blue bottle of Ensueño Max, a fabric softener that on its label held captive a smiling young woman dressed in a light pink shirt holding a happy lamb in her arms.

So then the woman had glanced over her manicurist's table examining some nail polish bottles that Gabriela had not bothered to put away after her morning clients. First being attracted by the light colors, French-manicure colors, and reading their labels, she had discovered there what she already knew—Fairy Princess-like sounding names: Platinum Cinders, Opal Moon, Snow Dreams. Then she had gone on examining others bottles that held down-to-business-working-girl-colors: Venus Dazzle, Cave Flame, Midnight Gold. She liked them all and had worn them all on different occasions.

And now, approaching the last rounds of the manicure, the heat seemed to really begin to close in on the women. Gabriela owned a small fan, which that day swayed side to side without cooling anybody, but stoically, both women had gone on playing their part in this ritual, struggling against the sleepiness that gathered up around them, fighting off the dense humidity, solid as a boxer's blow. In this hill-town, Mayagüez, namesake of a Taíno chief, in the late afternoons people know to hide in air-conditioned shops or government offices or fast food restaurants, or be condemned to loll the hours away, the slightest physical effort making their clothes constrict round their bodies. But Gabriela labored on, applying peach oil and rubbing it into to the cuticles and, taking off her mask to allow her to breathe and speak freely, she began to remember her student days, her psych professors and textbooks, articles on child development, then the master's degree she never started, yet had hoped to finish years ago.

As Gabriela's words filled and filled the makeshift salon, images, sluggishly, had began to press forth in the mind of the woman sitting across from her... images that a long time ago she had let slither away, a piece of clothing she had thought lost, slipping out of reach, a memory showing a pretty neckline. But now, suddenly, she couldn't wait any longer to dive into her memories, so she pressed the latch, spilling forth soapy socks, the torn sleeve of a boy's shirt, the drooping hem of a skirt, and pushing her hand in, grasping...

I am four or five. No. I am only three and a half. I am walking, holding my mother's hand. She is tall, her hair short, black, falling in soft waves round her face. She wears a cotton dress, sandals, her small waist belted. I can see her peach-colored toe nails. Her lips are the same color, but darker. It is a bright morning and the sun is just beginning to burn on our skins. We walk by a low wall and then the small, branching tree... in the steady breeze its flowers fly away as torn, pink cobweb.

I slow down as we near it and my mother grips me tighter, but eventually she stops so I can choose a flower from the ground or low lying branches. Then we march, fast, away. But I hold it safe in my hand, waiting until I can take a deep breath again. That's when I open my fingers and look... fragile tendrils, an octopus-flower that flutters in the waves of the sea... then, a ballerina-flower and I pirouette—up side down, I lift my skirt of gossamer flights towards the sun—then I bend and jeté—the flower comes down into my palm as the yellow pollen falls to the grown—then I bow deeply. And while my mother hurries, the octopus-flower has disappeared in a dark flash, leaving a stain on the sea of my hand, and the imaginary ballerina has already begun to fade away.

But no, not me, not today. Today I am going somewhere. So my mother and I climb one last slope, we walk through a gate. We are on school grounds. No flowers, just grass, wild, everyday grass everywhere. Only ants and worms live on those bitter green blades. I know already. Bitter. I have tried it, my head bent down, chewed on it. The four brothers next door having dared made me to do it. But not today. Today I will try something else.

My mother and I approach an L-shaped building, two long lines of classrooms placed around a cement yard. The breeze pushes the papers and wrappers around, over the gray, rough surface. I hear children's voices as we walk along the classrooms, the windows open. The doors are open too, to let in the morning air, so I turn my head to look inside.

Then my mother takes me in, into one of the classrooms, and she walks away to check on my brother. The children are bigger than me and four or five women are helping them dress. I move closer to the wall. Which one is my brother's teacher, I ask myself, and then one of them comes up to me, "¡Qué niña bonita! ¿Cómo te llamas?"

I look over to my mother, and I call out, feebly, "¡Mami!"

She answers, introducing me to the other woman, "That's Meli, short for Melisa."

I go stand in a corner, near the back widow and I watch the one tree growing behind the school, a reina de las flores, just starting to cover its branches in yellow and purple. And above the school, clouds, rounded clouds, solid but unstable, changing in the steady breeze and gathering heat, changing shapes and guessing at today's game.

Masks, pointy-cone-shaped and cowboy hats, wings, red, black, and golden capes. Everywhere there are bags: brown paper, plastic, big square ones with handles. Near me one girl helps another put on her costume. One is dressed as a witch, the other as an angel. The witch-girl offers to help and she takes hold of the wings. The angel-girl is heavy-eyed, a silver halo atop her black hair. Then she turns, so her friend can place the wings on her back. But suddenly they fall, they lie on the colorless floor, broken.

She turns, and falling down too, cries, "No! Oh, no! ¿Qué pasó?"

"No sé. I don't know," lies the witch-girl.

From the corner I have seen the witch-girl's fingers press and bend too far, making the wings come apart. What should I do? Should I tell them? Tell who? I see my mother and brother; she is helping him with his costume.

On the floor, the angel-girl weeps. A teacher walks over and the other girl, holding unto her pointy witch hat, says, "The wings broke."

"Bueno, vamos. Let's get some tape." The teacher guides them towards a desk covered in plates and cups, juice and chocolate milk cartons. On the desk, too, next to a wide-eyed plastic pumpkin, sits the cake my mother baked the night before, when she had warned, "Meli, no toques, don't touch." And then had offered me the mixing bowls, with their sticky, sweet rawness, to lick clean.

And the teacher, now looking lost herself, shuffles around the crowded desk, pulling out a roll of tape from a drawer, cutting off a long piece and sticking it across the torn wings. "It makes them look old and dirty," I whisper in one breath that seems to travel across the room. So the teacher looks for something else in the desk, finds a wider, cleaner roll of tape. She places the two sides, carefully next to each other, on the floor and sticks another strip across. Then she turns the wings around, placing more tape on the other side. Slowly she picks up the wings, checking out the repair job, and they hold, so she tells the girl to turn around, face the other way. The teacher hooks them unto the back of the costume, and when the angel-girl feels, once more, the weight of the wings on her back, she smiles running off towards a boy dressed as Batman.

Then I feel how my tie-up shoes are cutting into my ankles and I sit myself, crossing my legs and spreading out my skirt over the ash-colored tiles. Finally one of the mothers walks over and looking down at me asks, "What are you doing on that dusty floor?"

I look up, uncertain.

"¿Quieres algo? Would you like something?" she asks me while pointing to the mounds of candy amassed on a nearby table.

I nod, "Sí."

She returns, offering me a plastic bag, the image of a friendly ghost flying across it, and I push my hand in, grasping... pressing my fingers shut and whispering, "Gracias."

"De nada," the woman says and begins to walk away.

My hand slides out of the bag, then my grip loosens, and I see them—bright, shiny, black and yellow and pumpkin orange. And as I lift my head to call out, I also see my brother coming towards me, my mother close behind him. So I straighten my back and bring my hand up to my mouth, open wide, and drop in all the pieces of candy.

"What color?" Gabriela suddenly had asked, noisily opening a large, plastic box filled with bottles and bottles of nail polish.

"Black and yellow and pumpkin orange," the older woman had sang out in response to her manicurist's question, an expression of wonder flashing over her hot, tired face.

And Gabriela, surprised by the sudden breeze that sometimes precedes an approaching late afternoon thunderstorm, began to look round her plastic box for the unusual colors as the woman sitting across from her closed her eyes and, deeply, breathed in the cooler air.

Little Brother
William Copeland

i.
I came home to find young
            Lee taller &
bigger than me

I came home
to find him still on
the carpet bloody
            upstairs

I came home to Detroit the city
            is a bullet in my brain
is the blood
   the ground
        open
book, the
            dropped
        awkward
The
                            angle

ii.
when my brother comes to
meet me in our dreaming

we fling our fists
into each other I wake

up to pain
the pain   all over

Fled My Father With
William Copeland

Fled my father with
chest caved in teaching
me don't let sis get too far
from sight, older trees witnessed

me: thirteen, gangly green
stayed silent secretly

seasons later leaves would bruise deep
red and fall away

Katherine Dunham
Tara Betts

Nine decades, seven years marked your
time here, so many lives fanning out
in the swirl and flutter of skirts
caught in the motion of snake, cake
walk, black bottom, Lindy hop, steps
that reveal the body as speaker saying
those before you needed to say now.

Gwendolyn Brooks
Tara Betts

If we had known in the Mecca
that world equals ghetto,
we would have reached for the blue
heavy tome called BLACKS—a guide telling
South Side folks how to love each
other, a map that insists we have
so much loving work to do.

A Soft, Bright Absence
Tara Betts

Oddly enough, relief rises when he opens the door.
The steady thud of his steps, a falling night stick.
He holds me & my heart thumps like the pulse
of red & blue lights. The helicopter whir of anxiety
slows its chopping in my chest. When he's late,
my searchlight does not go black. I breathe deeper
knowing that his rights have not been read.
His wrists cuffed only by crisp shirt & his father's
bracelet, shiny as a revolver just cleaned.
When he says hey baby, hey honey, it is
a soft, bright absence of siren and megaphone.

The Castle
thandiwe Dee Watts-Jones

The Duke and Duchess are regulars on my morning news show. Their latest outing is among the lead stories of the day, and I'm talking pre-pregnancy. Lithe, tender-fleshed lovers, measured in their regal way, Kate and William turn up the longings that whisper, perhaps gnaw inside us. For white horses to ride in and swoop us up from the humdrum, beasts that turn human and handsome, good and golden, the bullion bar kind, and sunsets that never end. Like bloodhounds on the scent of fox meat, the media know famine in their audience. So cameras chase. Voices hype, feeding and stoking the hunger for a breathing fairy tale. But before my eyes, their couture and courtly smiles come and go between images of chained limbs bound for labor and profit.

So kind and lovely as the royal couple may be, I yearn for more. For something weighted and mournfully rare, a perennial acknowledgement of the wretched legacy beneath the royal feet, the royal spread. An exquisite gem of accountability offered for the done and undone, its clarity soaked in violet.

Seven months after my mom became an ancestor, I boarded an evening flight out of New York to Accra, packed with Ghanaians. Younger adults kept watch on elders, steadied them to and from the rest room, pulled a blanket from overhead, or homemade food from bulging tote bags. Babies passed from one pair of dark hands to another, jostled and soothed. At least one missionary was aboard, an African-American man who sat next to me. Miraculously, we managed not to offend each other, and even found laughter in our banter. Rows back, a dear family friend, Bernadine, hugged the aisle.

My daughter, Maia, was scheduled to arrive a couple days after us with a cohort of doctors from the U.S., invited by the Ghana Health Service. Their mission was and is to help reduce maternal and newborn deaths there. She is a cardiac anesthesiologist with a specialty in critical care. Petite and with the face of an ingénue, she's grown accustomed to dubious looks and words from patients at first encounter, clueless that she's in her early thirties.

During mom's last weeks, Bernadine, Maia and I, among others, had sustained a "life watch," as mom's pastor-friend called it. A generous stream of people came by, bringing flowers of tribute while she could delight in the feast of color and fragrance. Students, colleagues, co-volunteers, break-of-dawn co-walkers, and family.

"I'm so happy," mom said, more than once, her 87-year-old face like a polished macadamia nut.

Through it all, Bernadine, a retired physician, stood like a sturdy oak, shading me from being an only child. Blunt, low-key and humorous in a parched sort of way, she grew up an Oklahoma farm girl, and was a graduate student when she met mom. Their relationship evolved from professor and mentor to a deep friendship over the years that blossomed into our family.

Sorting through mom's papers one day I'd found a black & white photo that sent me running to her bed and then to Bernadine.

"Mom, look what I found!" I said, my voice elevated and ripe.

Thirty or so well dressed people are standing for a group picture, professionals by their starched posture and the drab backdrop. Every face, white and male, each body, suited, except one. Mom stands in a dress, her arms folded across her chest, poised, her hair pulled back in a French roll, the Lone Woman. Solo Black. My emotions swelled, and her words at seeing me so moved are indelible.

"I never knew my family would be so proud of me."

After the gatherings and drawers had emptied, and Bernadine and I had returned to sleep in our own beds, something brewed in the silence and thunder of my grief – a desire to pay tribute backwards in time to the beginning of the ancestral line. I could not know the exact dungeon through which my blood ancestors had emerged, able still to lay the trail of daughters and sons to which I belong. But I could stand in one prison that marked the limbo between forebears living and dying as people with known smiles, village spaces and names in Twi, Ewe, Fante and Nzema, and living and dying as anonymous chattel.

From the moment Maia's dad and I first called her name, we held African beauty up to her like a handcrafted mirror. She'd twice done a stint at a hospital in Swaziland, and I'd once visited East and West Africa months before she was conceived. But I wanted to be on the Motherland with her, to share that return, and together bear witness for each and every ancestor. We would complete a circle, it seemed, and I was ready. Bernadine, on the other hand, had already been to Goree Island in Senegal for the same reason and was willing to join me.

When Maia was younger we'd taken a summer vacation in Charleston, South Carolina, known for the Gullah women who weave their baskets for sale, the fresh, kick-seasoned seafood and its historical sites. It was August, the sun lit up the place. We'd driven to a nearby plantation, walked through "The Big House," and stood in the doorway of the replica of the quarters of the enslaved, a dirt floor rectangle. We toured Fort Sumter, the site of a Civil War battle after South Carolina announced secession from the Union, and walked to the Slave Mart.

But nothing cut the numbness like the humid night along the Harbor, shrouded in a blanket of fog, everything stilled to an eerie quiet. I stood fixed on the darkness, waiting like the water, present. I could feel a ship approaching, barely visible, creeping, and its lost people, dazed with no bearings sailing into this mysterious, foreboding port. I could feel an unnerving energy, fear-strung, like prey sensing new evil in the air.

A mere 220 miles inland is Anderson, South Carolina, where my maternal grandmother was born. My mother took me a lot of places when I was a girl, but nowhere near a plantation. Nor would she have gone with me, as an adult, to any site of enslavement on any Continent.

"You like to pour salt on wounds," she'd say whenever I wanted to talk about something painful. She did not believe in re-visiting hurt. Sometimes I wondered if that's why she remained so bitter about my dad. But more than anything it frustrated me, her tendency to shut down a communication whenever the emotion in my voice rose past the low set point on her gauge.

"I'm through discussing this," she'd say, like a cleaver's ritual. Pretense was the only way around the bloody mess left behind, and I never played the part well or interminably.

But the time for words aloud between us had passed. Two days into Accra, the capital of Ghana, my skin had well absorbed the moist heat and softened away the dry patches of eczema that worsen every New York winter. Having dressed in white since mom's burial, I was thoroughly enjoying a return to my summer whites. At the Cultural Arts Center, vendors had already swamped Bernadine and me and my first bargaining venture had little bargain in it. We had eaten at the same Ghanaian outdoor restaurant back-to-back, and savored *jollofrice*, *red red* (a beans dish), and *kelewele* (spiced fried plantain). We'd also taken a day trip to a shrine in Kligor, a small village in the Volta region, and participated in a ritual of the Afa spiritual tradition, derived from Ifa in Nigeria.

I kept checking to see if I understood people correctly when they referred to the places where the enslaved Africans were kept.

"Elmina *Castle*?" "Cape Coast *Castle*?"

How could the splendorous home of royal people be a slave pen? Then I realized, some piece of that starry-eyed eleven year old had survived. *How could she?* I'd long ago re-learned British history, European history for that matter, the stories of royal booted footprints on brown to beige-kissed women and men, their land and rituals. Yet it was as if I didn't know, as if my notion of "castle" had been harbored, frozen in a child's snowdrift memory, unsullied.

I was eleven the summer mom and I flew to London, and stayed for the season. She had a research fellowship and I had school. For the first time, I learned British history, the stories of Queens and Kings. Tales of finery and pomp, bouffant gowns fanning out from cinched waists and commanding the floor, tiaras and gold crowns titillating above heads, lush velvet capes and daunting castles of impenetrable stone, cool to the touch, I imagined. Inside, a feast of rooms and a host of characters kept form and pace with the demands of protocol. And what drama!—power-plays in love and war, even beheadings, whose gruesomeness failed under the spell of glitter. I'd read for hours, and conjure.

Outside Buckingham Palace, the Iron Gate seemed to run forever. From the sidewalk where mom and I stood, we came as close to the Queen's abode as we'd ever be, inches from the frozen guards. We could have touched them, but wouldn't dare. Men in gold-buttoned scarlet jackets, their heads burdened with black furry drum major hats, their arms holding bayonets stiff against their chests. I stared, scanning for the slightest movement, a blink.

"How can they stay so still?" I asked mom, half-heartedly trying to ensure the men couldn't hear me.

"It's their job," she said, "I guess they have to."

A black girl from the South, I knew nothing of royalty or castles. Nothing of how enthralling they could be as their enchantment spun its threads across the mind. Before mom and I returned to the States, we toured Ireland, Italy, France, and Scotland, where we entered the Edinburgh castle.

It was harder than I knew to relinquish all the sparkles, like ashes to the wind. But to finally grasp *Elmina Castle*, I had to.

On Maia's first night, she was in no mood to take a chance on a restaurant where we had no first-hand data. No problem, we hit our usual spot. Despite our separate schedules and accommodations, it worked out for her to go with us to Elmina Castle in the Cape Coast region.

Felix, our always neatly attired driver, a serious Christian man in his early 60's with good humor and a halogen smile, arrived at our hotel at the set time—a first. Maia wore a jean skirt and sandals that day. I'd forgotten to tell her about the other stop, Kakum Forest, and the canopy walk—a squeaky, swinging plank of wood with a rope net on either side, high above the trees. Even in my sneakers, the steep climb proved daunting, and the thick heat piled on. I paused to catch my breath, and refresh my mosquito repellant. Once we started on the canopy, disembodied screams from those far ahead of us didn't help. Maia tackled it like a mission to be carefully expedited. Afterwards, her contained fury softened a bit with lunch by the ocean at the Coconut Grove resort. She later revealed that the call she made when she walked away from our table for privacy was to her brother.

"Mommy tried to kill me," she'd told him.

They had agreed it sounded like the movie *Temple of Doom*.

But once we arrived at the Castle, words escaped. Out of the car, we approached on foot as children swarmed around us pressing their wares. An unfathomable wonder came over me as the massive structure in peeling off-white paint and black trim loomed in front of us under a perfect azure sky. A wooden bridge crossed the moat, and my body braced as it came closer. I stepped across the boards feeling the wood against my heels, the curl of my foot, the flattening of my toes. The entrance, a dim cubby, awaited us. We paid to enter, and then extra, to use our cameras. Incensed, I thought to myself *why should I have to pay?* African-Americans should be granted free entrance as a small token of acknowledgement, of caring. We would donate generously anyway, to ensure the upkeep of this monument to the Maafa, a Swahili word that means catastrophe, and used to refer to Transatlantic Slavery and its aftermath.

I let the crazy thought go as I stepped through an arch into the central courtyard, flooded with light. My eyes circled the walls in a spiral, going up, around and then back down, drawn to the tall steps of the wide staircase in one corner. I could not tell until later when I climbed them that they were made of a polished white stone, marbled with tan. I followed them visually from the ground floor to the level where black wooden shutters dotted the facing wall. They reminded me of the outside of a home. Otherwise bare of trappings, the castle had none of what had mesmerized me as a girl, except its grand scale. We were asked to wait in the one room library for the tour to begin. Above the doorway hung a sign, "Portuguese Church," its former identity. I had not long been reading the display about the Asante people, the largest ethnic group among the Akan in Ghana, when our tour guide appeared.

A handsome young man of medium build, Kwesi looked to be in his early twenties. His skin had the satin of coffee beans. His shea-butter voice had a hint of British inlay in his distinct enunciation of 't' at the end of a word, and as he spoke, his hands often came together. Everything about him seemed natural and I felt his reverence through every ghastly detail. It occurred to me on our way back to Accra how difficult it must be for him to deliver this information over and again.

Inside the narrow enclosed space that ran adjacent to the open courtyard, two small archways at opposite ends had cast a shadowy light for hundreds of women that had been packed there. "Three months they were kept here with minimal care to their bodily needs, women who menstruated ..." I drifted from the words, imagining me as one of them in that space—stunned, a woman stacked, musty, shackled, sticky wet ... but I could not keep going or stay. I came back, and envisioned my containment bursting. A mad woman's wail piercing the silence around Kwesi's voice for as loud and long as I could hold my breath, shattering the vise that clamped the tongues of millions for centuries, registering publicly the flesh inside the facts, even if a muffle of it ... "and above their heads, sounds of Dutch church services could be heard."

Tears streamed. No one would have known if I hadn't needed to blow my nose, which I resented, and resented resenting.

Back in the courtyard, Kwesi lifted up a square wooden cover over the concrete floor, revealing a deep well where rainwater collected. On occasion, a woman would be cleaned with it. The Governor, perched on the balcony, had chosen her from among the women below in the open space, corralled for his viewing. A private staircase unfolded from a discrete door a few feet from the stone steps, a part of the ritual. She'd ascend this wooden and rope ladder, monitored, as she made her way to the Governor's two-room suite. About ten of us stood there, mostly Ghanaians. Bernadine, Maia and I did not stay close or speak until the end. We were together, yet alone, like a dying family member surrounded by kin.

The Portuguese built the castle in 1482, the first holding pen in Africa in service to the Maafa. Though many others followed, Elmina is where it began. Later the Dutch took it over, followed by the British. The castle and the country have been in Ghanaian hands for only 53 years. Like our guide at the National Museum in Accra, Kwesi acknowledged that Africans had a hand in what transpired—the chiefs who used prisoners of war to barter with Europeans, and raiders who captured other Africans for the European merchants. Each time I heard this admission, I felt a certain solace. It's what I imagine a molested child may feel when an adult perpetrator stops resisting what has occurred or pasting over his actions and says, "I did it." It had sweetness to it as well, because these Africans and I both know that slavery in Africa could not string a bridge in the mind to the slavery practiced in the Americas.

We moved on.

"These are the steps that took the enslaved to their final moments in Elmina," Kwesi told us, as he revealed another wooden ladder, a downward one. We took a different route. In the dark cube we entered, three coffins side by side would have been a tight fit. The crowd had thinned and for the first time we stood close to each other.

"Here is where they were loaded onto the ship," Kwesi informed us, as he gripped the handle on a wooden square covering one of the walls. As he pulled the shutter back we could see it—a narrow rectangular opening of light—'the door of no return.' When my chance came I moved right up to it and looked out onto the loveliest and saddest blue. Sunlit water and sky. Had the millions who faced this door seen anything of God's beauty?

I had brought a piece of rose quartz from my ancestors' altar at home, hoping to leave it as an offering of love for those whose suffering ended here and those whose did not. I whispered to Kwesi, telling him of my desire. He gestured to a ledge on the wall opposite the light. I had not noticed it, or the wreath placed there.

"Some African-Americans left this," he said. "You can leave your offering here too, and say whatever you need to say."

I squatted down to say a prayer, and placed my pink crystal.

For sometime after, we all stood there, as though we couldn't pull away, leave behind the vessel soaked in our ancestors' final rupture from African land.

Kwesi caught our rhythm, and eased us on only after he sensed our readiness. We moved on to shoebox cells for troublemakers on the ground level, and the Dutch church and kitchen on the floor above it. They had refused to use those of the Portuguese. Near the end of our tour, we climbed to the roof. In the distance, the sprawling red roof of a fort set high on a hill stood out among its dotted surrounds. Kwesi identified it as a look out, a first line of defense against the approach of the unwelcome. Small canons sat poised at intervals along the edge of our roof, but neither they nor the fort could stop a succession of European flags over Elmina castle. I stood there, in the complete open, at the top of it all, able to see for miles over the Atlantic, its vast loneliness, estranged from contact, and the places where its waters nudged against Africa's sandy coastline.

Day gave way to dusk, as we again took to the road. Felix, who had waited by the car, confirmed that he too had once been inside the castle, his face aged in the absence of his smile.

"I found Goree Island harder to take. I couldn't even stand up in the space with the door of no return," Bernadine said, finally giving voice.

In that instant I knew I'd had my fill of castles. Anywhere.

Maia still had Kwesi on her mind, "He was so amazing. All that information he knew, and he was so respectful."

She had wanted to make an offering to him before leaving the castle, but he had disappeared with someone who'd dropped out earlier and wanted to make up for it. We had called his name aloud, and he soon jaunted down the lovely staircase.

"Thank you so much," she said, as her hand reached for his. "May God bless you."

"Oohh, thank you," he responded, his head and upper body tilting back.

Their smiles unfolded, wide and weathered.

Dusk bowed to night as Felix drove. Along the road, silhouettes walked in the dark, some balancing bundles on their heads. I wondered how far they had to go and thought of mom, how she kept her focus on the task at hand and on moving forward, just as those before her had done. How else could they have awakened to one sun break after another in the midst of civilized barbarity, except to have rationed their energy to the day before them or the dream ahead?

I wondered if what I'd taken for granted as the core of healing, befriending the pain, allowing its course, had for many been the very thing that exacted slavery's final severance. Maybe containment marked those who pulled forward the bloodlines. Maybe constriction is how mom got to be the lone Black, the singular woman among white men. I softened against her impervious side.

I never understood the weight of sorrow upon me, so much heavier than my life. But now, I am a willing vessel of undelivered grief, an offering to those whose sacrifices I cannot bear to surrender to all that is forgotten.

My Father's Ranch
Scott Hernandez

The grey barn
full of oily
chicken
feathers,
dirt so dry
hard
not even
blood
would soak
in.

What We Lost in the War
Scott Hernandez

English = house or home

Spanish = casa, dormitorio

Portuguese = casa

German = Hause (Haus)

French – Maison

Italian = Casa

Slovak = Dom

Arabic = Mazil (للذزننمم) or Bayt (تتيـب)

Breton = (a language of France): Ti

Haitian Creole = Kay

Icelandic = Hús

Sardinian (a language of Italy) = Dómmu

Welsh = Tŷ

Nahuatl = Calli

Dock Scribes
Hari Alluri, Cynthia Dewi Oka, & Sevé Torres

i.

black-&-mild ritual rite, this for dock scribes
and love that's old. smoke water blown free form
block calligraphy. humbled tricksters vision walk
to calm, ply under touch, melt tear tongue symphony.

some words need to be repeated: in prayers. we travel
breath. release worry to ash, circle flame burn petals
to white. birth tongue and flower supplicant to poets
kneeling. heat drying spine into thirst shouting

ii.

there are bodies made for water. to read and enter as sound
whipped by trade of journey you feet blood and smoke lines
no echo to rope the dusk profile tusked breath sleeved in elbows
the patience of knees scraped by just in time arrivals

thieve   whittle   pray   syncopate the language of kin
none anthems for home.   content with applause of fish
between sun and set the waves   veil you into verse   learn
to recite your name by first   taking off your shoes

iii.

and other moorings only touch can relay
never to be repeated alone
in the tenderness of casting
blessings not yours to scale with words

never to be repeated either
burn the white blossoms you picked
in offering or blow smoke into the quiet
you carve with your own ashes

Millie's Girl
Vanessa Mártir

I once punched a girl in the face for saying, "You're dirty like your lesbian moms." All because a boy she liked, liked me. I didn't think about it, I just swung. Then I dared her to say it again. She didn't. She knew better.

I was raised in a gay relationship in the 70s and 80s. Long before *Heather has Two Mommies* hit the mainstream in the 90s. And just a few years after the American Psychiatric Association took homosexuality off the list of mental disorders in 1973.

For years I was told that my family was living in sin. That my two mothers were immoral and disgusting and going to hell. That no one's born gay.

Still, when I went to boarding school at thirteen, I didn't tell anybody about my family. I convinced myself that I just didn't want to deal with it. What would people say? How would they treat me? I was carrying my own shame.

When California's Prop 8 was overturned in early 2012, I cheered with the crowds that stood outside the San Francisco courthouse, and I teared up watching the gay couples hug and cry. But the images that really shook me were those of kids, little kids like my daughter, seven, eight and nine years old, grinning and holding up signs and wearing t-shirts that read, "GAY means God Abhors You." Hatred like this is taught. It's learned. And it's vile.

Over the past ten years, thirty U.S. states have passed referendums defining marriage as a union between a man and woman. In mid-November, Uganda officially passed the "Kill the Gays" Bill, calling it a Christmas gift for the Ugandan people. The bill essentially equates homosexual acts to the same level as murder. In Uganda, my moms would have been killed for loving each other.

We've got a long way to go.

I was orphaned when my mother Millie died seven years ago. My biological mother went back to being a Jehovah's Witness, and now says she regrets being with Millie for twenty some odd years. "Les dí un mal ejémplo." That's bullshit. Millie is the reason I'm sane.

Millie always wore a kangol. A black kangol. And a pair of worn jeans. So worn they had the outline of her wallet on her left back pocket like someone had traced the square with chalk. She carried a ring with a thousand keys on the belt loop on her right hip. And, she always had beads of sweat on her lip and on the bridge of her pointy Castillian nose, no matter what season it was. Summer or winter. She smiled her chipped front tooth smile that was such a big part of her face, and she'd grab the brim of her hat and say, "Yo soy butch." But the way she said it, it was like she was dancing salsa, but just with her shoulders.

She was proud of who she was. Of being Boricua. Of being a butch. "Yo soy del monte. Yo soy Lares." At least that's what she showed me. Except when she and mom fought. And, when she was dying.

Mom and Millie were vicious to each other when they argued. They hurled hate like daggers. But when mom took out her uzi and called Millie a maricona, Millie shrank into herself. Her bottom lip trembled. Her eyes got watery. And, she'd pound her chest and yell, "¡Yo no soy maricona, coño! ¡Yo soy butch!" Her voice would crack and she'd cry. "Yo soy butch." Over and over. Like she was trying to convince herself. Then she wiped her face roughly with the front of her orange t-shirt, grabbed her keys and she was out. "Me voy pa'l carajo."

What must have been going through her mind? What was it like for her to grow up a lesbian in Lares in the 50s and 60s where the Pentecostal church is as deeply rooted as the wild mango trees? Is that why you left your querida isla, Millie?

When I came home from first grade and told her I was being bullied, she took me out to the backyard and taught me how to fight. How to throw an uppercut and a jab. "Pero ten cuida'o con esa manos de madera."

When I was obsessed with basketball, she fashioned a hoop out of a rusty tire rim, nailed it to a splintered piece of plywood and put it up in the backyard. Then she went out and bought me an official Spalding basketball.

When I wanted a bike, she went around and collected parts from her friends and neighborhood junkyards and built me my rainbow bike. One wheel yellow, the other blue, a white seat, peeling aqua grips on the handlebars. I rode that bike like it was a king's chariot.

And when I told her, excitedly, as she lay withering away from that mothafuckin disease, cancer, "I think I wanna write a book, Millie," she propped herself up on one arm, her breath raspy, and said, "Pero negra, you've always been a writer." And that night I went home and started writing my first novel.

I visited Millie everyday while she was in hospice. Calvary was just two miles from my house. I was home collecting unemployment while nursing Vasialys who was only months old. So every morning, I'd bundle up my nena, pack up the stroller, and walked my way over to the hospice, praying that Millie had a good night, that she'd be vibrant and laughing, her breathing smooth, her pain eased.

Millie had been diagnosed with breast cancer six years earlier. She had her right breast removed and repeated stints of chemotherapy. But the mastectomy and chemo were not meant to save her life. The cancer had already spread to her lymph nodes by the time she felt the lump in the shower, so Millie knew eventually she'd die from the disease. She carried her mortality like a heavy load that shrank her will and faith. And even her pride.

She said the breast that remained looked like a deflated whoopee cushion. She slapped it so it bounced and her double rolled belly jiggled. "Si yo fuera una mujer femenina, estó me molestaría," she said about the keloid gash, bubbled and sagging to one side.

I could tell that she was lying. She was covering up her sadness with jokes. I once caught her staring at her nude reflection in the mirror. She traced the wound with her finger and bit her lip. When she saw me watching, she laughed. "Yo si estoy gorda, negra."

When I cleaned the gash, she searched my face, looking for a reaction. Disgust, I think. I never showed it. This was the woman who cleaned me when I shat my pants that time I had a bad case of the runs when I was eight. This was the woman who carried me on her shoulders when I was just three and mom made us walk the two miles to Knickerbocker Park. This was the woman who taught me how to fight when I was being bullied. "Te tienes que aprender a defender. ¡Con puños Vanessa, con puños!" I was only doing for her what she'd done for me since I was two. I was loving her.

One day when I walked into the hospice, she was whimpering into her pillow. I ran to her. "What's wrong? Te duele algo?" I reached for the nurse button but she grabbed my arm with the hand that was forever swollen after the mastectomy so it looked like a blown up latex glove.

"No, I'm okay." She wiped the tear that clung to the tip of her nose. "Hi negra." She kissed and hugged me. She was trembling. "Pasame la nena." I put Vasia in her arms, sat on the chair next to the bed and watched.

I knew better than to ask any questions. Millie didn't talk much when she was emotional. She did so in her time.

After she drank the coffee (con leche y dos azucar) and ate the old fashioned donut I brought her every morning. After holding Vasialys and cooing at her. After explaining to Vasia what was going on in whatever show she was watching, in between her stories about life and love and how blessed

Vasia was to be my daughter "porque yo la crié," she looked at me. "Tengo miedo, negra."

"Why? What are you afraid of?"

"¿Te sacastes mas leche o le vas a tener que dar seno?" Millie preferred that I pump my breast milk so she could feed Vasialys until mom came in the early evening and sent me packing, telling me I needed to go home to my marido, though by then my daughter's father was more roommate than partner. But the hospice was no place to reveal that I had failed at yet another relationship.

"No, Millie. There are two bottles in the bag. Don't change the subject."

"Que subject, ni subject. Eh!" She shrugged. "Dos botellas no es suficiente."

"Millie, there's plenty of milk in these tetas." We laughed, staring at my swollen breasts that popped out of every top I owned. "And I brought the pump just in case." I pointed at the bag hanging from the carriage. "So, ¿que fue lo que tu diji'te?"

"Ay na'. It's nothing."

I grabbed the remote and turned off the TV. Only I could do that. Anybody else would have gotten an ice stare and something thrown at them. Usually the closest thing to her. I raised my eyebrow and waited. She looked down at Vasia who was sleeping on the bed next to her. She adjusted her onesie and rubbed her back. Her hand was trembling. "What if it's true? That I'm going to hell."

"What do you mean?"

"Vanessa, la Biblia dice…"

I cut her off like I always did when she brought up the Bible. These kinds of conversations never ended well between us. I'd listen for a while, rolling my eyes. Then I'd get frustrated and go on a rant about how the Bible didn't come to earth via fax, that it was biased, machista, and contradicted itself. She'd call me "atea" and we'd stop talking about it. But this conversation felt different so I held my tongue, or at least I tried to. "Millie, you're not going to hell."

"¿Y tú que sabes?" She stared out the window, one hand still stroking Vasia's head.

I leaned in and ran my fingers through Millie's hair. It had re-grown after her last chemo session, but now it was gray and wiry, not thick and jet black like it used to be. She started to cry softly. I held her head on my chest until she calmed down. "Tu huele a leche," she giggled. Comedy was how she kept her sanity.

"How can God send you to hell? You loved me, Millie."

She brushed the hair out of my face. "Tu eres mi negra, you know that?" I bit back the tears. She needed me to be strong. This was no time to get lost in my grief.

"You're really scared, aren't you?"

"Si negra. Yo viví en pecado."

"¿Quien dice? Who is this God you're talking about? The God I know loves you."

"Si, pero la Biblia dice que yo viví en pecado, Vanessa, y Papa Dio no perdona esa cosa."

"What sin Millie?" I was getting mad. I felt helpless. I knew there was nothing I could do to save Millie from what she learned as a kid en Lares. From her three brothers who were all pastors, especially the one who was extra self-righteous because he found God after being an alcoholic for twenty years. If he could give himself to God, anyone could. And then there was Millie's mother, who died begging her, "Deja esa vida, hija. Te quiero ver en el cielo un día."

My helplessness got the best of me. We didn't talk about it again. I found her a few times whimpering in the bathroom and sobbing into her pillow. She sometimes confessed to being scared, before an exam or after a really bad night. I held her until the shaking passed. It was all I could do.

I went to see Millie every day for nearly two months. I walked there. Every single day. Con la nena. During the dead of winter. Even if it was snowing or raining. I went. Eventually, Vasia got sick. Really sick. Fever. Cough. Congestion. So I couldn't see Millie for a week, though we talked every day. One day, I felt something off. When I called, no one answered. Finally, on my fifth or sixth try, the nurse answered. "She's sleeping. She's been sleeping all day."

A mi se me metió algo. I had to see her. So when my daughter's father got home, I insisted he take me. I screamed and yelled, wouldn't let him change his clothes. Stood over him, yelling while he ate the dinner I'd prepared. I flipped until he finally agreed, though he argued the entire ride there. He screeched off when I got out of the car.

Millie opened her eyes when I walked in. For the first time all day, Mom said. She was propped up on the pillow, resting her head on her arm. She had an oxygen mask on. The cancer had invaded her lungs by then. She pushed the mask down and patted the pillow. "Ponmela aqui." I placed the baby next to her. Tears dripped down onto the pillow. "Cuidamela." She played with Vasia's fingers and smiled while Vasia kicked and stared. Millie looked at me. "I love you, negra." It was the last thing she said.

I got the call the next morning. Millie died. By herself—like she wanted to.

In 2009, a Connecticut church posted a video of what church members called the exorcism of a "homosexual demon" from a teenager's body. In the twenty-minute clip, the boy is seen thrashing on the ground, crying, vomiting, while church leaders yell, "Right now in the name of Jesus, I call the homosexuality, right now in the name of Jesus," over and over.

Over the past few years, headlines have been wrought with stories of kids who killed themselves because of gay bullying. Children all coming to the same desperate conclusion: If you're gay or labeled gay, life just isn't worth living.

My Millie wasn't (and still isn't) alone in her desperation to reconcile her love for women with the messages she received from society. From her church. From her family. From the island she so adored. The world told her that her homosexuality was not, is not acceptable.

I once punched a girl in the face for saying, "You're dirty like your lesbian moms." I was twelve years old. We were playing where we always played, in the supermarket parking lot because the crack dealers and fiends had taken over the playgrounds. I already knew I had to stand up for my family. My Millie taught me early on I had to take on life "con puños, Vanessa, con puños." These fists now have words.

math problems (and other lessons)
teri elam

(after seeing the homework a teacher in norcross, georgia gave to combine math and a history lesson about frederick douglass)

i. *"each tree had 56 oranges. if 8 slaves pick them equally, then how much would each slave pick?"*

that they used *pick* present tense   not
picked past   in this calamity   mathematics
and history   this minstrel show nonsensicality   or
that the orange trees   *had* fruit   not *have*
so the correct answer   a big fat 0?   mathematics
is fine art   not inert   to subvert or pervert   but
puzzle   psychedelic patterns   red triangles inside
blue squares inside green circles   the aperture van der zee
dreamed and weems *dreams* through   or zen
like basho's haiku   *past* rite for wright   *present* sanchez
and a tanka   the exact amount of saffron needed
to infuse olive oil   seduce gin   it multiplies infinity
grows exponentially   slows time logarithmically   complex
and simple and imaginary   mathematics *is not* a slave.

ii. *"if frederick got two beatings per day, how many beatings did he get in 1 week?"*

a thorny rose   his
forearms bore prickles to guard
his language   his strength.

one october night in the bay
teri elam

near geary   where neimans coach saks meet
thru misplaced teeth   a graying bird-like man hisses
his tongue spitting venom into the indigo skyline
empty-palms open   false lashes rapid-flashing
his rage blistering   i swallow hysteria   the masses push
past us suspended in time—   we breathe

at a different bend off market street
in plastic cups baptized with grit & pee
coins clank   scrap-starved bellies stagger
aside bright pashmina-scarved swans
white earplugs silence serenades   protests pleas   saddled men
faces whittled in place   sad-breasted women
layered dirt   murmurings of lost fathers   sons   i watch in a hush
heart fragments slow-lifting into san franciscan-winds

at union square   a full moon hangs low   kindling
this crowded city   starlight spins on 8 wheels   a chimney sweep
rolls backwards pulling old speakers static-popping stevie wonder
in this stunning moment   the world loops into a pirouette
& gravity pushes us into the bodies next to us—   i grab you
hold tight   we slow drag lip-to-lip   breathe

El Diablo Bailarín
Vibiana Aparicio-Chamberlin

When I was a kid growing up in East L. A., I couldn't get enough of Ma's cuentos. Her Mexican folk tales with their moral lessons and warnings of disaster used to scare the hell out of me. I'm sure they caused my horrifying nightmares. Yet, I loved Ma's stories about ghosts and diablos. The scarier the better. One of her cuentos warned girls never to sneak out of the house at night because the world was full of dangerous handsome men who were múy catrines.

Ma said when she was a teenager; she never dared to go out dancing at night. She went to the afternoon tardeada dances with her girlfriends on the ten-cent P Line Trolley to the Salesian Dance Hall in China Town. Sometimes they went to the Lincoln Park Dance Pavilion on Mission Road to dance under the stars at the Boathouse.

One time Ma told us a story about Chata, a girl from the old Boyle Heights neighborhood by Hazard Park. She snuck out through her bedroom window one Saturday night to dance at the CYO Catholic Youth Organization Dance Hall on Brooklyn Avenue and Gage Street.

Chata came to a bad end because she took her sister Chicki's new dress without permission and cut it into a coqueta party dress. She was too ashamed to wear a homemade dress sewn by her mother on the old Singer sewing machine. Chicki's dress from Grayson's dress shop on Whittier Boulevard was made of indigo blue velveteen. The sinvergüensa Chata cut the sleeves off the dress, showing her bare arms. She shortened it so when she twirled you could see above her knees almost to her calzones. She wore her sisters black hose and ratted her hair up in a pompadour with a white gardenia at her ear. She even used her mother's lipstick and her "Evening In Paris" perfume. Chata broke the rules because she was a conceited and dance crazy teenager. She wanted to be the envy of all the girls with her makeup, stylish hair and short party dress. Her lips were painted with orange lipstick by Tangee. Chata's enticing shiny lips were ready for some slick kissing.

That night at the CYO dance, Chata got the scare of her life. A tall strong-featured man chose her among all the other girls to dance. She knew he asked her to dance because she looked so bonita with her new dress and her Tangerine Kewpie doll lips. The mysterious stranger had black wavy hair smoothed down by scented pomade. He wore a black suit with padded shoulders. It fit tightly at the waist so as to show off the smooth dancing dips and turns of his long legs and the slow gyrating of his hips. The dandified demon twirled her around so furiously she became bewitched by his spell and moved her hips and shoulders in suggestive rhythmic movements. Suddenly, she saw his feet burst out of his pointy black shoes and morph into rooster clawed toes. The Demon's smooth ivory hands formed into bristly sharp talons. They squeezed her body breathless. His boney fingers clawed her neck. From his body emanated the suffocating smell of evil sulfur. With a pitiful voice, she cried for mercy, gasping for air as he nearly choked the last gulp of air out of her.

She prayed, "Hail Mary, Hail Mary, Hail Mary."

Then Chata tore away from him. She screamed and fled frantically from the dance hall taking a desperate short cut home through Evergreen Cemetery. She was never seen again. Jamás. Never.

After Ma's story, I lay in bed trying to rid my mind of the Diablo Bailarín.

"It's only a story. It's only a story. Not real, not real. The Diablo doesn't exist. No existe. No existe," I said to myself.

I prayed that El Diablo Bailarín wouldn't pry into my dreams. After all I was just a kid. I never sneaked out of the house. I only wandered around after school in the hills of my City Terrace barrio, peeking over fences to see the neighbor's back yards. I prayed that my sister Concha wouldn't sneak out the window to go dancing. Ma sometimes let her go to the dances at Sacred Heart of Mary High School in Montebello. She gave Concha permission because the nuns chaperoned and watched the girls like hawks. Also, Concha went with her girlfriends, Sheila, Blinky and Eleanor. So she was safe. But I still worried. Maybe she might meet her boyfriend, Alex. I worried that El Diablo Bailarín would go to Montebello to get Concha for being up to no good.

Then I prepared to think good thoughts. As I lay in the bottom bunk bed on a new foam mattress, I prayed for Concha's safety. I expected another night of bad dreams, so I kept my mind off El Diablo by imagining myself sleeping on pillows, soft and warm as the dough of Ma's buttery dinner biscuits. I prayed that Our Lady of Guadalupe and the holy spirit of Grandma Emilia would protect me. At the foot of my bed I taped a holy card of St. Michael, the Archangel. Then I prayed.

"St. Michael, with your flaming sword, slay el Diablo Bailarín. Drag him to el infierno para siempre. St. Michael send el Diablo to hell forever."

As night fell, I caressed the worn wooden beads hanging from the end of my rosary while I recited the five decades of "Hail Marys" and "Our Fathers". I whispered thanks to baby Jesus and holy Mary for my warm bed and for Concha's satin-edged hand me down blanket. I felt confident and cozy under my new cream-colored chenille bedspread from the big Woolworth's Store on Broadway Street in downtown L.A. I gave thanks to Apá for my new sponge mattress with its waffle like texture but strangely sinking feeling. I knew he would say powerful prayers for me.

That night, Apá prayed for me on his knees; cradling the Bible with his thick brown hands. But I still had fears. My mind was filled with thoughts of El Diablo Bailarín and the girls he'd capture next. The buzz of the prayers on my lips brought me close to sleep.

Suddenly, the Diablo was dragging me down deep into the crevices of my sinking mattress. The smell of the diablo's azufre suffocated me as he clutched my legs and pulled me into a flaming pit. Its walls moved in closer and closer, squeezing me in. I couldn't move or breathe. But my mind cried out, Wake up! Wake up!

Then screams exploded out of my mouth. The thumping in my heart seemed to burst through my chest.

"Apá, Apá. Pray for me! Pray on your knees! Pray the rosary!"

Apá came quickly, followed my orders and prayed fervently. El Diablo loosened his grip on my ankles. The heat and sulfurous azufre smell of the inferno slowly dissipated. Apá gave me his brown scapular ribbon with Jesus's image on a small fabric square.

"Here mija, wear my scapular around your neck. Now you're safe."

Then he made a sign of the cross on my forehead and prayed me to sleep. A new day arrived, all sunny with the smell of Ma's handmade tortillas. The morning ritual sound of her hands patting and slapping the perfectly round flour tortillas onto the stove grill comforted me. Apá brought me a cup of warm yerba buena tea, brewed from the tender mint leaves growing under the dripping faucet at the side of our white wood-frame house. Then he took me outdoors to gather Ma's delicate pink roses of Castile that wove through the chain link fence by the garage. We took the bouquet ofrenda to the old church on Fisher Street and placed it at the feet of La Virgen de Guadalupe. I asked Apá to pray aloud to La Virgen, and to tell the Diablo to go away.

"Go away Diablo, be gone," Apá prayed. "Our Lady of Guadalupe and Holy Mary mother of Jesus, tell el Diablo to be gone. Yo, Elias Rodriguez Aparicio, el padre de Vibiana, I say be gone, Diablo. El bueno conquista el mal. Good conquers evil."

After church, Apá talked to Ma.

"Chabela," he said. "Stop telling the kids those scary stories. Vibiana believes them. They're making her sick. You're just like a child, making eerie sounds, and making the kid's room dark and spooky with candlelight."

"Caro," she said. "We don't have a phonograph player, a radio, or one of those fancy Philco television sets. We're just entertaining ourselves. You're never home. You leave for work early Monday morning before the sun comes up to go to Coachella to work construction. Then you come back late on Fridays, when the sun goes down. We feel triste and lonely. So I tell stories."

Another night came and I wanted to hear a story from Ma. But I needed more time to get over el susto, the terror from the story of El Diablo Bailarín.

"Not tonight", I thought. "Maybe tomorrow."

About Errant Drift

in response to Yael Villafranca
Kimberly Alidio

A vessel has a want,

a will and a design

but no power to stop

It should be powered by

steam in the radio age.

A steampunk ship, maybe

on a jah A tug boat in steam

drag. In the cinema age,

the inventor plays with

tub toys in a Jersey creek

to broadcast the war.

The favorite summer movie

to watch while bobbing in

Barton Springs is JAWS.

A ship is a siren, a femme

fatale, recalling the B&W

playing at the dock

in CINEMA PARADISO.

Monolinguist's Trick
Kimberly Alidio

The bodies I've had inside and out
Hiccup a series of notes
Over long-distance:
Scale a woman's Japanese and
Nasal out business Portuguese

My lovers' advanced vocabulary goes missing.

Twinning is obsessive research.

Since my days as a mini-device
Transliterating two giants' shadow-soundings

El La.
Meant to.
A thought.
Uh.
Round the mouth.
A race it.
As per the spire.
As fix it.
As dry is.
Cross it clever as need.

See me more grinning

The Book of Ant Bites
Kimberly Alidio

for every figure eight, infinite patience
bugged eyes, imprecise: press twice

companies, departments, interview committees
fancy potlucks and symposia
with lines out the back
trains v. HOV lanes
cluster cohort in windowless rooms

I hold tobacco in a two-fingered mudra
entering the arrivals of the dead
exiting dead on arrival

this language bitten out of me
and rubbed in mud
cheek to earth beneath stars and steam
each unconsciousness comes out in Spanish

I fall into the circle of anthropologists
one uttering my name
another feeding me
a Zyrtec

my entrails:
a trail
of refined sugar

Ashes
Jennifer De Leon

Graciela Ana Fernandez remembers everything, including her birth. She can still see the honey-colored walls of the sticky clinic birth room in Mexico where a dozen women in various stages of labor formed an L shape with their cots. Some shared the company with their own mothers clutching their hands. A few had no one but an indigenous nurse to trace the length of their brows with an ice cube. Then there was the old midwife lady who hovered over Graciela's mother and her perfect, round belly. From inside her mother's womb, Graciela could hear the little old lady say, "She is almost here, so get ready Señora, in two minutes you will hold your daughter in your arms." A shriek broke from Graciela's mother and echoed into Graciela's ears, which at the time resembled two dried apricots. Graciela hesitated to kick her feet away from her mother's core and nudge her head toward the heat of the opening that led to the rest of the world. Her mother grunted in horror as she pushed a hairy head out of her, along with a sprinkling of urine. This was normal, the indigenous nurse assured her, sensing her possible embarrassment. One hundred and one years later and Graciela still remembers the cold air that felt almost wet on her scalp as she slid centimeter by centimeter out from the centerfolds of her mother.

The memory of that cold air will return in her second year of primary school, when Graciela is asked to write a paragraph to the prompt: Where I Come From. She will write the first sentence: I am from the dark hole in between my mother's legs, a never-ending spool of thread that connects me to God. What will follow minutes later are the icy smacks of tree branches on the backs of her thighs as the school Director makes her pink and swollen for all the students to see, including Alden, the German boy whose parents were in Mexico for PhD research. For Graciela, this will be the worst part: Alden's laughter during the school Director's interrogation. Where did you hear that? From where did you copy this kind of language? Graciela would try to answer these questions for the rest of her life. And each time, she remembers the midwife.

On the day of her birth, the little old midwife lady spit in the palm of her hand and mumbled a prayer into it before smearing the warm liquid on Graciela's milky torso. Even the woman on the cot to the left turned toward baby Graciela. She was kneeling on all fours and wore only a stretched out pale blue tank top, while another, younger midwife cupped her hands underneath the woman's naked end as if she were to catch a slippery fish.

Outside, the sun spilled light over the sea. The unforgiving rays caked the dirt paths that connected like veins to the main artery of town. Even the ancestors stayed in the shade of the plaza's shadows. Inside, for a room full of women about to be ripped open, it was rather quiet. Only breathing sounds waved in and out the spaces between them all. The old lady midwife giggled and pressed her old lady wrinkled lips to Graciela's nostrils, two dots the size of raindrops, and whispered in it a prayer.

After a final prayer, the midwife left the room. No one ever saw her again. You were the last baby she delivered, they would tell Graciela when she was older. She left you her gift: being able to remember everything. Every detail, memory, billboard sign, secret, direction of the wind on a given tree on any Sunday after church, all of it. Even those conversations you'll wish you hadn't heard.

Of those, there is one that stands out from the one hundred and one years that will be Graciela's life: the conversation she had with her father the last time she saw him. She can still hear him singing to her while they sat under the lime tree in the central park in Mazatlan when she was just four years old, the way the melody coupled with the afternoon sun lulled them both to sleep. Never could she imagine her father leaving her the way they said he did—resting on her side on the wooden park bench, in such a deep sleep that she ignored the tingles developing in her forearm that she had used as a pillow. It was the last time anyone saw him, before he vanished like a participant in a stage magician's show, leaving behind only his sweat rimmed caballero hat, browned with the last scent of him.

Graciela's mother refused to believe that her daughter, now ten, does not remember where he was going and why.

"You remember everything."

"But I can't remember what did not happen."

Like this, it went on for hours, then days, then weeks, then years and centuries.

"What did you do to him? Where did he go? With whom?"

Her mother spanked her with any item she could summon every Sunday: wooden spoon, sandal, cat. Rather than dig it out, her mother only stuffed the information in deeper.

On Christmas that year, Graciela's mother played boleros on the record player. It snowed. It had only done so once in Mexico, fifty years ago. The Indians thought it was the ashes of their ancestors falling down. This year, this time, Graciela collects the snow with a broom outside in the street and slow dances with the ghosts of the past.

A Thing Called Exodus
Ky-Phong Tran

The war ended three weeks ago. You know because the hills have stopped quaking with cannon fire and you cannot remember the last time you saw a French soldier. Today, you are walking home from school when you hear the low moan of a plane overhead. You look up but see nothing, only an overcast sky, reddish-gray like the silt of the river that runs through town. Down by church and its small lake, small shadows begin to speckle the sky. At first it looks like a large flock of birds swooping down, but then you realize it is paper, thousands of sheets, each the size of a hand, rustling in the air, fluttering lazily to the earth. The leaflets land everywhere, whitening the trees and floating atop the lake's light green water. Around the lake, townspeople scatter. Fearful elders duck into doorways. Children pretend it is raining. You grab one from the air. You read it. It says, "God has moved south."

You rush home to your father, your white ao dai flapping behind you like the tail of a kite. On the way, you pass the cemetery where your mom was recently buried. It has only been six months but it feels so much longer. If she were alive, she would say, *You are becoming a woman now.* She would tease you, measure your new hips with her palms, pinch your small breasts and say, *The mangoes are not ripe yet.* But she isn't, so you keep running.

When you arrive home, you find your father sitting beneath the soft shade of Old Man, the white oak tree that spreads his massive arms in the center of the courtyard. Your father works at a table, tying bamboo rods together and cutting paper mache.

"I'm making you a lantern," he says. "For the Mid-Autumn Festival next month."

You hand your father a flyer and say, "These came from the sky."

He takes it from you.

"What does it mean?" you ask.

Since mom died, he has been a quiet father and you a quiet daughter. You speak little to one another and *never* about her. Silence, in your home, is a language.

"Nothing," he says. "This news is for big people."

***

The soldiers come the next day. You are at the lake with your friend Thu, though both of you should head straight home after class to start dinner and do chores. She is tall and lanky like a palm tree and has a pretty, two-dimples-on-one-cheek smile that makes all the boys in school like her.

"Did you see the flyers?" she asks.

"I wish I knew what was going on," you say. "No one ever tells us kids anything."

"Yeah," Thu says. "It's always orders or questions. Never answers."

"It's a tradition," you say and both of you laugh at that.

Thu turns to you and says, "Come here, let me braid your hair."

You go and sit in her lap, your elbows resting on her knees. She pulls a comb from her school bag and slowly brushes your hair. She is gentle, but sometimes the teeth of the comb scrape along your back and tickle you. You arch your back and giggle. It has been too long since your hair has been brushed by someone and it feels so wonderful, like a kind of love. Mom used to comb your hair every morning before school, family gatherings, church. She liked to try different styles, a pony tail with a white ribbon or one side pulled back with a butterfly clip, but always neat and sharp. *God is in the details*, she'd say.

You hear and feel the soldiers' arrival before you see it, the clang of metal on metal, the rumble of a diesel engine.

"They're here," Thu says to you in a low voice.

"Who?" You ask.

You open your eyes to the bright day, and as they adjust, the view looks like the inside of the kaleidoscope at school. Over the wash of colors, dark figures grow bigger. One by one dozens of soldiers jump out of a flat-bed truck as if it were giving birth to them. They are tired-looking and dirty, fresh sweat making rivulets in the caked-on dirt of their faces.

When the dirtiest one notices the lake outside the church, he takes off his shirt, rolls up his pant legs, and jumps in for an impromptu bath. Soon a group of them are in the water, splashing about like boys, unaware or unconcerned by the stone statue of Jesus watching over them.

While you watch the men, two soldiers approach you from the other side of the lake. They stop right in front of you and Thu and their bodies block the sun, making long shadows that cover your face. They look at you with hungry, animal expressions on their faces. You do not like it. It makes you feel indecent, like you've done something wrong when you have not.

One of them looks dead at Thu. He has a long whisker growing out of a mole on his cheek. "Hello ladies," he says. "Can I get my hair braided next?"

Thu looks down and says, "You hair is too short."

"I know, I was just kidding" he says. "I just wanted to—"

"—be between your legs," the other soldier laughs. He smokes a cigarette, and up close his teeth are yellow.

Mole-Face turns to him and you hear him say, "Motherfucker, this is not how we planned it."

"Quit the games," Yellow-Teeth replies back. "When a guy wants some pussy, I say, be up front about it."

You have never heard men talk like this. You both stand quickly and begin to walk away.

"Where are you going?" Mole-Face asks. "We're just playing, trying to make new friends."

"We have to go home," you say.

As you go, Yellow-Teeth grabs your wrist. His grip is strong. You cannot break his hold and despise the feeling. "No harm in just talking to a fellow is there?" he says leaning in to smell you. You can tell he hasn't bathed in days and his sour stench makes you want to vomit.

Just then, a jeep pulls up driven by a white-haired soldier. "Stop!" he shouts and Mole-Face promptly releases you. From his voice and posture, you know he is their commander. He steps from his jeep. "Forgive my men," he says. "We've been away in battle and have lost some of our manners."

White-Hair nods his head and stiffens his body like a statute. He yells an order and all the soldiers—even the ones in the water—stand at attention. He returns their salute with a casual flick of his wrist. "Now that the war is over," White-Hair says, "we've been ordered to secure this town. We're here to protect you."

***

That Sunday, church is unusually crowded, as if it was Christmas or Easter, and not a regular August mass. Before the service begins, you kneel before the Virgin Mary and light a candle for your mom like you do every week.

When you are done praying, you return to your seat, a comfortable length from your father. Distance is your way of mourning. You did not tell him about the incident with the troops. It's been this way since mom's funeral, which was your first one ever. Most of that day is a haze, perhaps because of the incense smoke that hung in the air like a fog. You remember your family, everyone with a white cloth tied around their forehead looking like they'd returned wounded and bandaged from some far-off battle. You remember the hole in the ground, deeper and darker than you could have imagined. But most of all, you remember mom being lowered into the ground. The squeak-squeak of the pulley and ropes. You were crying so hard you bit your lip until it bled. You looked to your father, standing next to you as mom steadily descended. He wore a blank, stoic face. He did not cry. Instead, white-robed mourners, ghostly women he had *hired*, wailed like crows and threw their bodies atop the coffin. Not one tear. You have not forgiven him since.

Now mass begins. An organ plays, the choir sings, and the procession slowly enters. The altar boys hold a gold cross and flickering candles; the deacon holds the bible aloft; the priest, whom you don't recognize, carries only a solemn look on his face.

After the readings, the new priest takes the lectern. He wears dark-rimmed glasses and is almost handsome. You expect him to address the papers that fell from the sky. But he doesn't. While he speaks, his eyes scan the audience and it is obvious he is nervous because he repeatedly wipes his forehead with a cloth and it is not even a hot day. For three days, you have wondered about the bird-like flyers and their odd message. But the priest talks only about lambs and shepherds, valleys and summits, his voice bouncing off the stone ceiling and back down through the wood beams. Then he tells a story from the bible. It is about a man named Moses and a thing called Exodus. The priest concludes his sermon by saying, "Our faith is all we have. It is our passage to freedom."

Almost in unison, everyone in the church says "Uh, uh." Your father nods and makes the sign of the cross. From the side of the altar a small cackle rises out and, for the first time, you see what has made the priest so edgy: a half-dozen soldiers, feet up on the wooden pews. One of them applauds, slow and off-beat. It is White-Hair. Mass continues, quiet, uncomfortable. You receive communion. The soldiers do not.

***

A few days later at school, you turn to ask Thu what color ao dai she will wear for the festival and what kind of lantern she will have. She is not there. Not the day after or the day after that. Because she is tall and pretty and popular, she is readily missed. Rumors about her attendance spark and burn quickly through school. *She was attacked by the soldiers. Walking home from her aunt's house on the edge of town. Raped. What is that? I don't know, I overheard my parents say it.*

You never see her again. The following week at school, you notice that a classmate or two is missing every few days. *Where is everyone? I hear the soldiers are putting them in secret prisons. I hear they are running away in the middle of the night. To where? Saigon. That's so far. I've never even been down there.*

The stories unsettle you and you decide to tell your father about the things you have heard at school: Thu, the soldiers, families running away. Remembering the flyers, you ask, "How can God move? Isn't he everywhere?"

"You ask too many questions," he says.

Two weeks later, when you walk home from the market and it is obvious that people are missing, you ask your father, "Are we going to too?

"No," he says. In your family, lying is how you protect one another.

***

The night before the Mid-Autumn Festival, your father comes into your bedroom. "After the evening parade," he says," I will be hosting a big party at the house. For the whole town. The other respectable families are gone and it's my duty to keep the tradition."

You are groggy and his words blur and mean even less than usual.

"A lot of people will be here and it will be very busy. But listen to me, child, make sure you sleep in your bed tomorrow night. No one else's. I will need to find you. It is very important. Do you understand?"

You nod.

"Say it," he commands.

"Yes, father. I will sleep in my bed."

He tells you that your lantern is hanging on Old Man out in the courtyard. "Do not forget it," he says. "Now get some rest. Tomorrow, we'll need it."

That night, you sleep but do not dream.

***

The next evening, everyone in town gathers in front of church for the parade. You are alone. Your father is at home getting ready for the party afterwards. It is dusk, the sun asleep for the night, and the sky glows a feint orange from the full moon just above the tree line. Packs of children mill about, holding lanterns in all sorts of shapes: birds and fish and butterflies. Your father never finished making your lantern. Instead he bought you a common star-shaped one, red mache with gold trim. Mom used to make your lanterns. Your first was a unicorn. Last year, a phoenix. She would make the prettiest ones in town, from special paper she had brought back from Hanoi, and then tell everyone you made them yourself. At times, your lanterns were so much nicer than everyone else's, you felt ridiculous, but you held them high anyway, just to make her happy. When the parade begins, a man comes by and lights the candle that is tucked inside the lantern. Within minutes, the street glows in blues and reds and yellows.

The parade ends with a firework show down by the big river, explosions turning night into day. Through the forest of bodies, you see a child crying on the ground. A little boy has tripped and skinned his hands. Because of the noise, no one can hear him crying. After one particularly bright flash of light, you see that his hands are bleeding. During the finale, a woman finds the boy. She has black hair that almost reaches her waist. She kneels down and comforts the boy. When she notices his cuts, she rubs the boy's hands on her pant legs, red handprints permanently streaking down white silk. Then she lovingly takes each hand and licks the remaining blood from them. The little boy smiles and runs off. You will never be more jealous.

After the show of lights, you walk towards the river. It is alive and the moon reflects off it like shards of glass. You take your lantern and lay it on the water. It floats. *The Mid-Autumn Festival,* mom once told you, *is a children's festival.* Slowly, it drifts out with the currents. A few meters out, the mache catches fire, a small crackling burst. Standing at the river's edge, you wonder, What is a children's festival without your parents? As the flames reach the water, they are extinguished and the lantern sinks into the black.

***

When you arrive home, the party is in full swing. Lanterns hang from the walls and turn the courtyard a soft pink. Old Man has white streamers hanging off his arms. There is a horde of people in attendance, so many that it seems the whole town is there. Some surround a banquet table, picking at catered dishes and a roasted pig. Others stand by the bar and toast drinks. A group to the side plays cards and throws dice. In the center of it all, a record player plays and young people dance around Old Man.

"Glad you could make it," your father says. "Greetings and well wishes."

He smells like alcohol.

"Hello, father," you say.

"Enjoy yourself, but don't stray too far. It looks like a hectic night."

"Yes, father."

At that moment, a jeep pulls up with a dozen soldiers hanging off of it. They are wearing their dress uniforms and it looks like the whole brigade is there. The first to approach are White Hair, Mole Face, and Yellow Teeth.

"Welcome, welcome," your father says. "Our protectors are here!"

He shakes each and every one of their hands and leads them to the bar. You find it curious that your father would invite these men into your home.

"Drinks for our troops," he tells the bartender. "Their duty keeps them away from home, so let us be their new home."

When they all have a drink in their hands, your father offers up a toast. "For our country," he says.

"For our country!" they reply.

After the drink, White Hair walks up to your father and says, "You're not so bad—for a Catholic!"

Your father looks at him, smiles, and downs his drink. Soon, the whole brigade is laughing.

The scene makes everything seem upside down and you feel dizzy. Your father is, again, doing the wrong thing. To retaliate, you decide you will not participate. You will not dance. You will not play. You will not eat any of the food. Instead, you slip through the crowd and over to Old Man. In the middle of the commotion, no one notices you climbing up his trunk and into the nook where all his branches begin. You lay atop in the blanket you keep there and watch the festivities below. You are above it, not of it. Beneath a canopy of leaves you watch couples dance, suits and ao dais swaying to the music.

Throughout the night, this is what you see: your father leaves and returns with a truckload of beer, two soldiers toast two glasses apiece, drink them with their heads tossed back, and pass out on the ground; your father leaves again and returns with more alcohol; a group of soldiers throw up in the bushes.

The night grows older, dew chilling the air, and soon it is past your bedtime. Your head feels heavy and your eyes weary. Instead of climbing down and sleeping in your bed like your father told you, you will sleep where you want to. Above the party, amongst the branches, with music and laughter and voices drifting up to you like smoke, you fall asleep. And for whatever reason—Old Man's blessing, because you miss her so badly, your anger towards your father—you dream of mom this night.

You are still a child, five or six years old. You wake early one morning, the air still cold, a dim gray light in your bedroom. You wake because you feel a human gravity, as if someone is tugging you. When you sit up, you rub your eyes and then see mom. She sits in a chair next to your bed. She has a calm, peaceful look on her face and you can tell she has been there for some time. At that moment, you know, unequivocally, that anyone who sits and watches you sleep must surely adore you and you have never felt more loved.

***

You wake to your father's voice and a cloak of cold, night air.

"Tien," he says. "Tien, where are you?"

There is something strange about his voice.

"Daughter. Where is my daughter?"

When you look down, you see him walking through the courtyard, scanning for you, carefully avoiding the passed-out bodies of party-goers and soldiers.

"Tien oi," he whispers. "Tien oi."

Why is his voice so strange?

"Come out, Tien. Daddy is not mad. Please just come out."

As he calls for you, you realize what is off in his voice: It has fear in it. It warbles. It hesitates. You have never seen him like this. You like watching him worry and you let him call your name two, three, four more times before you climb down from the tree.

You walk to your father, head down and arms folded across your chest. "Yes, father," you say, expecting to be reprimanded.

"Shhhhhhhhhhh," he says, putting a finger to his lips. "Don't wake up our guests."

He takes your hand, firmly, and pulls you toward him. "Let's go," he says.

But instead of walking you into the house, he walks you through the courtyard to a side gate. Everything is a dark mess now, the lanterns having burned out long ago, plates with leftovers scattered all over, empty beer cans and wine bottles littering the courtyard. The record player spins but plays no music, only the monotonous dead end of an album. Just before the gate, you see White Hair, Mole Face, and Yellow Teeth passed out around a table.

Your father bends over, looks at you, and points his finger right between your eyes. "Do not make a sound," he says. He tip toes past the soldiers and you follow his every move. When you make it out and into a field behind your house, he says. "Good girl. Let's keep moving."

The two of you continue walking through tall reeds, beneath a moon so full the whole field glows white. All around you the crickets chirp so loud it sounds like they are in your ear. When your feet get stuck in the mud for the third time, your father picks you up and carries you.

"Almost there," he says. He is exhausted and you can feel dread in the way his chest heaves up and down like mom's old, worn sewing machine.

By now, you know better than to ask where you are headed.

Soon, you notice that the ground slopes down and you are at the banks of the small river at the edge of the field. There you see a small fishing boat, as long as a house with a thatched roof, tethered to a pole. From inside, whispered voices leak out.

"Hurry up! We were about to leave you."

Your father sets you down on the bank and pulls you into the river. The water shocks you. It is colder than you expected, biting into your feet and calves. The two of you slosh through it towards the boat.

"I had to find my daughter," he says, his voice hard like a stone. "Without me, this doesn't happen, remember?"

Your father picks you up and hands you to a man inside. When you get close, you see the man is wearing dark-rimmed glasses and recognize the priest from mass.

"Welcome my child," he says.

When your eyes adjust to the darkness beneath the palm roof, you look around and see the shadows of a dozen or so people crammed into the boat.

"Let's go," your father says. He is still in the water, untying the boat and then shoving it deeper into the river. At first, the water is only up to his knees. When it is at waist level, he pushes the boat along the river, along the mangroves that slither by like snakes. Eventually, only his head is above the water and he swims along side the boat. He shivers fiercely. When the boat is completely away from shore, the lights of the town sparkling far off like fireflies, he swings a leg over the boat and pulls himself in.

"Thanks be to God," he says.

"How was the party?" the priest asks him.

"Those boys will be drunk until New Year's," your father says.

"Morning is fine with me," the priest says.

Soon, the boat gets caught by the current and picks up speed. Beneath the full moon, now low and a brooding orange, the jagged shadows of the shore pass quickly. Everyone is silent. The only sound is the boat as it cuts through the river's small waves. At one point, someone whispers "patrol boat" and everyone sinks deeper into the belly of the boat, covering themselves with blankets and straw mats. You hide too, though you are not sure what you are hiding for or who you are hiding from. Out in the water, a dark shadow, possibly a boat, looms close. The tension on the boat is airless, everyone holding their breath, afraid to exhale.

A few seconds seems like a few hours. Finally, someone lets out a laugh. "Heaven and earth, it was only a log. Motherfucker, only a damn tree," a voice says.

When all seems safe, everyone crawls out from their hiding. The priest says, "Listen carefully. God is with us tonight. The current is strong and we will be at the port by morning. French ships are taking people to Saigon, I assure you. This is my fourth trip. Stay low in the boat and no talking, voices carry a long way on the river. Remember, we're just fishermen going home from a party."

You turn to your father and ask, "When will we go back?"

"I don't know."

"I don't want to go."

"This isn't a choice."

"I want to go home."

When he says nothing, you look at the people tucked between boxes and suitcases and know you will never return. You think of your friends and house and clothes and books and Old Man. You imagine mom, buried in the ground, and are afraid she'll be washed away in the next big storm. You begin to cry. At first, you shed quiet tears but when you think of mom, dead in the ground with no one to hold her one-year death memorial, you sob loudly.

"Me oi, me oi," you cry.

"Shut her up or she's going overboard," an angry voice says.

"She's my daughter, I'll take care of it," father says.

You expect him to slap you. He has done it for lesser transgressions. Instead, he ruffles through a sack and pulls something out. He creeps toward you slowly, careful not to rock the boat, and hands you a small envelope.

"Your mother is here," he says.

The envelope is full of photographs. In a sliver of moonlight that comes through the palm roof, you flip through them. There are only photos of mom: the day she received her first communion, hands held out, palms side by side, ready to receive the Eucharist. Mom in her wedding ao dai, a white veil misting over her round cheeks, kneeling next to dad in church. Mom holding a baby at a baptism, it's you, bundled in blankets like a caterpillar's cocoon.

You look over to your father. He is at the back of the boat going over a map with the priest. You do not understand him and fear you never will. But when you settle in Saigon, you will learn to read him by his actions and inactions. He never remarries. At your engagement ceremony, fifteen years later, he will greet your fiancé at the door. Alone. In the United States, after you've fled another war, you will wake to use the bathroom and find him in the kitchen, head down, drinking cognac alone. He will be humming along to a static-filled love song on the radio and staring at these very photos. You will come to understand that for some pains, there are no words. In your family, denial is a habit of survival.

But for now, you are just a girl fleeing your home in the middle of the night. It is September, 1954. The province and town of Ninh Binh. The river you are on too small to have a name. You are twelve years old and you clutch the photos to your chest like they are the most precious thing in the world.

Living in the World (whose world?)
David Mura

Author's note: This is a shortened version of a longer essay. I wrote it in 1993, when the word "multiculturalism" was at the center of cultural debates concerning artistic standards and practices. Since then the word has fallen into disuse, though the issues that surrounded it are still very much alive. Similarly, the term "Third World" has become dated; but again the issues of post-colonial and post–post colonial writing still remain. Unfortunately, the difficulties I faced as a student of color in an MFA program are similar to those still facing current students of color.

I

When I first began traveling the country to give readings, I noticed the reception of my poems differed depending on the racial mixture of the audience. A poem which seemed difficult or extreme to white audiences did not seem so to audiences of color. I was forced to question whether I could write for both audiences at once. And I had to ask, what were the differences in the lives of people of color that could explain their responses? I realized that the deeper I went into my own life and into the lives of my community, the further away I traveled from the preconceptions of a white audience. I would not exclude the lives of whites nor the white audience from my writings, but I also would not write for their approval or in fear of their responses. There was a choice I had to make.

If I had not grown up in a white middle class suburb with Japanese American parents who wished to assimilate, I would not have been as surprised by these choices. But I had grown up very white-identified, with a view of writers of color as a literary ghetto. As a result I can understand why white writers cling to a view of literature and their lives that excludes, often unconsciously, the realities of people of color. I can see when they refuse to interrogate their own whiteness, as I did not wish to interrogate my identity as a Japanese American. I too wanted my art to be universal. I wanted it to possess "quality," to live up to the literary standards I had been taught. I could not conceive that the universal was chimerical, and that the standards were often arbitrary and intimately tied to issues of power. I didn't want to enter a realm where I would have to discover my own way and invent new standards, where I would have to change my life and my cherished certainties, my comforts.

II

When I went to an almost all white graduate program a few years ago, a black student poet won an NEA. Upon hearing this, a white poet professor remarked to a white student, "You know, us white guys didn't have a chance. There were so many minority judges on the panel this year." Later, when this black poet gave his final semester seminar on black aesthetics, another white poet professor muttered in the back of the room, "That's not aesthetics, that's paranoia." (Such a remark was not surprising, since this same white professor had told the black poet, "Literature which drops the 'g' from 'ing' words doesn't last.") The next period, this same white poet introduced his seminar on the ode by saying, "Horace didn't write for special interest groups" (tell that to the Roman slaves). When I confronted the director of the program about these remarks and suggested he bring in a woman who did diversity training workshops for Fortune 500 companies, the director replied, "These are writers, you can't tell them what to do." At the time there were no faculty of color among the sixteen professors.

Thus, while race could be considered an essential issue in a Fortune 500 company, it could not be discussed or considered a problem in an MFA program. The director viewed the issue on an individual level, on the level of creative freedom. He didn't consider it as an institutional issue, a problem of social practice. But racism is not simply the conscious— or unconscious— belief that other people are inferior because of their skin. Racism is a system through which power is distributed unequally.

Multicultural art concerns itself with the lives and realities institutions shut out. It is the end of one world, and the recognition that another world is gaining power, a world that has always existed but has been silenced. It is about celebrating the voices at the margins, their power and courage. It is about recognizing that the margins are no longer the margins, that there are centers within the margins and margins within the center. It is about abandoning my loyalties to those racist, sexist and homophobic people and institutions that formed me—family, friends, the university. It is about creating a culture where the complexities and issues in the work of authors from marginalized groups are appreciated and understood. It is about writers from marginalized groups writing for their communities rather than for the voices of power in the culture.

III

Writers of color tend to question many traditional European assumptions about the relationship between the group and the individual, about the separation of politics and literature, about colonialism, about our relationship to history, and about realism or the nature of spiritual reality. I am not here arguing that subject matter per se is a criterion for assessing literary quality, but I am arguing that, partly because of their subject matter and their experiences, the visions and strategies of writers of color in this country and many Third World writers add to our sense of the world's complexity and create new possibilities in our writing of, and approaches to, the text; therefore, they widen the criteria by which we judge the text.

What follows below are notes concerning this shift in aesthetics; a broad mapping of how the literary landscape is being transformed. The reader may or may not agree with this shift or the following arguments, but the views I'm sketching are driving a vast number of multicultural writers and artists. The bottom line is that the function and standards of art are changing in our culture. Whatever label these changes are gathered under, however they may be attacked or derided, they characterize what is unique about this cultural moment. As Eliot, the arch conservative knew, an artist cannot change the historical conditions he or she has been given. These conditions dictate, in many ways, what type of art is possible at a given time.

IV

In many ways, American culture conceives of the self mainly as an individual rather than as a member of a group. When the subject of race comes up, many whites seize on this perspective as the solution to the problems of race. "If we all just treat each other as individuals ..."

But many people of color see themselves simultaneously as an individual and a member of a group. That is because if you are black in this country, a significant part of your life experience is determined by your membership in that group. As the gay black poet Essex Hemphill remarks, "It doesn't matter if I go around wearing a dress, wherever I go in this country, I am first and foremost a black man."

We all live in groups—families, churches, schools, class, etc., but once you begin to label people by race many liberal whites suddenly don't understand why this concept represents an essential turning point. I recall talking with one of the three black poets in my MFA program about race, when a white poet sat down with us. We told him we were talking about how we viewed our lives as members of groups. His immediate response was, "But doesn't that divide people? Aren't we all the same?"

The white poet thought he was offering a symbol of solidarity. In fact, he was marking his ignorance not only of how race affects the lives of people of color in this country, but also how it has affected his life.

I have come to see that this denial is not ultimately a matter of intellect. It is a psychological, spiritual, and political response. Part of the protest against multiculturalism has to do with the way multicultural art challenges the denials and comforts of being a member of a privileged group, whether that group be whites or men or heterosexuals or middle or upper class. As Langston Hughes put it in his poem, "Evil":

Looks like what drives me crazy

Don't have no effect on you.

But I'm gonna keep at it

Until it drives you crazy too.

This was also evident when I taught a course on Third World Literature. I found that all the authors recognized race was crucial to an understanding of history and the present.

V

"I'll tell you a little story ...There's an elegant lady in England ...getting on now. She wrote a novel about a lady with a lover; the lady had a moral crisis—"Should I condemn others when I'm immoral ...", you know that kind of thing, all very delicate and beautiful. And this novel came out a few days before the pound took its enormous dive—it seemed it was going to touch one dollar fifty. And I thought, the dive of the pound—the extended event—has destroyed the value of this novel, which implies that this world is of value, that values are steady and are going to go on. But when your pound crashes, you cannot make those assumptions anymore."

—V.S. Naipaul (from an interview)

A novelist like Naipaul deals with societies where values are in flux, where what was deemed beautiful or moral yesterday, is seen today as ugly and immoral, where traits that once seemed admirable or innocent are now seen as proof of one's emptiness or guilt. The causes for these shifts in American society are many—demographics; the decline of our economy and the rise of other economies, such as that of the Japanese; the breakdown of the Communist world and a common perceived international threat; the rise of a middle class of color ... the list goes on.

For many writers of color, the changes of this moment involve a strengthening of community and purpose, an embrace of the historical flux. They perceive that this flux is somehow bestowing on them a power they have been denied. They aren't as afraid of changes in the status quo, since the status quo was designed to keep them out. They don't display the same nostalgia for a halcyon past that many white writers do. Thus, the reason why they don't write poems about Henry James or Tintoretto is not that they necessarily see such art as lacking in value, but that the world that produced such art still excludes them. Homage to a European past increases not only the prestige of that tradition but also the white writers in the present who see themselves as the legitimate heirs of that tradition. Such homage almost invariably places the artist of color in a position of a latecomer, of secondary status.

Even when a white critic may be praising a writer of color, the critic's approach can still betray a bias. Lucille Clifton has remarked of her poetry, "I'm a Black woman poet and I sound like one." In his essay on *Clifton in Contemporary American Poets*, A. Poulin acknowledges that Clifton shares similarities with other woman writers and other African American writers. However, what he chooses to emphasize is her singularity: "But no other poet of her generation (regardless of gender or race) sounds quite like Clifton. Why that is, however, is rather difficult to identify in the standard language of literary criticism." Poulin never questions whether or not a deeper knowledge of black culture on his part might enable him to analyze the sources of Clifton's individuality. Instead, he deliberately deemphasizes the focus of Clifton's remarks and her clear sense of being a member of a group. This resembles a maneuver many successful people of color hear. It's the "you're an exception" badge. The Asian American poet Garrett Hongo has remarked that some white poets will praise him, saying, "I'm so glad you didn't go the ethnic route."

Why is it so important for white writers and critics to downplay this connection with the group? The focus on the poet as individual is seen by whites as an attempt to get beyond racism, to a spot where we are all judged by our "merits." But what if this focus on the individual is, in part, an ethnocentric bias? What if it ignores the fundamental way the writer of color looks at her work? On another level, if the critic can ignore issues triggered by race, then it really doesn't matter whether a poet is writing on Tintoretto or the internment camps, on Malcolm X or Henry James, on Cape Cod or Pine Ridge. The value and politics of content and vision can be pushed aside in favor of discussions of technique. In this way, a critic or poet surveys the landscape of American writing and its institutions without confronting the question of whether or not racism or sexism or homophobia affects our judgments of literary quality.

VI

The writer of color does not discard the Anglo/European tradition, but rather, reads that tradition from a troubling angle. Such a writer calls attention to the exclusionary nature of that tradition, the political history upon which it was built. In *No Name in the Street*, James Baldwin wrote:

> The South African coal miner, or the African digging for roots in the bush, or the Algerian mason working in Paris, not only have no reason to bow down before Shakespeare, or Descartes, or Westminster Abbey, or the cathedral at Chartres: they have, once these monuments intrude on their attention, no honorable access to them. Their apprehension of this history cannot fail to reveal to them that they have been robbed, maligned, and rejected: to bow down before that history is to accept that history's arrogant and unjust judgment.

When the poet Li-Young Lee was interviewed on PBS, he talked about reading Lord Jim and identifying with the novel's protagonist. At a certain point, Lee thought, "Why I am doing this? I have more in common with the natives than with Lord Jim."

This realization by a writer of color of how the tradition has excluded his own group is crucial to the discovery of the writer's own subject and underlying world vision. It requires that the Eros the writer has turned towards the European tradition be redirected towards those left out of that tradition. The writer is forced then to wonder what has not been represented in the social imagination. The writer's task here is imaginative reclamation.

VII

For those at the margins, history carries a different meaning than for those at the center.

In The Battle of Algiers, one of the movies I showed to my Third World Literature class, the head of the Algerian revolutionary organization says to Colonel Matthieu, the head of the French colonial forces, "We have a better chance of defeating the French than the French have of defeating history." In J.M.Coetzee's *Waiting for the Barbarians*, the white magistrate protagonist remarks: "Empire dooms itself to live in history and plot against history.

One thought alone preoccupies the submerged mind of Empire: how not to end, how not to die, how to prolong its Empire." Later, the magistrate adds: "I wanted to live outside history. I wanted to live outside the history that Empire imposes on its subjects, even its lost subjects. I never wished it for the barbarians that they should have the history of Empire laid upon them. How can I believe that is cause for shame?"

History is an inexorable process. It destroys, it judges and condemns, it tells us who is on the wane and who is on the rise. In the works of some neo-colonial writers, history speaks the language of justice and morality; in others it speaks of power and amorality. In either case, there is a desire to tell what the victors in the past or the present have left out.

VIII

Multiculturalism involves a radical alteration of the American cultural fabric, a redistribution of power within this country. Multiculturalism cannot be separated from the existence of racism, homophobia, and sexism in our society. You cannot engage yourself with a work by a person of color, by a gay man or a lesbian, by a woman, without acknowledging the social, political, economic and cultural forces allied against each person in those groups. And many of the artists from those groups consciously see themselves as fighting those forces. But beyond this, the mind by which you absorb this art has been shaped by a society that is racist, homophobic, and sexist. It is not a mind that stands above the work of art, in objective neutrality. It is a mind that is formed by a certain history, a certain set of assumptions, that has been shaped by race, sex and sexual preference, by class and ethnic background. We each start from different places. And the art we produce reflects those differences in ways we have only begun to recognize.

Jazz Trio on the Uptown Metro
for Gil Scott-Heron
David Maduli

solo ends   spotlight empties
the light remains
on the edges of a solar system
drummer bass player and keyboardist
drive a city bus full of survivors
through the rain
let the rain come now let it
waterfall

no traffic lights now
no traffic we ride now

no city   no street
three musicians and wind

no bus now they steer us forward
steel water our eyes concrete air our throats
a river of wounds rolling down

no band now
drum becomes a hand smoothing hair
bass crumbles into gravel
keys snow flurries

no bodies now
no clouds   no sky
we are whispers

Eastmont Still Life
David Maduli

The license plate slumps gutter low
Out front our house, steel glinting

As stars fade. Golden State's
Emblem spilled under winter

Leaves and soda cups, candy foils—
This relic of a felony—lost.

At what time last dusk
Or night, gloves or bare hands

Beneath curb then ghost.
Headlights cloaked

In Seminary Ave's thunder.
Clouds pull back a quiet loss, a morning

Surprise. Nearby,
Couple blocks closer to sunrise

Under the day's new thirst, a fresh body
Rusts in a storm drain.

Trimester One
David Maduli

june sunken noon sun, unsets
come second son wind, unzipped
love under guns run, come sprint

bombs enter moms wombs, called sick
lawns under cops laws, hollow tipped
jaws soften god's flaws, full clip

draw trigger squeeze leaves, clack click
sleeve stuffed with queens breathe, bluff quick
slaves in the pavement graves, unstick

gum chewing tongues just, one kiss
more for the thirty floors, i've been
lived in the last give, to forgive

skin of my past lives, once loved
mud of the river blood, covered rib
cage for the ages veins, beat blue

soon as fate blooms truth, come true
truth in eight moons soon, come you

Native Language
Kenji Liu

out there is gone to, pōn!
riding a cup, goes up the river,
jiiiito looking, very dreamer boy is.

ん, fragments remembering does,
when speaking, inward bones lean do.
chō important is, these mono.

why these mono recall happen doesn't?
sounds away slide, nyoro nyoro-like:
matta miru, miso shiru.

gūtto! thinking does but itai itai comes
so sometimes forgetting better is, ん or
boat in, roretsu roretsu roretsu,

stream ni yukuri down float,
waku waku waku ureshii ni
life wa dream desu, ne. ん.

To My Future Son
Kenji Liu

inside concrete, men spin and flex
like WWF wrestlers, hollow and fearsome

and always performing. son, you do not have
to empty yourself like them, fists squeezed

so tightly your tenderness becomes
a sickness, constricted and hard

in your liver. this is the price
of manhood, to be a stone quivering

inside an egg. you will be told
to choose from a stir fried lineup

of kung fu gangsters, dumb-asses and
anti-sexy uncle tongs. these are men

made from the politics of other men
who only worship themselves.

if you choose manhood, many
will reward you, but really, who wants

to be a plastic action figure, muscular
yet with only one move: a head slam?

Outword

Dismantle: An Anthology of Writing from the VONA/Voices Writer's Workshop is both a gift and a necessity. This first collection of work by participants of the VONA/Voices workshop highlights the talent that has come through the program. Mixing faculty and student work, this anthology emphasizes the need for the scope to widen in our literature to a vision of inclusion and urgency, and to recognize that writers of color are the writers of a missing history, of an America that has been whitewashed and excluded. Or even worse—we are represented by a handful of talents that have specific experiences that could not possible give the multiplicity of our experiences. We are not a category, or a field; a subject or a theme—we have a canon that radiates backwards into the worlds from which these writers originate.

We thank Marissa Johnson-Valenzuela, of Thread Makes Blanket Press and a VONA alum, for her vision of creating this anthology and for assembling an editorial team to help see it through. Andrea Walls, Adriana Ramirez, Marco Fernando Navarro and Camille Acker joined Marissa in reading hundreds of manuscripts and making difficult decisions.

We give gratitude to the writers here—they are the mirrors that reflect successes from fourteen years of the VONA/Voices workshop. Many have moved forward to publishing their own volumes and that, in turn, keeps us alive. Our life brings breath to more writers in the margins, more unheard/unseen words, yet to be discovered.

VONA/Voices continues to follow its mandate to support writers-of-color through our workshops. This anthology reaches beyond the circle of our workshops. It invites all readers to transform and appreciate American literature that cannot always be seen.

La Luz!

Voices of Our Nations Arts Foundation Co-Founders

Diem Jones, Executive Director
Elmaz Abinader, Director of Programs

Learn more at www.voicesatvona.org

Acknowledgements

The editors would like to thank the VONA/Voices founders, board, and staff. In particular, thank you to Elmaz Abinader and Diem Jones for trusting us with this book, and supporting us through the long process of compilation and production. Thank you to all of the writers included in *Dismantle*. Without your support of this project, it would not exist. Thanks go out to Eric Kane for his preliminary layout and design work. We also thank Maori Karmael Holmes for finalizing the design of this book. Her talent and expertise were essential to the completion of *Dismantle*. Thank you to Damon Locks for the beautiful cover art. His early involvement and cover drafting provided us with a guiding light that helped see this project through. Immense thanks to Rebecca Peters-Golden, Nico Amador, and Ben Goldstein for assistance with copy-editing.

Thread Makes Blanket would like to thank Nico Amador, Roger Reeves, Irit Reinheimer, David Mura, Chris Abani, and Minal Hajratwala for their feedback and advice. Thanks to Ezra Berkley Nepon for helping strengthen Thread Makes Blanket, and to AK Press for agreeing to distribute this book long before completion. Thanks to Kaffa Crossing, Cindergarden, and Fancyhouse (in particular Danielle Redden) who all tolerated de-facto office hours and meetings. Thanks to the Leeway Foundation for their support via an Art and Change Grant to editor Marissa Johnson-Valenzuela.

Finally, thank you to every VONA alum. Our only mission is to exhibit the range and beauty of the VONA/Voices workshop and larger community.

Contributors

Chris Abani is a poet and novelist who has received many awards, including a Guggenheim fellowship in creative writing. His most recent book is *The Secret History of Las Vegas* (Penguin, 2014). Since 2005, he has regularly taught at VONA.

Elmaz Abinader is a memoirist, poet, playwright. An avid performer and celebrated teacher, Elmaz is a mentor, friend and champion of VONA/Voices students. She teaches at Mills College, and is one of the founders of VONA.

Camille Acker is a writer living in Chicago, Illinois. Her heart, however, can always be found on the east coast, sprinkled liberally in Washington, DC and Brooklyn. She has attended workshops around the country and can't help that VONA will always be her favorite.

Faith Adiele (www.adiele.com) is author of an award-winning spiritual memoir; writer/narrator of a PBS documentary about her mixed family; and co-editor of an anthology of international coming of age stories. She's taught travel and memoir writing around the world, but teaching at VONA is it.

Kimberly Alidio has a chapbook, *Solitude Being Alien*, forthcoming from Dancing Girl Press. Recent publications include *Bone Bouquet, Drunken Boat, ESQUE, Fact-Simile, Spiral Orb*, and in the anthology *Philippine Palimpsests*. She received a UIUC Asian American Studies Postdoc and a Zora Neale Hurston Scholarship. VONA is the lyric.

Hari Alluri is a poet, community builder and filmmaker who immigrated to south Vancouver, Musqueam Territory at age 12. A member of cinder block, he has work in several publications. VONA is foundational to his ongoing personal and collaborative journey in descendant, brown, migrante storytelling.

Li Yun Alvarado is a Puerto Rican poet, writer, and educator. Her chapbook *Nuyorico, CA* was published in 2013 and her poems have appeared in several journals including *MiPOesias*, *The Acentos Review*, *PALABRA*, and *PMS Poemmemoirstory*. The first poetry workshop Li Yun ever attended was Suheir Hammad's VONA workshop in 2006; the experience emboldened her as a writer—she hasn't stopped creating since. www.liyunalvarado.com

Anna Alves is a NYC-born and California-bred writer who lives in Jersey City. Her work has appeared in several journals and anthologies, including *Kartika Journal* and *Kuwento for Lost Things*, and been supported by PEN USA and Hedgebrook. Always, VONA brings her home.

Vibiana Aparicio-Chamberlin has performed her stories at museums, universities and libraries throughout California. "I am influenced by my mother's Mexican folk tales and childhood surrealistic dreams growing up in East Los Angeles. At VONA I created among writers of color who demanded arduous excellence."

Adam Balm is an attorney, musician, and married father of two (cats). He recently completed his first novel, "Knucklehead". His wife learned about VONA in 2006 and encouraged him to apply. He has been active in the community ever since.

Born in Ecuador and raised in the Bronx, **Oscar Bermeo** is the author of four poetry chapbooks, most recently *To the Break of Dawn*. Oscar is grateful to VONA for the opportunity to study with mentor and friend Willie Perdomo. Palabra. For more information about Oscar's poetry, please visit www.oscarbermeo.com.

Tara Betts is the author of *Arc & Hue* and the libretto *THE GREATEST!: A Tribute to Muhammad Ali*. Tara is a Ph.D. candidate in English/Creative Writing at SUNY Binghamton University. Her work appears in numerous journals, anthologies, and interdisciplinary projects, and you can find her online at www.tarabetts.net.

Amalia B. Bueno is a poet, writer and graduate student at the University of Hawai'i. Her poems and stories have appeared in various journals, magazines and anthologies, most recently in Bamboo Ridge, Hawai'i Review and Tinfish. She tips her haku lei to Willie and Junot for the VONA love and inspiration.

New Orleans writer **jewel bush** has covered assignments in Haiti and Palestine. Her work has appeared in *The Courier, The Times-Picayune* and *The Washington Post.* She writes a weekly column for the *Uptown Messenger.* In 2010, she founded MelaNated Writers Collective to inspire writers of color just like VONA.

Ching-In Chen is author of *The Heart's Traffic* and co-editor of *The Revolution Starts at Home: Confronting Intimate Violence Within Activist Communities.* A Kundiman and Lambda Fellow, they belong to Macondo and Theatrical Jazz writing communities. At VONA, Ching-In discovered their writing voice. www.chinginchen.com

Sharline Chiang is a writer who lives in Berkeley, and co-founder of haikoozdesigns.com. Her work has appeared in Shout Out, Calliope, school, and 580 Split, among others. She has received support from Soapstone. A VONA O.G. since 2002, she thanks VONA teachers, founders and all VONAstics for family, funk and pan dulce. So much gratitude.

Monét Cooper is a teacher and writer from Georgia, who lives in Washington, D.C. She attended VONA in the summer of 2011 and found the first home for her work there. Thankfully, her writing life has not been the same since.

William Copeland iis a poet, MC, and cultural organizer from Detroit. He has been published in *Drumvoices Revue, the Listen zine,* and The Museum Of Contemporary Arts Detroit's *Telegraph.* His first VONA workshop experience rocked his world; his second shook his relationship with self and craft.

Jennifer De Leon writes fiction, nonfiction, and poetry. She is the editor of *Wise Latinas: Writers on Higher Education* (University of Nebraska Press, 2014) and teaches in Boston Public Schools and Grub Street. Her essay, "The White Space," was listed notable in *Best American Essays 2013*. For her, VONA was a Godsend.

Junot Díaz is the Dominican-born, New Jersey-raised, Rutgers and Cornell-educated, Pulitzer Prize and MacArthur-winning author of *Drown, The Brief Wondrous Life of Oscar Wao*, and *This Is How You Lose Her*. He is on the board of Freedom University and one of the original founders of VONA.

Gail M. Dottin = Storyteller + VONA disciple (has attended five times) + Columbia University MFA + Fulbright Scholar, Panama + completing *Where There Is Pride In Belonging*, about family's connection to construction of Panama Canal. VONA remains the most significant force in shaping her work.

teri elam lives in Atlanta. She has work forthcoming in *Electronic Corpse: Poems From A Digital Salon* and published in *The Ringing Ear: Black Poets Lean South, The Lion Speaks* and *Chemistry of Color*. When asked, her ancestors hymned that VONA translates into love, healing, home…

Born in Port-au-Prince, **M.J. Fievre** is an expat whose short stories and poems have appeared in numerous publications, including *Haiti Noir* (Akashic Books, 2011) and *The Beautiful Anthology* (TNB, 2012). She's the editor of *Sliver of Stone Magazine* and a VONA alumna.

Nikky Finney is the winner of the 2011 National Book Award for poetry. She is the author of four books, *On Wings Made of Gauze, Rice, The World is Round,* and *Head Off and Split*. She is the John H. Bennett, Jr. Chair in Southern Letters and Literature at the University of South Carolina. She taught at VONA.

Cristina Garcia is the author of six novels, including *King of Cuba* and *Dreaming in Cuban*, Latina/o anthologies, children's books, and poetry. Her work has been nominated for a National Book Award and translated into fourteen languages. She was among VONA's early teachers.

Minal Hajratwala is the author of the award-winning epic *Leaving India: My Family's Journey From Five Villages to Five Continents* (2009), and editor of *Out! Stories From the New Queer India* (2012). Teaching memoir at VONA 2012 is a high of her teaching/coaching life thus far.

Tatiana Richards Hanebutte grew up in Greenville, Alabama (pop. 8,000). A graduate of the University of Alabama, she currently lives in Wolfsburg, Germany where she writes about life as an expat at tatianainflux.com. She is a 2008 alum of the VONA writers workshop.

Scott Hernandez is a writer, poet and filmmaker. He has lived among the vanishing farms and orange groves of the Inland Empire all of his life. His recent work appears in *American Poetry Review* and *Connotation Press*. VONA feels like home.

Maori Karmael Holmes is a designer, filmmaker, curator, and producer originally from Los Angeles. Her films include the award-winning *Scene Not Heard: Women in Philadelphia Hip Hop*. Maori is the founder of the BlackStar Film Festival and previously designed *(1)ne Drop: Shifting the Lens on Race* published by BLACKprint Press.

Sasha Hom lives in a 10 X 12 cabin with their three daughters, husband and wolf dog. The only contest she ever won was a scholarship to VONA twelve years ago. She hasn't won anything since, but she's been published often.

Ashaki M. Jackson is a social psychologist and writer living in Los Angeles. She is a Cave Canem fellow whose work has been included in *Eleven Eleven, Suisun Valley Review*, and Cave Canem anthologies among other publications. VONA remains her essential and living writing community.

Mitchell S. Jackson is a Portland, Oregon native who lives in Brooklyn, New York. He is the author of *The Residue Years* (Bloomsbury, 2013). He is a 2007 alumnus of the VONA workshop. Visit him at www.mitchellsjackson.com

Mat Johnson is the author of *Pym* and other novels and graphic novels. He is a Professor and the University of Houston Creative Writing Program. Johnson has been leading workshops at VONA since 2007.

Marissa Johnson-Valenzuela is a writer, educator and semi-retired DJ who lives in Philadelphia. Her writing has appeared in *Make/shift, Aster(ix), The Rust Belt Rising, Apiary, As/Us* and elsewhere, and has been recognized by The Leeway Foundation, Hedgebrook, and others. She teaches at Community College of Philadelphia, and is a founder of Thread Makes Blanket press. For her, finding VONA was finding family.

Diem Jones is a writer, educator, activist, musician, photographer, and visionary. A fearless advocate of emerging artists, Diem is the beating heart of VONA/Voices. He is a co-founder of VONA.

Jourdan Imani Keith fellowships in creative non-fiction and poetry include VONA, Wildbranch, Santa Fe Science Writing workshop and Hedgebrook. Her work is possible because of funding from Artist Trust, 4Culture and Seattle's Office of Arts & Culture and the courage she receives from VONA love.

Mūthoni Kiarie is an Oakland-based Kenyan writer. Her work has been published in *Generations Literature Magazine* and in *Narrative Magazine* where she was a finalist in the Spring 2012 Short Story Contest. She has found a comfort in VONA that feels like home.

Alan King is an author, poet, and journalist. He is a Cave Canem fellow, a two-time Best of the Net-nominee, and a Pushcart Prize nominee. *Drift* (Aquarius Press, 2012) is his first book. For him, VONA helped him continue to build a circle of poets.

Laila Lalami is the author of *Hope and Other Dangerous Pursuits*, a finalist for the Oregon Book Awards and *Secret Son*, which was on the Orange Prize longlist. She attended the VONA workshop in 2004.

Alberto Ledesma is a cartoonist, writer, and educator who works at UC Berkeley's Student Learning Center. His work has appeared in *New American Media*, *Colorlines*, and *Con/Safos*. He lives in Castro Valley, California. For Alberto, VONA's Residency in Non-Fiction and Sandra Cisneros' Macondo Writing Workshop have set him on a path towards (re)writing what being an undocumented immigrant artist, student, and scholar is all about.

Kenji C. Liu is a 1.5-generation immigrant from New Jersey. His poetry chapbook *You Left Without Your Shoes* was nominated for a 2009 California Book Award. A Pushcart Prize nominee and first runner-up finalist for the Poets & Writers 2013 California Writers Exchange Award, his writing has appeared in numerous journals. He is a three-time VONA alumnus.

Damon Locks is a visual artist operating in the Chicago area where he received his BFA in Fine Arts at The School of The Art Institute in Chicago. His work is a combination of, but not limited to: drawing, photography, digital manipulation and silk screen. **www.damonlocks.com/art2**

David S. Maduli is a writer, veteran public school teacher, established deejay, and father. Born in San Francisco and raised all over, he is a longtime resident of Oakland and winner of the 2011 Joy Harjo Poetry Prize. He is a proud alumni of Las Dos Brujas and VONA, through which he co-founded the poetry collective Cinder Block.

Mia Ayumi Malhotra is the associate editor of Lantern Review. Her most recent work has appeared in *Best New Poets 2012*, *DIAGRAM*, *The Collagist*, *Volta*, and others. Currently, she lives and teaches in the San Francisco Bay Area. She was a VONA Fellow in 2010.

Vanessa Mártir is a NYC based writer and teaching artist. She is currently completing her first memoir, *A Dim Capacity for Wings*, and chronicles the journey in her blog vanessamartir.wordpress.com. Vanessa is a five-time VONA alumna and the newsletter editor.

Maaza Mengiste is the author of *Beneath the Lion's Gaze* and was a writer for the documentary Girl Rising. She teaches at Queens College, New York University, Princeton and Callaloo. Maaza's career as a fiction writer began at VONA.

Rajiv Mohabir is a poet and teacher living in New York. Author of three chapbooks he is the current Editor in Chief of *Ozone Park Journal* run by the MFA students at CUNY Queens College. For him VONA is a community of the heart.

Janine Mogannam is a San Francisco-based writer and librarian. She is a PoetsEleven contest winner, and her work has been featured in *580 Split* and *Kweli Journal*. VONA turned her world upside down, taught her who she is, and defined the meaning of home.

David Mura has authored memoirs, *Turning Japanese* and *Where the Body Meets Memory*, poetry volumes, *After We Lost Our Way*, *Colors of Desire* and *Angels for Burning*, a novel, *Famous Suicides of the Japanese Empire*, and a book of criticism *Song for Uncle Tom, Tonto & Mr. Moto: Poetry & Identity*. He is on the faculty of the Stonecoast MFA program.

Marco Fernando Navarro's fiction has appeared in *Word River, Dossier Journal* and once placed third for a *Glimmertrain* Short Story Award for New Writers. He is currently pursuing a Ph.D. in Rhetoric and Communication from Rensselaer Polytechnic Institute. As for VONA, that *Glimmertrain* thing happened after a week with Elmaz.

Cynthia Dewi Oka is a poet, mother, educator and author of the poetry collection *nomad of salt and hard water* (Dinah Press, 2012). Her poems have appeared in *Kweli Journal, 580 Split, Briarpatch Magazine, Borderline Poetry, Zocalo Poets, Generations Literary Journal, Ozone Park Journal* and *Boxcar Poetry Review*. For her VONA is voice, family and revelation.

Rae Paris is from Carson, California. She lives and writes mostly in East Lansing, Michigan where she is Assistant Professor of Creative Writing at Michigan State University. She attended VONA the first summer of her MFA program and it changed everything. More at blackspaceblog.com; @rae_paris.

Part of the global cultural arts movements within NYC, Los Angeles, and abroad, **Mai Perkins** has nurtured her intellectual and artistic talents at Howard University and Sarah Lawrence College. Mai credits her first poetry workshop with VONA as the catalyst to her crafted skill in writing.

Roopa Ramamoorthi is a biotech scientist and poet from India who now calls Berkeley home. Her poetry, short stories and essays have appeared including on NPR, the book '*She is such a Geek*', *India currents* and *Berkeley Daily Planet*. VONA is her writing shelter.

Adriana E. Ramirez tells stories, performs poems, and investigates violence. She teaches, edits, and dreams about the written word. She once gave a speech at TEDx and wore too small a sweater; this is not her fault as it was cold. VONA made her cry, but in a good way.

Jo Reyes-Boitel is a poet, activist, hand drummer, lover and mother living in San Antonio, TX. For Jo, VONA is a practice in the embodiment of insistent voice, despite upheaval.

Linda María Rodríguez Guglielmoni born in Puerto Rico, Linda María is a Raymond Carver Best Story Award winner and in 2011 "First Memory" won Honorable Mention at Glimmer Train's Family Matters Competition. In 2013 she was awarded The David Hough Literary Prize by The Caribbean Writer. At VONA she has worked with Elmaz Abinader and Willie Perdomo.

Born in South Korea and raised in the Mountain West, **Leah Silvieus** has received residencies from Kundiman and the Voices of Our Nation Arts Foundation. Her work has appeared in several journals, including *CURA, diode, Melusine, Rock & Sling,* and *CaKe.*

Anastacia Tolbert's work is a trellis of twilight, ultramarine ache and lowercase loam. She is a writer, performance artist, documentarian, creative writing workshop facilitator, cameo's as superwoman occasionally and is a full time mother raising feminist boys. Her VONA experience had a deep rooted impact on her in both her artistic and personal life.

Justin Torres is author of the novel *We the Animals.* His fiction has appeared in *The New Yorker, Harper's, Granta, Tin House,* and other publications. He is an admirer of VONA.

Sevé Torres is a poet and teacher currently based in New Jersey. He earned his B.A. in Sociology at UC Berkeley and is currently completing his MFA at Rutgers-Camden. For him, VONA means community, family, and a place of rigorous craft, a home where a nomad can rest before travel.

Ky-Phong Tran and his family fled to the United States at the end of the Vietnam War--his mother six months pregnant with him at the time. A New America Media Award honoree and Bread Loaf scholar, his work has been featured in the *San Francisco Chronicle,* the *Orange County Register,* and *Hyphen Magazine.* His writing career began in Cristina Garcia's indelible novel-writing workshop (VONA, 2004).

Torric Valentine is a VONA Alum and Cave Canem fellow whose work appeared in *Cavalier Literary Couture, Boston Review, Mythium*, among others. For Torrie, VONA is home. "It is the place where I gave myself permission to be myself, because I knew I was safe in that space."

Norma Liliana Valdez is an educator and writer whose work has appeared in *Calyx Journal, The Acentos Review, As It Ought To Be*, and *La Bloga*. Her poems recently received honorable mention by the San Miguel Writers' Conference. VONA taught her the courage to call herself a poet.

Andrea Walls lives in the "invincible city." She hopes it will rain today and be sunny tomorrow. Once, she was the lucky seat winner at a Phillies game. Her favorite dinner is pancakes. VONA is the cryptic answer to her unintelligible question. She says hello.

thandiwe Dee Watts-Jones is an African-American writer, poet, psychologist, and a member of the Earth clan in the Dagara tradition. Her work has been published in the *New York Times* and *Essence* and supported by Ragdale and Renaissance House. VONA has been coconut water/home made ginger beer.

Previously Published Credits